HELP WANTED

HELP WANTED

Tales from the First Job Front

SYDNEY LEWIS

The New Press
New York

Published in the United States by The New Press, New York, 2000
Distributed by W. W. Norton & Company, Inc., New York

LIBRARY OF CONGRESS CATALOGING-IN-PUBLICATION DATA

Lewis, Sydney
    Help wanted : tales from the first job front / Sydney Lewis.
        p.   cm.
    ISBN 1-56584-369-X (hc.)
    1. Job hunting. 2. Work. 3. Youth—Employment. 4. Youth—
Attitudes. I. Title.
    HF5382.7.L484   2001
    331.3'4'0973—dc21   00–036165

The New Press was established in 1990 as a not-for-profit alternative to the large, commercial publishing houses currently dominating the book publishing industry. The New Press operates in the public interest rather than for private gain, and is committed to publishing, in innovative ways, works of educational, cultural, and community value that are often deemed insufficiently profitable.

The New Press, 450 West 41st Street, 6th floor, New York, NY 10036

www.thenewpress.com

Printed in the United States of America

2 4 6 8 9 7 5 3 1

For Jane Jacobs

CONTENTS

INTRODUCTION

Whether you teach, trade, labor, paint, care-take, program, doctor, dissect, sell, organize, legislate, research, hammer, manage or sing, whether you join the nine-to-five world, work out of your home, become a wildly successful entrepreneur or an altruistic volunteer, the move from the world of school to the world of work involves a major transition, a change from one way of being to another.

In these pages, young people talk about what it's like to enter the workforce: to search for a job, encounter great bosses, survive horrible ones, face ethical questions, market themselves, network, succeed, fail, move on, flail around, find direction, wonder where it's hiding, sink or swim. It is my hope that their stories, observations, and insights, their questions and quandaries, may prove instructive and enlightening to those for whom having a good or any job is an oceanic mystery, as well as to those whose feet are wet but who have yet to experience the rapture of coordinating head, hands, and heart in an effort to navigate work journeys, to walk those mysterious waters.

How you get to "work" is a series of big and small questions. How do you? How do you apply for a job, how do you find a job to apply for? How do you manage to get to work on time, wear appropriate clothes, behave in acceptable ways? How do you find a job you'll like and want to keep? How do you know when it's time to move on? How do you find work that makes sense to you, that connects to your life and makes you feel that your involvement matters? Why do you need to?

In the introduction to *Working*, Studs Terkel's moving, illuminating, encyclopedic inquiry into what people do all day and the way they feel about what they do, he describes his book as being, "by its very nature about violence—to the spirit as well as to the body. . . . It is about a search, too, for daily meaning as well as daily bread, for recognition as well as cash, for astonishment rather than torpor."

For the much smaller grouping represented in this book, which is about first work experiences, it is the search that most resonates. For the most part unencumbered by the obligation to care for the needs of children, parents, mortgages, or health crises, their focus is on finding what Mick Betancourt, who toils as a Home Depot driver while honing his comedic skills, calls "the real job. . . . the job that makes you happy." But making one's way to the real job can take time, and as music promoter Ray Mancison says, "Sometimes you have to learn through finding out what isn't right, what doesn't fit, to get to what does."

Recently, an acquaintance told me he was amazed by the change in young people's ideas about work. He'd been a child during the Great Depression. "In my day you got a job, you did a job, no big deal. You didn't worry about whether it was personally fulfilling, you didn't expect it to feed your soul." Twenty-seven-year-old Emily Hanford strongly disagrees. "Work *should* matter. Work should be a creative and constituting kind of practice, not something you do just for the money."

A recent increase in efforts to prepare young people for the world of work suggested a useful endeavor: sharing, with high school and college students, conversations with people thirty and under about their first jobs. "Why under thirty?" asked several talkative friends and acquaintances, all eager to volunteer, all over thirty. (People love to, *need* to talk about their work.)

Because with the passage of time, the excitement, confusion, anxiety, wonder, disillusion, gratification, fear, and *newness* of the work world wear off. We take for granted our possession of sometimes hard-won organizational skills; the grace of a good phone manner; the sense of appropriate dress and behavior; the ability to solve problems. We forget what it's like to first nervously wade into those churning waters. As journalist Marc Spiegler explains, "The first three or four weeks at a new job you're always exhausted. Your brain is processing stuff: 'Where's the copier, how do I use the phone system, who is this person and why do they hate that person, is it OK for me to wear jeans?' It's sensory overload, it wipes you out."

It seemed to me that those interviewed would need to be relatively close in age to the uninitiated reader. If you've never held a job, it helps to hear about the work world from someone who shares your generational sensibilities. More importantly, it helps to hear from someone who actually *remembers* the raw, shocking, exciting intensity of being new on the job. As time passes, we tend to turn early moments of triumph and humiliation into amusing anecdotes, don't fully recall our pure soaring joy at having done a really good job or our acute shame and anxiety at having done the exact opposite. Julie Baxter, in talking about her law firm internship, describes a specifically new-to-work anxiety. "The first time you really screw up, it's difficult to know what to do. This is not your mom. Your boss doesn't have to forgive you." As we progress and our skills increase, we develop calluses to such things as shabby, unfair treatment or work accomplishments that go seriously unappreciated. In remembering youthful triumphs, a financial analyst notes, "You start work with a school background: if you did really well on the SATs you got patted on the head, you got a prize. It's not at all like that in the workplace."

But the nature of work and the texture of the work experience have changed from century to century, from decade to decade, and even, in recent technological and economic boom times, from year to year. Growing and harvesting crops that feed your own community, or building and installing a window frame in a neighbor's house, are very different activities from erecting iron bridges, logging acres of forest, designing aeronautical equipment, or managing a computerized payroll. This is not to judge any activity better or more worthwhile than the other. But to mill flour and see about you those whose hands have turned that flour into sustaining bread may feel like a "creative and constituting kind of practice" far different from the rushed grocery-packing in a large and largely anonymous supermarket about which teenager T. J. Devoe speaks.

In describing a high-school carpentry and construction job, the young journalist Marc Spiegler harks back to the kind of craftsmanlike work more widely done in decades past—at least by men, given women's then narrowly constricted work opportunities. He emphasizes the role that carpentry played in his developing attitudes about work: "That job created in me this faith that there's a value to working hard and focusing, that there's a return on the investment of time . . . When you build something, there's a physical result to your effort. When you build something, it's *built*." His words do not romanticize physical labor, but point out the profound value of a connection between your actions, exactly what it is you toil at, and your feeling about work itself. "It would be much harder to feel that satisfaction flipping burgers, or waitressing, or stocking shelves."

The feeding of the soul need not stem from grandiose work. In truth, it stems from the feeling you have about what you do. And everything from the nature of the work itself, to the design, lighting, sounds, and air of the workplace, the time allotted your task, the level of repetition, the demands and opportunities for creative thinking and problem-solving, the time of day, and the amount of human interaction, affect that feeling.

Though laboring at a steel-forging plant or on an automobile assembly line is not the same as designing a webpage or processing health-insurance claims, the feelings such seemingly different kinds of work evoke can be remarkably the same. Gabrielle Lyon describes working on an apple-packing assembly line. "At night, that's what I'd dream about. The *sounds* get into your blood, you feel them in your body . . . That job gave me a real sympathy for what working on an assembly line does to you as a human being, to the human spirit." But a less physically exhausting and much higher-paying city job was equally draining to Karen Hurley. "I felt that if I stayed, I was going to become like the people around me. I was starting to pick up the phone on the fifth ring instead of the first. . . . It was killing my spirit."

For those in this book, finding work that they can feel connected to and engaged by, feeling that what they do is in some way significant, is an important part of their search. Their yearning makes them especially sensitive to the emotionally disturbing disjunction, the spirit-shattering estrangement of time spent doing things that seem to have no meaning. T. J. Devoe shudders when describing his supermarket stint. "I *hated* that job 'cause it was just standing around the whole time, putting food in bags. It was empty labor to me—it wasn't *doing* anything." After a series of internships, Julie Baxter's point of view is much the same. "You spend so much of your day at work that to do something that's *just* a job, just ten vacuous hours you're not doing much with . . ." The disheartened expression on her face finished her sentence quite eloquently.

For some, feeling that they're "doing" something, that their work has value and meaning, is more than important, it's crucial. A young woman looking back at her time as a volunteer Emergency Medical Technician says, "For me, it's important to interact with people and have an impact and see it. . . . That's what I loved about working on the ambulance—that passion." A teacher reflecting on her approach to work says, "My mother is a Quaker, but even before I had any concept of what that meant, I remember feeling that to help others was your duty." Even if the emphasis is on personal satisfaction, still, the work must matter. Troy Graham, who hopes to move up the corporate ladder, speaks of the importance of a "bond with your work. Enough of a bond to say, 'I want to do this, I want to be here. It's *worth* my being here.' "

In most of these interviews, college attendance was a given—almost everyone had taken or was about to take college courses. Society's message that a B.A. is a necessity for earning a decent living seems to have registered with the young, at least the academically empowered and hopeful young. Says political operative Robert Richman, who took seven years to graduate due to work interruptions: "You need the paper." For others, who for any number of reasons lack a solid education or the financial means to attend college, this information gives rise to visions of gigantic gates closing against them. There is not much to be hopeful about.

The two teenagers interviewed in this book each planned to attend college, but chose to take a time-out after high school: T. J. Devoe, to earn money as a housepainter and floral-shop employee; Max Leonard to join the City Year volunteer program. The way Leonard sees it, "For some people, seventeen or twenty years of school in a row is right . . . But others get a lot out of mixing different experiences: volunteering, working for money, traveling. I would encourage each person to think for themselves." Both young men are now enrolled in college.

People's reasons for going to university were varied and sometimes conflicted. Their career aspirations ran the range from vague to specific, and of course, included big looming question marks. Mary Henderson had no career goals when she exited high school. "It was just, you take piano lessons, you go to college." Some knew, or thought they knew, what career they wanted; others went solely to learn. Gabe Lyon flat-out enjoyed school. "I felt no pressure to come out of it with a job. But I dated a guy who was being beaten over the head by his parents, who told him, 'Take economics, that's why we sent you to this place.' Yet his real passion was classical Greek literature."

While several had, over time, defined specific career goals, two in particular had grown up intuitively knowing what they wanted their work to involve. Gina Parks, a twenty-four-year-old guidance counselor, always wanted to do just that. She now chooses to work with inner-city school kids. "It's interesting to get the kids thinking about people who affect their lives as people who have *jobs*. Like, to them, I'm Miss Parks, this person they know, not a possible job prospect." Gil Santoscoy, Jr., began acting in grade school, and spent his high-school years co-hosting a children's television show. At the time we met, he worked as an inventory taker. "I'll just keep doing whatever until I find an acting job . . . anything you do helps you understand something a little better, whether it be about yourself, or about humanity, or society."

A larger number of those interviewed left college unsure of where they were headed. Jenny Petrow, a recent graduate, says, "I always tell people I know the *components* of my dream job—like it's a jigsaw puzzle and I just can't find the box cover." Karen Hurley's search landed her, for a time, in the National Guard where she underwent basic training. "It's hard to be targeted arbitrarily. For *no reason* told to stop what you're doing and do fifty pushups . . . Somebody says, 'Drop,' you *drop*." For Mary Henderson, at times frustrated by her lack of direction, a temporary job evolved into a satisfying career direction—that of social worker.

Like most of the young people I spoke with, my own first lessons about work came from my parents. My mother, a registered nurse, was good at her job, although she didn't love it, and the failure of the nurses' union-organizing effort she led nearly broke her spirit. My father, a court reporter, never enjoyed his job. While I was at work on this book he said, "I always felt I should be doing something else, but I never figured out what the something else was." He retired early and became a painter; not a successful painter by any commercial standard, but certainly a more fulfilled human being. When I was a teenager, his advice to me was, "Never work at something just for the money; find work you can care about." I have taken those words to heart.

The effects of parental words, actions, and values are laced throughout these interviews. Ray Mancison was haunted by the knowledge that his father gave up a musical career to sell real estate. "The idea that he didn't do what he wanted to do drove me insane." Conversely, Isabel Lucero's politically active mother established the template for her own commitment to public-policy work, as did Iliana Roman's blue-collar father, whose hard-working example she intends to repeat for her own children.

But what defines where a person comes from is more than the matter of immediate family; it's also a matter of class. My parents made it into the lower middle class, but at school and in college I was exposed to people of other classes, both lower and higher. This gave me the chance to talk with people who had widely different experiences and knowledge, and I benefited by my exposure to all that was outside my realm. Those connections fed my imagination and sense of possibility about a wide range of matters, including what work could mean in a person's life.

Mick Betancourt ruminates on class while pondering a way out of his blue collar background and job. "What it boils down to is connections and people you know . . . That's a force in the work world, definitely." Chico Pinex, raised and still living in an inner-city housing project, sees the world from a slightly different angle. For him, having a job is a matter of survival and dignity. "A lot of people, they look at me like, 'Yeah, I see you've found something better to do than just selling drugs.' . . . This job has changed my life."

The journey into the work world almost always involves learning about oneself, and at times those lessons can be bruising. Julie Baxter's internships resulted in more than realigned career plans: she found herself growing up on the job. "You really can't separate your personal growth from your growth in business." Of getting fired she says, "When it happens, you're really shaken. You might start to think, 'Nobody else could do this job,' but there's plenty of people who can." Wounded in a different way, Gillian Moore left a teaching job she loved because of harassment by her supervisor. "Even though I feel like a victim, I feel like a failure too, because I did make some key mistakes."

There is no way to underestimate the effect on your life of the person you work for. Very important, those bosses. They come in all kinds of shapes, colors, and sizes, and exhibit varying degrees of sanity and civilized behavior. After life under a number of different bosses, Kate Mc-Fadyen seriously evaluates any prospective employer. "This person is going to have a great effect on my life, well-being, and happiness over the next X amount of time. You have to work for awhile before you start to recognize qualities of people in organizations."

After graduating from high school, Credell Walls worked at a small grocery store where his employers offered him an important "bad boss" lesson. "If I was supposed to get ninety-six bucks, they'd pay me eighty-four. It was up to me to step up and say, 'This is how much I'm *supposed* to have.' If I don't say that, I'm not going to get my right amount. In a way, they were teaching me to stand up for myself—but that's not what they meant to do." Grace Tilsit earned an MBA and found a job in health-care administration, but suffered under a boss who repeatedly embarrassed her after she made an unfortunate work error. Eventually, she stood up to him and ironed things out, but she plans on leaving the administration field anyway. "It's great on your résumé and it's a great experience and people respect it. But does it fill me with satisfaction? No."

She is following Kate McFadyen's advice: "Never stay in a situation where you're unhappy. Never . . . It's not worth it . . . Keep looking and be inventive . . . Always look for more." I did the same back in the mid-seventies when young, restless, and dissatisfied, I dropped out of college junior year after having switched majors every other term, and went to work for a newly launched small alternative newspaper in Eugene, Oregon. But after a year or so, again restless, I moved to Chicago because one friend offered a place to stay and another hired me as a music club waitress. While figuring out what to do next, I found work through a temp agency. A week-long stint at a large food/luggage/and-I-don't-know-what-all-else corporation proved valuable. In my first exposure to "big business," I made an important discovery: that particular climate was not my kind of scene. Its culture was most definitely not my cup of tea.

My workplace, an enormous room filled with desks and female secretaries, was ringed by offices inhabited by middle-manager men. One day, a manager whose door stood near my desk, paused as I sat reading the newspaper during a lunch break. I looked up to find him eyeballing the orange peel I'd set on a paper towel. "Sometimes we have clients coming through," he admonished, nodding at the offensive display. I smiled, wrapped the orange peel in the paper towel, opened an empty drawer and put it inside . . . "Just till my lunch break is over," I assured him. "Don't you have a wastebasket?" He was impatient, irritated. I smiled again and offered an "I'm-just-a-temp" shrug. "No . . . Do you think you could get me one?" His narrowed eyes told me all I needed to know about my future in corporate America. To use the current lingo, there was "no fit."

My reaction was immature but sincere: I understood the validity of Mr. Management's concern about appearances, but I just couldn't bring myself to care, and frankly, hoped never to have to. And as journalist Marc Spiegler observes, "Who you are as a person is not going to change that much. You're not going to suddenly develop a great organizational skill or become someone who loves a routine. Figure out who you are in relationship to work and then look for a career that fits, rather than trying to *bend* yourself into a career." Me, I tend to stay out of a particular kind of corporate office as much as possible.

Both Spiegler and Robert Richman have forged self-tailored careers. Spiegler by seeking a new direction in journalism after a chance conversation with a woman reporter. Richman, by continuing along a path first trod in high school, where he involved himself in student government and community service. He says, "I always felt school should be about more than just books." They each stress the importance of being flexible, and Spiegler especially advises not rushing into just any career. "Time spent considering what you want to do is a good investment."

In many ways, I feel I'm still taking that time. Over the years I've waitressed and bartended, and also worked as an administrative assistant for politicians, screenwriters, and museum consultants. For a long stretch I worked at a radio station where fate plunked me down just a few feet from the office of radio host and oral historian Studs Terkel. Oddly enough, years earlier Studs had been one of my first customers at the music club. Daily contact with Studs eventually led to my own work in oral history; but, to put it mildly, I didn't exactly walk a straight line down my "career path."

Meandering has likewise been the path of Emily Hanford who, feeling pressured, dropped out of college for a time. "By not getting my degree, I put off getting the 'real job,' making the real choice. I was afraid of getting stuck." Carl Valentin is another whose career goal took time to come into focus. For years, his dream was to be a professional bike racer. "It was always work *so I could* . . . do whatever, usually race." But as time passed he realized, "I was fulfilling the dream of a fourteen-year-old, and as a twenty-four-year-old I had a different agenda."

In this book's first interview, T. J. Devoe, eighteen, speaks directly to the heart of the matter: "I think you have to know yourself, know what you want to do, and what you want for yourself in the future . . . Sometimes that knowledge doesn't come to you right away. You gotta experience, you gotta live, you gotta *do*."

But sometimes "doing" can be confusing. Educator Gabe Lyon poses her dilemma: "The long-term question is, where do you have an impact? Is it in a classroom where you see thirty kids a day? Is it with a whole school, working with the teachers who are seeing thirty kids a day? Is it writing so that perhaps lots of teachers read it? Do I work at a university and train teachers? What's going to let me combine the things that I really enjoy doing?"

Troy Graham sees his retail career path as a series of steps: "The computer company was my first step; the pet store was my second step; I'm looking for my third step, a bigger step." For Jeff Marcus, it's a matter of finding a way to combine his interests in wildlife and education. And Kate McFadyen, who went through college without a career plan—"Didn't care, didn't really think about it"—journeys her way through instructive internships, agonizing job searches and good and bad times at work on the way to crafting a career. "A lot of people's mistake is they don't keep their eyes open, they pigeonhole themselves . . . It's important for people to realize, 'Hey—life is fluid.'"

During this group's formative years, American business culture was in a frenzy of downsizing. I'm amused when I hear reports of old-school employers who describe the under-thirty generation as ruthless, disloyal, impatient job-hoppers. These so-called work mercenaries didn't come out of nowhere: their noses may have been sunk into algebra or English books, their attention focused on sports or computer games, but they weren't entirely oblivious to what was going on in the larger world. Julie Baxter recalls watching her stepfather's joy in his work fade. "I remember the tension in the house when he had to lay off one of his oldest and dearest friends. It did a lot to shape my views on corporate America." Even more disillusioned is the music promoter who himself survived waves of corporate downsizing. "The day comes when you realize that a corporation is an emotionless, unfeeling entity whose function is to make more money than it made the day before. That's when you understand that business, although it is run by humans, is not human."

While few of the young women recounted stories of out-and-out gender discrimination, readings of continued inequality surface. Says the guidance counselor: "There's lots of frustrations about being new, being young, and being a woman . . . It's like you have to speak louder than anybody else just to have an idea heard. . . ." When considering a career as a banker, Kate McFadyen noted, "You look at the people who are at the higher levels, ninety percent of them are men." Gabe Lyon, who says she benefited greatly from an internship at a women-owned and -run business says, "The idea that there's a glass ceiling, which is a reality for *lots* and *lots* of women, is not a factor in the way I think about things. I haven't run into one. Or I have and I didn't notice."

As for men claiming the role of provider, only Mick Betancourt and Chico Pinex, both from working-class families, expressed anything like concern about that. While talking about his future, and future wife, Betancourt worried aloud. "I can live on a box of rice for a week and a half—I've done that, it doesn't matter to me. But am I gonna be a good provider for Kate? I don't want her to see what I've seen, *ever*. When I have a family, I want to have money in the bank, I want security." Of his current job, Pinex matter-of-factly states, "It supports me, it helps support my kids, it puts food on our table." No one, male or female, said anything about men being the *sole* source of support in a family. Those days are long gone.

For adults, as we fax and e-mail, or cell phone chatter while shopping, dining, walking, driving in ever-increasing traffic, as we cram as many activities as we can into our semiconscious, sleep-deprived days, rushing to our job or jobs, rushing home, always rushing, it becomes harder and harder to hold on to or even catch sight of moments of meaning—much less to accumulate them into a substantial sense of connection with our daily lives as arenas filled with significant action. May the young, against all odds, push themselves toward significant action, take notice of what they are doing with their labor and why. Take notice also of whom it benefits, whom it damages; whom it enriches and empowers, whom it exploits and exhausts. May they look into themselves to discover what they're drawn to, good at, or simply have a need to do, and look outside of themselves to find out what might need doing in the world around them.

Whatever their experience, this group's sense of engagement is powerful. For many of the people I spoke with, work is not merely something to be gotten through: it is a thing to be grabbed, shaken and examined, to be fashioned and re-fashioned and re-fashioned again. On my desk as I write these words are my own college transcripts (I sent for them shortly before I began writing this introduction). My acquaintances had gotten me thinking, Maybe it's time for *me* to graduate. Maybe there are other kinds of work I can do, and maybe a return to school will lead me their way.

I study my college transcripts, think back to myself in my twenties, think about those in this book, and wish I'd known then what they know now. Jenny Petrow is one who has already learned the most important lesson. "In my senior year of college, I thought it just sort of happens upon you: this flow of light angel comes down and says, 'You will be a . . .' I don't think that's the way it is. You have to work it out yourself."

I

"No Timetable": Testing the Waters

G raduating from high school or college is an exciting, occasionally even traumatic event. Your identity changes as you move from being a high-school teenager to a university student or a worker; your connection to home loosens as you attend school elsewhere, move to a place of your own, or simply exercise your right to stay out later. You suddenly find yourself doing different things, thinking different thoughts, fretting about different matters. As recent high-school graduate T. J. Devoe puts it, "I wasn't really scared, but having this vast range of opportunity made me uneasy. I didn't know *what* was gonna happen." Jenny Petrow, in describing her first year out of college observes, "It's a tough year. It was for all my friends."

There are different ways to approach this transitory time. Some choose to pause before gathering their energies to pursue their intended goals. In high school, Devoe decided what kind of work he wanted to do, and he understood that higher education would play a role in achieving his goals. But he made the decision to postpone college in order to take a break from school and earn some money. At work, he paid attention to how different people approach their jobs. This helped give him a fuller notion of how he might develop his own career.

Gina Parks knew from the time she was a small child what she wanted her work to be, and in high school she researched how to prepare for her chosen field. She sees talking to people as one of the best ways to get information or assistance. "What I've found is that if you need a job or anything, tell *everybody* and someone is going to hook you up."

Troy Graham could have gone straight from college into the family business. But, as much as he emulates and respects his father's work and work style, he's chosen to strike out in his own direction. Through early work experiences he's learned a great deal about relating to customers and co-workers. According to Graham, "How to read people and how to talk to people isn't something you learn by reading a book."

Like Devoe, Max Leonard decided to postpone college in order to work. He's unsure what his career will be, but to Leonard all jobs are learning experiences, and he particularly appreciates opportunities to work with people who aren't like him. He urges young people to recognize that "each individual has to look at what's important to them, what interests them." Like Parks, he encourages people to "explore fields, investigate . . . When you meet people, think about where they are in the world and what experiences they have."

There is pressure to choose a direction; there is also one's own desire to make it the right direction. Unsure of her career path, Jenny Petrow struggles to find "something that I love, something that's me, *my* job. . . . People make me feel like I have to know what I'm going to be doing for the rest of my life . . . It might be difficult, but it's OK not to know, it's OK to try a bunch of different things."

For all the young people in this section, sure or unsure of their career directions, their early work experiences provided occasions for them to learn more about their own interests, skills, and perceptions—to learn some things about what it is like to be part of the world of work.

T. J. DEVOE

When T. J., eighteen, discovered music, he felt he'd found his calling. "I play drums in a band, and that's my dream, to be in music." He decided to take a semester off and earn money before entering college to pursue music studies. "I don't know anything. I can barely read music. I'm looking to learn different types of techniques so I can better myself as a musician." T. J.'s first job was at a supermarket. From the agony of being bored to the annoyance of conforming to the corporate image, "It shattered my idea of work a little bit." A mental-health facility data-entry job better suited him and increased his compassion for others. A summer house-painting stint was hard work, and he feels work at a flower store where he's currently a part-time employee is "the coolest job." Seeing a successful small business has given him ideas about what he might someday achieve. T. J. was in his first term of college when we spoke.

When I graduated from high school I was overwhelmed. People go through high school and they get to be seniors and they're like, I'm *huge* now. And then it's over and you've got a whole new life. I wasn't really scared, but having this vast range of opportunity made me uneasy. I didn't know *what* was gonna happen. But then I took the attitude that whatever happens, what matters is what I make of it.

When I was a kid, work was the farthest thing from my mind. I was thinking more about what it would be like going to high school. In grade school, I got into drawing and doing art. When I was fifteen, I found music, and that just *took* me, I fell in love. I used to write rhymes, and I rapped with these guys in a band. We didn't have a drummer, so I'd fill in. I didn't know how to play: it was just stick banging and loud noise, like what mothers hate.

I messed around with the drums a bunch, and then one day I found out I could separate, keep different beats and times. It's like being ambidextrous: you do two different things with your hands.

I didn't start loving music until I found out I could be good at it. I looked at music and thought, "I could do something with this." But it's not a perfect world, you don't always get what you want, it's not guaranteed. I needed to think about something a *little* more practical to fall back on. I looked at my choices and thought, "What do I want to do? Am I serious about music?" I had to ask myself realistic questions: What if I'm not good enough? So I'm majoring in sound recording and acoustics—I can work in recording studios. If I can't be performing, I want to be close to the business. But I worried, what if the recording thing turns out to be completely boring?

My band recorded something in a little studio last year, and it's buttons and knobs, thousands of them. I'm going to have to learn what every one of them does. But now that I'm in school, I realize it's not as drab as I feared. And my attitude is that I *have* to learn this to make the music sound good. It's for the music and that's what I love.

My mom and dad separated when I was real young. My mom's white, my dad's black, but people think I'm Mexican or Greek. I guess I don't talk like people's stereotype of a black man. My dad's been a cook in a hotel for ten years now and seems to enjoy it. My mom works at a place that has something to do with workers' unions, and also at a mental-health facility, doing stuff with client information.

I was fifteen when I got my first job. I needed money and my mom was always telling me, "Get a job"—typical parent thing. So I was like, I gotta do it, be responsible, and then I can buy things for myself. I got hired at the supermarket down the road. But I *hated* that job 'cause it was just standing around the whole time, putting food in bags. It was empty labor to me—it wasn't *doing* anything. I worked from around four until ten on school nights, and on the weekends till one in the morning. Basically, I'd punch in, stand at the register, put food in bags and give them to people. And then I'd go outside and get carts. We'd have to do that in freezing-cold weather and on blistering-hot days.

People would give me attitude and expect me to be all *happy*. "Oh, here you go, here's your food, enjoy it!" And look at this job I'm doing. People wouldn't be happy if *they* were at this end.

At the orientation, you spent the whole day sitting in the lounge where employees take their breaks. You watched movies on how to be a good bagger and then you went out and you were *bagging* . . . A good bagger packs the food without crushing fragile things, like fruits and bread. Cereal boxes go on the ends, so you have room in the middle. Just little tricks. That was interesting for, like, a split second. That's pretty much *it*.

They had their whole code of *smile* and *do this, don't do that*. And the outfit! For orientation you were supposed to wear a white shirt and black jeans. I didn't know, so I went kind of casual. I wore black jeans, but I had a white shirt with little black designs. When I went into the store for training, all the other employees were looking at me like "who's *this* guy?" One of the customer-service desk people said, "Tell that kid if he wants to keep this job, he's gotta wear the right outfit." I was embarrassed, but I didn't *know*.

Plus, I had crazy hair. It was long, but shaved on the side. I'd pull it back in a ponytail for work. Some of the customers looked at me like I was this big freak. It was weird 'cause I was just trying to be myself. I thought I could be myself and still do a good job. But they wanted this corporate company image, so being uniform and conforming was like a *big* deal to them.

There were older people there, in their twenties. They were all friends and had been working at the store for five or six years. They had their own little life together outside of the store, they'd socialize. It was obnoxious, 'cause they'd talk about this person or that person. You'd get tired of hearing the gossip, you wanted to hear something *else*. And I'm thinking, "How could you want to be a cashier for eight or nine hours a day and just stand there and get sore feet?" [He shakes his head in disbelief.] I quit because it was getting in the way of school and I just couldn't *stand* it.

Then I didn't work for awhile 'cause I was kind of iffy after that grocery store. After about six months, I was desperate for money. I got a job at the mental-health facility where my mom works—from the summer before my senior year all the way through that year. That job gave me a better outlook. My mom had worked there for fifteen, sixteen years, so everyone knew about me and they were real nice people. The only downside was that *everyone* knew about me—I felt like I had to live up to this image. People heard stories from my mom, "Oh, he's in art, he's in music," and then I would come in and would be like, "Here I am." It seemed to confuse people. They expected this huge vibrant personality, you know, and I don't talk that much, I kind of keep to myself.

The job was doing data entry—I learned how to type in school. Most of the time I was alone in a room. Sometimes I like to work by myself because then I don't feel I have to work *and* provide conversation, I can get down to business. I entered information about clients, their names and where they lived, and sometimes information about why they were in the mental-health facility—like if they had drug problems or were schizophrenic.

I'd look at people on the street and wonder what kind of problems they might have. Are they mentally healthy? You don't usually think about that. You get an idea that everyone's OK from the people you deal with, and from what you see on TV. You start thinking people who *do* have problems are just scummy and evil. But there are *so many* people with problems. I liked that the job gave me a different view. I'm a good listener, and when something's bothering someone I try and help. That job made me want to help people more.

The summer after high school, I took a house-painting job with someone in my band. I took it for the experience and to do something different. We painted for a national franchise that hires college students. We woke up every morning around six o'clock and went to job sites and worked on houses all day. At first I didn't like it 'cause of the routine. That was probably the most strenuous job I ever had. I'd come home with paint all over me, every day, sore feet, *dead* tired. But then I got into it and was like, "You gotta wake up every morning, you have to do this, stop complaining and *do* it."

My manager was really strict. You weren't allowed to get paint droplets *anywhere*. When you scraped paint, everything had to be clean, otherwise you'd have to do it over again, and spend extra hours cleaning what you messed up. We worked on a time budget. If you didn't get the house painted in a certain amount of time, you'd have to work on it without getting paid. It made you hustle. You had to maintain a constant speed, you had to pace yourself. [He claps rapidly.]

I enjoyed being outside all day . . . in good weather. Being with my friend, listening to music while we worked. Old people brought us lemonade, pitchers of root beer, brownies. They pretty much kept to themselves, just let us do our work. But we had houses where people were really picky and they would stand outside and watch. Or, like, if we were painting a window, they'd be on the inside looking out. When people are staring at you, expecting you to do a perfect job, that makes you more prone to mess up.

I never thought house-painting could be so *interesting*. I got into all the different tools you use. You have a "five-in-one," this little scraper tool that does five different things—cleans paint rollers, scrapes paint, it's a putty knife—and you have big scrapers and rollers. We'd go to the store and look all these paints and the way they mix them, so I got an idea of different paint textures.

I developed an extreme hatred for oil-based paint. [Smiles.] I had to paint all these iron rails with black oil paint . . . on one of the hottest days of the summer. I was a messy painter—not on the job site, but on myself. If I got paint on my hands, I would wipe it wherever. And I got this stuff *all over* me. My foreman said, "That's *oil* paint, that's not coming off for a while." I went home for lunch and showered—it didn't come off. On the hottest day of the summer, it's not great to have black on because it absorbs heat. That black paint was stuck on me for a week.

The foreman was twenty-one, and he was cool. He was on the job site all the time. As long as we kept to the time budget and got our work done, he let us take breaks, even when we weren't supposed to. But the franchise manager, he was a complete *jerk*. He only came on the job site every once in a while, to monitor our progress. When I first started, he talked to me like I was some sort of idiot. I'm painting, and he's like, "Oh, you want to do it like this and like this. And I'm like, "Well, the way I'm doing it, it still looks good." I don't always do it the textbook way, I form my own ways.

This job was full-time, five days a week. When I started, I was told we didn't have to work on the weekends. But sometimes we went over-budget on houses, and even when we didn't, the manager made us come in on Saturdays. The first three times I didn't say anything, but then it got to be *every* Saturday. Sometimes it would be on Sundays too . . . *NO*. I understand that I'm giving this guy my time and it's a job that has to be done. But when it's every weekend, and it's summer, and I just graduated . . . I wanted to have some fun, too. It was strenuous work and I needed a break. If you overwork people, they're not going to do as good a job.

I asked my foreman, "What's going on? I thought we got weekends off, I thought that's how it's supposed to be." And he said, "Yeah, it is." I felt like I was some kind of pawn, like *all* of us were. The manager would say, "I'm thinking about getting these houses done, I've got jobs lined up." I understood his position: he's got all these jobs lined up and he wants them done so *he* makes *his* money. He was selfish, just thinking about how everything's gonna work for him. Sometimes he scheduled budgets that were ridiculous, and those were the ones we would go over on. He wasn't thinking about our needs, or how if you want us to do a house in this little amount of time it's gonna look like *crap*.

We had this porch job—the worst job we had. Our foreman went back to school three days into the job. That left just me and my friend. We went over budget by a week. Our manager knew the foreman was leaving, he knew me and my friend were first-year painters. He should have known the job would take longer, he should have allowed more time. But he would say, "See this right here? That should take about two hours. And this over here, the soffit and the ceiling, that should take three hours." I guess he thought, "If there were two of me doing this job, we could do it in this amount of time." And I'm like, "Well, you gotta remember we're still rookies—we're not as good as you are."

An old lady lived in the basement and she would try and direct us without having any *idea* what she was talking about. It was sort of the blind leading the blind. She always called us by our names and it got to where I was sick of hearing my own name. "T. J., there's paint chips over *there*." She's an old lady, I guess you can't be too hard on her, but it was a nightmare, that porch, a big three-floor monster.

We had to paint everything: the posts, the roofs for each level, the floors, the stairs. We made a lot of sloppy mistakes 'cause we were over budget and we weren't getting paid for *any* of this. That made it worse. Each morning I dreaded going back because we weren't doing the quality we were supposed to do, the quality we really enjoyed doing. It was just painting. [Mimes slopping paint on.] Not taking any pride at all.

That bothered me because I liked making peoples' houses look nice, bettering them. We had some houses that were in terrible shape—ratty paint, peeling everywhere. And when we're done, the house has a sort of glow. You can stand back and look. *I* did that masterpiece—I made that house look *great*.

After the summer, I started working at a flower shop. A friend's parents own it—his mother does the designing, his father manages the store. I got hired around Christmas because they needed extra help. I put labels on mailers and the manager showed me how to wrap and do basic things around the store. I didn't know that jobs like this existed. I always think of work as serious, but this is fun. There are days when I'm wrapping packages and doing odds and ends around the store and it doesn't feel like I'm working. It's not at all like the supermarket job. I deliver flowers to people's houses and to hospitals and places all over the area. Flowers have an effect. I deliver to people that are sick or in nursing homes, and when they see flowers coming, everyone gets all happy and cheery. Offices are the craziest, everyone loses their mind— "Oh, is that for *me*?"

I never thought you could make so much money running a flower shop. My friend's mother is a great floral designer, and that was her dream. She's always studying flowers. She has meetings with other designers across the globe—she's been to Bangkok, in Thailand, and to Japan. I never thought you could do all these great things just by running a tiny little business. I'm looking at them and how they're living: as their own bosses, doing what they want. That makes me look at *my* situation and what I want to do. It makes me think about having goals.

I'd like to be my own boss. Maybe open my own recording studio, depending on how things go with my studies and music. I could rent an apartment and have the studio right in there, soundproof it and all that. All you really need are the resources and the knowledge. It's easier to think about the recording studio than wonder, "Am I gonna make it? Am I gonna be a superstar?" Taking a more realistic view is comforting. It makes my future more definite.

I want to do something that's gonna make me happy. I don't want to spend the rest of my life thinking, "What could I have done?" I don't want to sit back and think about all the things I could've been. I want to at least *try*, I want to take the chance. So, now I see what I want to do. I'm just striving for the goal.

I think you have to know yourself, know what you want to do, and what you want for yourself in the future, and then take the steps necessary to provide that. You have to go into every new situation thinking of how you want it to work for you. Sometimes that knowledge doesn't come to you right away. You gotta experience, you gotta live, you gotta *do*.

GINA PARKS

From the time she was in high school, Gina knew she wanted to be a guidance counselor. "My own guidance counselor had done very little. I wanted to do what she could *have done, but didn't." During a college internship, she worked at a facility for the severely retarded. Though it was demanding and occasionally frightening, "It gave me a total appreciation for life and for a lot of little things we take for granted." A public-school internship in a university counseling program gave her the opportunity to create a special program for ninth graders. That work eventually led to her current position at the same school (referred to here as Delaney High School, a pseudonym). But there were detours along the way, involving lessons about power, politics, and persistence. "It happens a lot of places, this whole struggle of being new to the job." From dealing with school-work problems to serious emotional issues, Gina, twenty-four, thrives on working in a diverse urban school setting.*

When I was growing up, my mother was a schoolteacher and loved her work. *I* loved her work. I'd go to school with her and help her correct papers. My father was a salesman, often on the road. They divorced when I was nine, and my mom went back to school to get a degree in computer programming. She was eventually rehired by the school system.

In high school, I took a battery of career awareness tests, but I already knew I wanted to be a guidance counselor in a school. The tests suggested careers like teacher, counselor, social worker, coach—all of which I now do. I went to someone who would know and asked, "If I want to be a guidance counselor and work with older kids, what do I do?"—because there's no undergraduate program in guidance. She told me to get a degree in education.

I did a lot of research on my own: I sought out information, I talked to lots of people. The thing that happens is you get motivated on one track. OK, you're on this guidance-counselor track. What about other things? What about child psychology? I went a roundabout way, but ended up where I'd intended to go. I now have a masters in education and counseling. I could work in a community agency, but I choose to work in a school.

In college, once I got into taking psychology, I had to do an internship. I worked at an organization for severely retarded male adults. I thought, "Oh my God, here I want to work with teens in school and instead I'm doing recreational counseling with twenty-one to forty-year-old men who have been in this home for most of their lives." It was scary, but I'm glad I worked there, and at some points it was great. They hired me to work one summer, but I continued working weekends throughout college.

At first it was tough because I was young, eighteen, and I was a woman—the place was mostly staffed by men. It wasn't so much a gender issue, except the patients were *all* male. [Laughs.] They'd been in this home for a *long* time and they looked at me like '*Whoooo*.' We tried to integrate the men into the community. I'd take them on trips, take them bowling, that sort of thing. It would be me and eight men, and some of them were *big*. I'm only five foot.

Once, we were going to a baseball game and I was driving the van, listening to some really corny love song and looking at these guys who would *never* experience that . . . I value my relationships with my family, my friends, and that's something they just didn't have. Sometimes I felt sad, but I didn't spend my entire time feeling sorry for them; it wouldn't have been productive.

I was attacked twice, which was very scary, because both men were what's called dually diagnosed: they were severely retarded on top of being autistic, or depressed, or something else. They could deal with the autism in some ways, but the retardation prevented them from thinking right and realizing, "Oh my goodness, this girl's here to help us and here I'm ripping her hair out."

The first time was on one of my fall weekend shifts, so I'd already been working there for a while. We were in a cafeteria. I'd been teaching them to put cans into the recycling bin. This one man had thrown his can in the garbage and I said, "That doesn't belong there. Do you remember where that belongs?" He said, "I don't *want* to put it there." I'm trying to explain things to him and the next thing I know he runs at me and grabs my hair. The others got him off of me, but I was petrified, very freaked out.

I didn't have to work till the next weekend, so I had time to think about what happened. My first thought was, "Wow, he hates me, he's angry at me." You don't want to work in a place where people don't like you or don't appreciate what you're doing. But I had gotten attached to some of the guys, and it would have been really unfair to *them* to let him drive me away—so I stayed. It took me a while to say, "He wasn't looking to hurt *me*." He was angry and he has all these different problems. You learn you can't take it personally.

The next time I saw him, he was like, "*Ahhh*"—like he was my best friend. Which was really hard because I was flinching. In your normal life, when one of your friends does something, you need an apology before you're ready to say, "We're friends again." And with someone like him, that won't happen. And because I was attached to so many of the men, it was hard to depersonalize *one*. But I think you have to do that in a lot of work—even in school. You want to make a connection, you want to care about the kids, but not so much that you're going home crying every night.

I never did any student teaching, so when I applied to the university's school counseling program, I hadn't had too much school experience. The way my university's program works is you're *thrown* in: you take your full load of course work, you go to school three days a week and you graduate in a year. At first they sent me to a middle school. I wanted to also be at a high school, but they couldn't find me one. I went to a friend and said, "Get me into your school one day a week—tell them I'll do *anything*." Delaney High School took me because they heard I

had computer skills. [Laughs.] I had a computer . . . My *skills* are still
limited. . . .

My own high-school graduation class was fifty-seven kids. You knew
what they had for lunch, what kind of gas they bought, everything.
This was my first experience in urban schools, and I was like jaw-on-
the-ground for the first three days: "You did *what*?!" An eighth grader
told me she had an abortion. That floored me. I was not mentally prepared for the urban nature or for the politics. They don't teach you
about that in the counseling program.

They teach you how to be a counselor, how to do therapy, and how
to work with different theories of development. You don't learn that
guidance counselors are disliked for this or that reason, or that teachers
have a certain attitude. Being an intern can be tough, because you have
this feeling of not knowing where you're supposed to be, what you can
do, what you can't do . . . It's a step that people *should* take before
going into the work field, because you can mess up and it's not the end
of the world.

At Delaney, most of the school population is Haitian, Vietnamese,
Hispanic, maybe three percent white. The diversity didn't hit me nearly
as much as the lives and the cultures that came along with it. While an
intern, I had a family come to me about a child who was having a hard
time at home and at school. The father said, "We discipline our child as
we feel necessary. This is our culture." They were Haitian and for them
discipline is *physical*. I'm looking out for this child and thinking maybe I
need to file some kind of report. I'm looking at this child like, I'm here
to help you, but . . . I mean, it's their culture. And, then, you also
don't want to totally disrupt a family.

In urban schools, you have people coming from so many different
countries. The kids act one way in Saint Lucia, but they get here and
they're put in a city and they're gonna act out. The family needs to adjust. Maybe they're living in a community of all Vietnamese families, so
in a way, the parents are still in their own community. Whereas at
school, the kids are immersed in something different all day long.
There's a constant pull. I see it in gang involvement and I see it in different kinds of substance abuse.

I found I was dealing with *families*, and it's tough. You're there to be the advocate for the kid, but sometimes the parents need more help. Sometimes, you want to tell the kid, "Hold on, I can't help you yet. First I've got to deal with your mom, or your dad, or your uncle, or your grandmother—whoever is taking care of you." You become an advocate for the kid, but the process can take time.

As I was finishing my internship, the school got a grant for a new transition program for ninth graders. They asked me and another new teacher to write it. They said, "Here's the idea—make it work." The program was to introduce ninth graders to college by bringing them to a university campus on Saturday mornings. Sort of college exploration, so they wouldn't be like, "College *schmollege*, I'll deal with it in eleventh grade." Because you *can't* deal with it in eleventh grade if you've screwed up your ninth and tenth grades. I explain to the kids how many points you need to graduate, what all this means. It's sad when you hear someone in their junior or senior year say, "What is that about? I didn't know!"

Through this program, I wanted the kids to get a feel for what college was like, that it was a life and a community, not just classes and a degree. One day we had a campus scavenger hunt. We sent them different places on campus: the bookstore, the health desk, the police station. They explored the campus, but they also had a goal, to get back first. It was fun, it was a game.

The idea was to use undergraduates as team leaders. I thought the kids should be in small groups, so they'd have a chance to get to know their team leaders well. Kids are intimidated by large groups and they'll cling to each other, not to the team leader. I knew it had to be fun. I knew that if you were going to get them there, you needed food. That's what gets me there on a Saturday morning! [Laughs.] We did a brochure, we recruited kids. I feel really proud because I know the program works well.

I worked on this with a woman from the university, and her concept was reading, writing, arithmetic. I'd say, "No, it's Saturday morning." She'd say, "I know, but you've got to give them *something*." I'd say,

"Believe me, if they're here from nine to twelve instead of at home, we've *already* given them something." The woman I worked with is the director of this whole program, and I'm more the program coordinator who's making it happen and recruits the kids—they come because they know me. She and I have different styles, but we talk about it, and we know that both approaches are good for the kids. I say, "You know a lot because you've been around." I need to respect that because there's so much I don't know. But while I may not be in touch with things like the state and federal educational standards, I'm *with* the kids, I'm *for* the kids and I'm *close* to the kids.

There's lots of frustrations about being new in a school, and there's lots of frustrations about being new, being young, and being a woman. It's like you have to speak louder than anybody else just to have an idea heard, and it could be a *great* idea. People are threatened: "If she does good, I look *bad*. If she does good, they'll like her, not me . . ." There's so much distrust. I don't know that *all* schools and businesses are like this. . . .

When Delaney High School found out that they were getting money for more guidance counselors, they decided to hire me as their ninth-grade counselor. And, as it turns out, the middle-school experience I had has been so helpful. I know what the eighth graders feel, I've worked with them. One of my jobs now is to go to middle schools and recruit—it's just like college, you want them to go to *your* high school. I want to show the kids the neighborhood of high school in order to lower their intimidation. I know what they're used to, and I can make comparisons between high school and middle school to ease their fear of new things.

I was glad to be hired at Delaney because I wanted to run the program I'd written. I was attached to it, I wanted to see it work. And I *really* wanted to work in an urban school. Kids in any school are needy. In most of the suburban schools, if their needs don't get met at school, someone else will meet them. Whereas in urban schools, sometimes school is the *only* place some of these kids will get resources and have their needs met. I felt like, if *I* don't do this no one else will.

And I really love the diversity. I love running into a student: "I'm new, I'm from Somalia." Of course, I'm like, "*Really?* Forget the schedule—tell me what's it like!" I love hearing about their lives, I ask a lot of questions. If you immerse yourself, you just get so much more out of this kind of work.

I worked there for a year and then was told somebody more senior wanted my position. This was about politics. I had experienced some of that as an intern, but this was *huge.* I was angry, because the kids I'd recruited were now going to get stuck with this guy and I knew he would do very little. I'd heard about him—he'd worked there before. I'd worked my butt off and coached track and done the mentoring program. I was doing a lot. I thought, "And this guy's gonna come in and just because he's been around longer, he has the *right* to this job?!"

But there wasn't anything I could do about it, and I had the summer off, so I decided to go abroad and worry about a new job when I got back. But I needed someone else to pay for my trip. [Laughs.] I called every organization I could think of. Someone I knew worked for the Soros Foundation and had heard through the grapevine that I wanted to go to Europe. She called and said, "You have a degree in counseling. We're sending people to Eastern Europe to facilitate workshops on peer counseling, conflict resolution, nutrition, health education. Would you like to go?" *Oh yeah.* What I've found is that if you need a job or anything, tell *everybody* and someone is going to hook you up. It's held true for me.

When I returned, I decided to use the same approach for getting a job. I told everyone. The principal at Delaney was wonderful. She said, "I'll find you something." I was hired by a school my principal had a good relationship with. The first day of school I called over to Delaney to see if the man who took my job had showed up. He hadn't. I'd suspected all along that he had another agenda—maybe it was just to piss someone off, who knows. I called the second day, he didn't show. I called the school where he used to work and sure enough he was still there. He had *no* intention of taking this job. The Delaney principal called my new principal and said, "I want her *back.*"

Earlier, when I found out I was losing my job, I called in a couple of ninth graders I'd become very attached to, to tell them I was leaving. Kids are kept in the dark about a lot of these kind of things and it's awful. They might not know that you had no intention of leaving, that you didn't even *want* to leave. Well, one day I'm sitting in my office and these same two girls come in. They give me this paper, it's like seven pages long: "To whom it may concern, we the ninth grade class feel . . ." It was a "Miss Parks Stay in School" petition.

I'm looking at it and I turn it over and they've got *hundreds* of signatures. They'd taken it to the superintendent of the entire school system and to the director of guidance for the whole city. They'd cut school to do this. I said, "Go tell the principal *right now,* because if she doesn't know when the superintendent calls . . ." [Laughs.] When I was hired back as the ninth-grade counselor I think the girls had a sense of "we *did* something!"

Ninth grade is tough because, first of all, they used to be the big kids, now they're the little kids again. Their bodies are growing, their hormones are going, they're like *vrrrooom.* They want to get jobs, they want to hang with the big kids. As long as kids have some sort of adult role model *somewhere,* they're in pretty good shape. The best thing a school can do is provide those role models every which way, through programs. And it's important to be a *good* role model, because everything you do, you're modeling.

I deal with everything from someone whose parents aren't taking care of them to kids meeting their parents' expectations in terms of grades. When the parent comes in and says, "How's my child doing at school?" they're often sent to the guidance counselor. Half of what I do is deal with kids that are cutting school, acting out, not doing their work. I like to hear from teachers, "So-and-so's not doing any work, but he's a bright kid—what's going on?" The chances are that behind all of that is the personal piece, and you're not going to help one side till you help the other. Everyone says there's guidance and there's counseling—but I think they go together.

The population I work with has had so many people come in and out of their lives that they need someone to say, "This is what I'm going to do for you and this is what I *can't* do for you." I deal with kids who are sexually active, not taking precautions, not getting enough information, kids with babies. I tell the kids they can trust me, and explain what confidentiality means. But I also say that if they tell me about something that puts them in danger, I *have* to take certain actions. Even if they say, "Please don't tell my mom, please don't tell my mom," I tell them, "It's my *job* to look out for you."

And there should be very clear limits: you have to set boundaries. I'm not their buddy, but I am young—and of course it feels better to have them like you than not. What I am is their advocate, and an advocate teaches and guides and does a lot of other things. But I don't think an advocate disciplines, because then they don't trust you. If the kids trust you, they may share something. If they don't trust anyone, they're going to live with it on their own. Sometimes you sense something's going on and you dig and dig and dig, trying to get some words out of them.

There was a student who rarely came to school and one day we had her in the office. She said, "I'm not happy with myself. No wonder I don't want to live, no wonder I don't want to . . ." Things like that. She led us to think she might hurt herself. We ended up calling someone and she's since been hospitalized. It probably made a lot of things really difficult for her, but it could have been a lot worse. If I can develop enough trust for someone to say, "I'm having sex with my boyfriend and I know this isn't right. I think I should talk to someone," then I feel I've made a difference.

There are kids I don't especially *like*, but I have to help them—it's my job, I'm their *advocate*. When drug dealers come into the hospital, nurses don't say, "You were selling drugs to first graders—I don't think I'll help you." When kids are with me and need help, they need it regardless of how awful they've been. There are kids who've said some awfully mean things to me. The ones that tell me to F – – off. Some of them can't help it, they have so much anger in them. I dislike it when they're rude to the girls; I dislike it if they do harm. I think to myself, "The reason I don't like you is because of *this*, and I've got to help you change or nobody else is going to like you."

When someone is hard to deal with, hard to take, and hard to *want* to help it's because they're not helping themselves. And some kids are just mean, they're bullies from the playground. You sit there thinking, "You know what? I'm going home stressing over this and you're not." I don't have a lot of work to bring home, but I do bring home the emotions of the kids. But if you don't have compassion, you're just not going to be effective.

So much depends on the school, and the system. As a counselor, you can go in and do paperwork and help fill out college applications and give career interest inventories and that's it. But in a school with kids with a lot of needs, you end up doing much more. I end up doing a lot of counseling because I *want* to. What's great is that you can make of the job what you want.

We have a guidance day and I do goal-setting with the kids, encouraging them to set very small, short-term goals. Their goals are always big: doctor, lawyer, professional sports player, media star. So to tone down or relate it to tomorrow is the best thing. "OK, where do you want to be?" They all write something down on note cards. "OK, if that's up there and you're down here, what's in between? What can you work on now? Can you work on your college applications? Not really. Can you work on your SATs? No, not in the ninth grade. But in the tenth grade you can get a book and you can start practicing."

I've been in classes where someone says, "Why should I bother doing this? I won't be alive in five years." You look at them and say, "I know that's a reality for you, I know that's something you're faced with, but you have *tomorrow*, and you have to do this." What's helpful to kids is when they get to see someone who *was* them, and see what that person's doing now.

We try to get the kids to think about careers besides the standard top five. So in school we do an activity where they build their own community and find jobs in that community—like mayor. People's perceptions about work are so limited. One time a friend of mine said, "It must be tough to sit behind a desk and fill out college applications all day long." I was mad—I had to educate her! Not about my job, but about how you don't *know* all that people are doing. She's a nurse and I said, "I guess it's kind of like taking people's temperatures all day long."

It's interesting to get the kids thinking about people who affect their lives as being people who have *jobs*. Like, to them, I'm Miss Parks, this person they know, not a possible job prospect. One student said, "Education this, education that—it's so important. But how much money do *you* make?" I said, "Nada." She said, "And business people and stock-brokers, they make tons of money." The kids know if they sit in the middle of downtown, they're going to see women in nice suits. They see the car I pull up in, the way I dress, they *know* I'm not making the big bucks. But I think I have a great job. I don't like the politics, and I don't like the way the system is—but the *work* I love.

I don't think you can keep doing guidance for too long and still be a service to kids. The first year I was like, "I'm going to do it *all*." Now I plan on being here five years, and that's *it*. Then I'm going somewhere else, to do different work. One reason is that I see all these burned out people and I don't want to be them; I don't want anyone thinking of me what I think of them.

As much as it's grueling, it's really fun looking for a job, because there are so many things you can do. And as I realized when I wanted to go to Europe, if you want to do something, there's a job for you to do; if it's gonna help somebody, someone needs it done. My advice would be to just head somewhere and you're going to find something. If it's not what you like, go to the next place. Eventually you'll find something or some place you like.

People get stuck on going after a job because they've met someone who does it, which can be great. But there are so many other jobs, jobs that you don't *see* people doing. You can major in something in college and then use that time to explore other areas. Talk to professors. Use the people there. *People* are the best resource.

TROY GRAHAM

Troy, twenty-four, grew up in the small town where his family runs a business. His father set an example of a good employer and satisfied businessman. After college, Troy was hired by a computer company where he benefited from his employer's interest in teaching him negotiating and sales skills. But after reaching the end of his learning curve, he left. "What isn't good for me is to get bored, because if I get bored then I don't work as hard, I don't have any drive to serve." Troy took a job managing the fish section of a local pet store and later helped manage the entire store. Being trusted for his expertise and honesty rewarded him; dealing with unhappy customers, hiring and firing staff, and the responsibility of managing educated him. He left the fish store a week ago and is now on the hunt for a new job. "The computer company was my first step; the pet store was my second step; I'm looking for my third step, a bigger step."

I grew up in southern Maine, pretty close to the water. From our house, you could see the lighthouses. It was a nice town, small. My high school was maybe five hundred people. My father and his father own a business that sells construction and paving equipment. My grandmother worked there for a while, and my mom and older brother work there now.

I sort of take after my father: he was always working, always doing something. When I was little I helped him around the yard and around the house. I've always had a strong work ethic. Helping out felt like something I should do; I didn't mind at all. My father definitely enjoys his work and he's good at it. I wanted to be like him. He was basically a salesman, and I figured that's where I would start out, in sales, talking to people. He's his own business owner, his own boss. Seemed like the way to go. [Laughs.] Still does, eventually.

In high school, I was a lacrosse player, and I went to a college with a lacrosse team. I looked at it as a way to keep playing and still get a legitimate career going. I studied business management, and in my junior year did a concentration in marketing. I thought it'd be interesting and might give me a small advantage when I went looking for a job. I thought, "I've gotta have a little something extra to get noticed." That comes from watching my father: he always seemed to know what was going on, he was always thinking ahead.

When I graduated, I didn't want to go back to Maine right off the bat. A friend of a friend needed roommates, and that's how I ended up in Boston. I had connections to people there who probably could have gotten me work, but I wanted to find something on my own. I didn't want to get a job, be unhappy in it and then feel obligated to the person who got me the job. I started looking for technically oriented entry-level jobs. I applied to small software, computer, marketing, advertising companies. I had some computer skills, but more interest than knowledge. I sent out lots and lots of résumés.

When I went on interviews, I bought a suit and got all dressed up. I was nervous at first. I worried, "What are they going to talk about?" and "What are they going to ask me?" and "Am I going to sound like an idiot?" In college, I read books about the basics of interviews and they gave examples of interview questions. But I was still nervous.

I hoped to find a place on the smaller side, where they wouldn't be afraid to say, "We'll show you what you need to know to get you going." I lucked out and was hired by a real small computer company. When I first started, there were two other people: the owner, who was from the Middle East, and a girl who ran the shop for him. She didn't have a big formal education, but she was very smart technically, she worked hard and she loved computers. She showed me around, showed me how everything went.

My boss was a nice guy. He was a business owner, so once in a while he'd get mad—but mostly he was right there beside you, and he'd help you with anything, from dumb stuff to something major. He liked to show me what he was doing and how he was dealing with this and that in the company. We were small, but with our dealers we'd have credit lines of $100,000. That overwhelmed me at first, that amount of money.

We sold everything: software, hardware, monitors. Most of our clients were in the Middle East. They'd call us up: "We're going to do this project and this is what equipment we need. Find it, price it, find out what it costs to ship it to us." That's how we spent most of our day, developing quotes of project machinery and equipment. We had seven or eight main suppliers, giant warehouses that basically had everything. And when the clients wanted oddball stuff, we'd go find it. We bought a car for someone's daughter; we also sent him a waterbed. We used the internet a lot.

More than anything, I learned computer skills, and how to deal with sales reps. I learned how they worked, and how our margins worked. You go through and look at the catalog price, and then you fight with them a bit, you learn what range they'll give you. You learn how to negotiate. I learned from listening to my boss and hearing what he'd say and how he'd say it. How to read people and how to talk to people isn't something you learn by reading a book. But we didn't actually speak with most of our clients due to time differences. Everything was through the fax machine, it was very impersonal. I wanted to be more hands-on—I feel more comfortable if I can talk on the phone or in person, I come across better that way.

That was a good first work experience, but after a while, I thought, "Well, I've gained quite a bit of knowledge, quite a bit of experience, but I've gone as far as I want to in this environment." By the sixth month, the job was getting more repetitive and less enjoyable. I was making as much as my friends were—it wasn't a lot, but it was enough to pay rent and have a little left over. I wanted to make more money. I explained to my boss that long-term, this wasn't what I wanted to do. He said, "I really like you and I'll give you a raise, if that's what you need." That was nice, but it made it harder for me to leave. He was good to the people that worked for him—if a big deal went through, he'd give us a bonus. I felt a loyalty to him and wanted to go out of my way to help him, and they counted on me. But I left, even though I didn't know what I wanted to do next, *where* I wanted to find a job, what field, what industry, what I *really* wanted. I just knew this wasn't the right place for me.

When I got out of college, I got interested in having fish tanks. I didn't know about water chemistry, so I did a lot of reading, trying to learn how to take living pieces of coral and keep them growing and alive. And how to take care of these very delicate fish that are shipped across the world. There's a big pet store not far from my house. I used to go down there all the time and one day I asked if they were hiring. I figured I could work there for a couple of months while looking around. The owner said, "We need people—you're hired. You can read and catch up on what you need to know."

The owner reminded me quite a bit of my father. He was a strong person and gave the impression that he knew what he was doing. He offered me a job as manager of the fish department. I was pretty excited because it was a lot to take care of: 15,000 gallons of water, *thousands* of dollars worth of fish to keep alive. The owner was breathing down my neck a bit because this was his baby of the whole operation—he *loved* fish. I planned on selling fish and tanks for maybe six months. It's retail, so people are always moving on. You don't get paid well and you work long hours.

Managing the fish department wasn't very hard to do; I didn't have to make a schedule or do anything with pay, or hiring. The work was all out on the floor. There were three or four guys, and it was basically, "You have to clean this, you have to clean that." Most of the workers were good, they were nice young kids. My biggest responsibility was taking care of the salt-water stuff to make sure the filters ran right. If pumps died, pipes broke, that sort of thing had to be fixed. It wasn't hard, it was just a matter of noticing. You gotta go through and clean everything, check for fish that are dead, not doing well. Once in awhile you'd come in and a pipe would have broken. Our store is 40,000 square feet, and we went in one day and had water on the floor from one wall halfway to another wall. We spent two and half hours cleaning up water, ruined dog food, all sorts of things . . .

We made house calls, we helped set up tanks. We'd get calls like, "My tank broke in the middle of the night." A guy that had 180-gallon tank, cracked in the middle! How does a tank crack in the middle of the night? Somebody hits it. So you get the van, load a new one up, and take it over.

We got a lot of, "All my fish seem to be dying. What do I do?" We'd be in at eight, the store opened at nine, and the phone would be ringing and ringing. People would come in and look for me, call and find out if I was there. That was exciting: it said I was being trusted and listened to, making an impact. The advice I gave people was good and solid and honest and open, so they said, "Hey, this kid knows what he's talking about."

When people would ask me, "What's a nice fish?" I'd steer them to ones that I liked. We had salt-water fish that would be in a bag for almost thirty-six hours, so it was amazing that *any* of them would live, let alone on a good shipment, ninety-five percent. Our tanks were way overcrowded, 'cause it was basically a holding facility. You wanted to get the fish out of a jammed-in area and find 'em a good home. You'd feel bad when you got somebody that didn't know what they were doing and didn't want to listen to you at all. I'd steer 'em towards stuff that was *real* durable, and try and teach them as much as I could.

We had a guy come in, he bought salt-water fish. He didn't want to talk to us, he wanted to buy *this*, *this*, and *this*—big, expensive fish. Salt-water fish are *delicate*. When things go wrong, they don't just get sick, they *die*. That happens a lot because they're hard to medicate. We asked him, "Is your tank set up?" Tried to get an idea of whether these fish would work out for him. He probably spent $350, $400 in one day. He killed off everything in a week or two and came back really mad. It was *our* fault, the fish were bad . . .

As a manager, I had to deal with customers who'd come in mad. I said, "I can test your water and then I'd like to talk to you about how the tank is set up and how it runs." There are big signs around the store saying, *no guarantee on fish*. If somebody comes through the door, they've killed their fish, if they act real nice, they bring us water to test, they listen to us, we have the liberty to say, "OK, I'll make the judgment—we'll give you credit." If they come in with a real bad attitude, we have the liberty to say, "Listen, you didn't want to talk to us before you took the fish home, so no deal." I told the guy, "We can't do anything." And he called and he called and he called, and he complained and he complained.

One day the owner comes out of his office. "This guy called me. What happened?" The guy had told him this big story that was quite a bit different from my story. The owner sort of laughed and said, "I'm not surprised." He called the guy back and said, "Listen, I'm getting a different story. I tend to believe the story on *this* end, but come in and I'll talk to you."

I saw the guy coming through the door and said, "I'll take you back." He was *really* mad and he didn't want to talk to me. Finally the owner calls me in and says, "We discovered what happened. We found out that Mr. So-and-so made some mistakes. He admitted that and said you did a good job. So we're going to give him a partial credit." I asked later, "What'd you do?" He said the guy kept trying to blame it on me, but the boss stood up for me and said, "No, he *didn't* tell you that." And the guy eventually just said, "Forget it, it's not worth it." The boss gave me a good piece of advice for retail: just because somebody gets in a fight with their wife at home, comes in and yells at you, that doesn't make it your fault. So don't worry about it, don't take it personally. I always remembered that.

I managed the fish department for about a year, and then they asked me to be an assistant manager in the whole store. The promotion was because they needed help. It wasn't, "Do you want to?" It was, "You *have to*." But I got put on a salary and my hours were cut back a little. In an industry that pays terribly, I started making more than people who'd worked for our company for a long time.

When I started as assistant store manager I was nervous. I'd had my little group in the fish department, but I knew more than them, so they sort of looked up to me. Now I had a lot more people to deal with. To be a good manager, you need to be able to read people. They don't always react the same way, you have to approach them differently. So it was much harder, but it was also good because it was a little more challenging, it didn't come quite as quickly, it didn't seem as easy to do.

I had to learn how to drive a forklift, and how to get things off the top storage units. I knew a lot about the store itself, I knew where things were. But I didn't know much about reptiles and birds, and dogs even. If somebody said, "I want a rabbit—what exactly do I need for a rabbit?" or had a question about snakes, I'd say, "Here's the book section, let's go find out." I think people were happier than if I'd made stuff up.

My group in the fish department was very dedicated to "yes, I'm going to show up when I'm supposed to show up, be there on time." In the rest of the store, we had high-school kids that enjoyed it but didn't really care a lot. So at the last minute, two people would call up and say they were going to a concert instead of coming to work, and it would be, "Great, now *I've* got to stay." I'd have been there since eight, now it's four and I want to go home, but I gotta work till ten—and then I gotta be back the next morning at eight. Last summer, three or four of us ended up working seventy-five hours a week a *lot*.

I had a hard time with people that really didn't care about what they were doing. I wasn't used to saying, "Go do this," and then having to check, make sure it was done. Somebody would say, "Oh, can I go on lunch break?" I'd say, "Well, I asked you to do something twenty-minutes ago, you didn't do it. You gotta do that before you can go to lunch." That was hard, because some of these people were older than me, or had been there a lot longer.

The hardest part was if somebody was really screwing up. The first person I fired was a kid who wouldn't do what you'd tell him to do. One day, another kid who worked part-time said, "What's *he* doing working here?" I said, "What do you mean? He's doing alright." It was his first couple of weeks. The kid said, "He shouldn't be working here, he steals stuff." He told me the guy had worked at another store, and that his friends would come in on his break—they'd be wearing big jackets and he'd give them stuff to take out. After that, we kept an eye on him. He'd call in, not show up, come in late. Then we started seeing his girlfriend come in when he was on his break, but we'd never see her leave. Finally I said, "You're not working out." He was mad about it, but I guess from his reputation, being fired wasn't new to him.

When we'd be hiring, the most important thing was someone's personality. We had people that weren't at all like myself, people with nose rings and lots of tattoos. I didn't look for somebody that knew everything. I looked for somebody who was outgoing, who would look you in the eye and be able to carry on a conversation. I looked for a real open, honest type of person. We'd always ask, "Are you willing to learn?" And everybody's gonna tell you they are—but do they sound sincere? 'Cause those people you can deal with and train. We had a kid come in, he said he was the best person in the world and knew everything. But he rubbed everybody the wrong way and he didn't get hired. Being arrogant doesn't work in a retail situation.

If I wasn't in a good mood I'd be very quiet and go clean tanks or something, try to get off by myself. Sometimes with employees I'd say, "I'm just not having a good day." If anybody had a problem, they could say, "Listen, I gotta get out of here and take a walk." If you really had to, you could. Everybody understood that. Especially at first, people are afraid to let anybody know they're having a bad day.

The owner was a good salesman. Obviously, not everything he sold was *essential*. He would sell people more things than I would. I'd be more likely to think, "they don't really need this." I definitely felt a loyalty to him, because he worked so hard. You'd see him climbing a shelf to get something down for somebody, which was impressive to me.

Most of our staff was scared to death of him, which I never understood. You'd walk through the store with him and you'd see people going the other way. He would tell you, "This is wrong, this has to be cleaned up," whatever . . . He wouldn't do it to be mean or spiteful, he'd do it because he wanted his store cleaned up. And it wasn't his personality to go out of his way and tell you, "You're doing a real good job."

I'm ninety-five percent sure I don't want to be in retail my whole life, and after a year and a half there, I wanted to do something else. I don't mind working a lot of hours, but I want to do it where there's a chance for growth. We had people get mad and quit, saying, "I hate this person, that person. I'm quitting, I'm outta here." That's not a good way to leave. I told my boss, "It's just not where I want to be for the rest of my life." He said, "You did a real good job and we don't have any problems with you. I'm sorry to see you go."

Now is the scary time. I quit without having another job. I said, "I'm going to look," every day for about a month. But it's way too easy not to look, or not to look very hard. At first, I'd look through the paper and not send any résumés. Now I send résumés every single day. I've probably sent out twenty. In about a month I'll *have* to take something, even if it's some crummy job, just to get by. I'm not too worried yet. People have been suggesting temp agencies and recruiters. I'm hearing that a lot of companies are going to headhunters, hiring people through recruiting companies.

You have to try things, and if they make you happy, *great*. I say eventually I want to be my own boss, and ideally I do. But I don't have enough real direction to rule anything out yet. At the moment, I want to get onboard someplace where I can grow, start putting my time in, do well, and go up the ladder. Someplace where I can make good money. I'd love to have my next job be my job for ten years, twenty years, thirty years. I'd like to get into a company, or even just a field that I want to stay in for a *long* time.

You have bad days, and sometimes it's hard, but you have to have some sort of bond with your work. Enough of a bond to say, "I want to do this, I want to be here. It's *worth* my being here." The biggest thing, I think, is to figure out what you really want to do.

So no, I'm not going back to Maine, not yet. I couldn't go work for my father right now. My brother, he really enjoys it, he's happy there— but I'm not sure I would be. If I went back it would be real easy for me to say, "This is where I'm going to be for the rest of my life." I want to make sure that I don't want to be somewhere else first.

MAX LEONARD

Before leaving high school, Max worked at an office and as an apprentice carpenter, both useful work experiences. For Max, nineteen, everything is a learning experience. "I don't feel that going to school for four years is an education that prepares you for the world. I'm trying to construct that type of education for myself." Max decided to take a year off before college, despite pressure from peers and others. He spent that time participating in City Year, which is essentially an urban peace corps, about which he says, "I have inspiration for years saved up from this experience." Working in a public-school classroom, organizing a volunteer project at a homeless shelter, speaking to groups about City Year, and being a role model to younger kids, are just a few of the things he did. But there were also frustrations and disappointments, as well as hard lessons about group dynamics and priorities. Max is open to almost any experience, as long as it's fully engaging. "My one real hate in life is wasted time."

I don't look at jobs as *just* jobs, I look at them as learning experiences. I really want to get the message out to high-school students and guidance counselors: there are lots of ways to learn through employment. You have to be careful though, because you can also *not* learn through employment. I have friends who work full-time in a video store. It's not that I judge them, because they may be doing great things with their free time and learning a lot that way. But these are valuable years, years where you need to be exploring. If not through books or lectures, then maybe through traveling the world, or exploring one's city, or trying different jobs.

I'm a big supporter of internships because the amount you gain from hands-on work is valuable and important. I've done City Year, and when I get into college and am studying social, urban, and poverty issues, I won't be talking out of some notion I've developed after thirteen years of school—from my teachers' opinions, my classmates, books, my parents, wherever. I can talk from my experience working in the public schools in Boston, volunteering at soup kitchens.

My parents both work in education, and I learned a lot about work from their way of approaching everything in life: asking a lot of questions, trying to completely understand the situation. My first job was when I was fourteen, working for an education review. My mother's office was on their floor and she heard they needed somebody to do mailings. I did office work, stuffed envelopes, things like that. I came up with all kinds of little systems and they appreciated that. They said people who had previously done the job, people a lot older, came in and did the same thing the same way every day. I've done mailings for other jobs and still use some of those techniques. Whenever I do a job, I try to do it the most efficient way; I keep revising my methods and looking at the results. That's just how I operate.

The people at the review were really nice. They'd give me a little Christmas bonus and tell me, "You don't have to work so hard, take some breaks." But I'd go in and challenge myself. "I bet I can get this whole pile done by five." I would time my work, to keep from getting bored. If I had just sat there, hadn't thought about how to improve things, I'd feel like I'd wasted my time.

At pretty much every job, I've had a good relationship with my employer. One reason is that I make an effort to be responsible and honest—if I forget what they told me to do, I ask questions. And I've been lucky to have reasonable bosses—I've heard stories about bosses who aren't. So those qualities, being honest and responsible, and trying to come up with better ways of doing things, have been the keys to my success with employers. I've found most of my jobs through connections, but for City Year, I applied. You *had* to apply to be part of the program.

A few summers ago, I accepted a job that paid very little, as an apprentice to a cabinet builder, and I worked for him again the following summer. Some people were like, "Well, how does that expand your mind? It's just labor." And, in a way, it is—it's physical work, there's no doubt. But that was great for me. I grew up in an intellectual community and working in a carpentry shop, getting to understand a whole different mentality about work, was educational. Plus, you make measurements, use mathematics, learn to use the tools. I learned things that may end up being more valuable in my life than some of the intellectual stuff I've learned. If I ever have a house and access to tools, I can build furniture, tables, cabinets. I'm looking for jobs in New York, and carpentry is a good experience to have had. Last summer I did construction work because I wanted to get a sense of that field.

After high school, I took a year off before going to college. People said, "Oh, you should go straight to college." I was *blown away* by that reaction. People pressured me, everyone from my barber to kids at school. "I thought *you* got good grades." I was like, "Yeah, I did, and I got into every college I applied to." They couldn't understand why I'd want to take a year off. But also a lot of people said, "I wish I'd done that." Even if no one had opened their mouth, it would have been a difficult decision. All my friends were leaving and going to school, and I wasn't. I would argue that's a more responsible position, sometimes, than just saying, "OK, college next." So on one hand, I pat myself on the back, but, on the other hand, if my parents hadn't been supportive I might not have done it. It was scary.

How I got involved with City Year was I did the City Year Servathon, which is like the walk for hunger, the walk for peace. People pledge money, but instead of walking, you do service. At the end of the day, money is raised and your city is a nicer city. That's the idea behind it. It's a youth community service program committed to being diverse economically, racially, and in terms of age and gender. Part of its mission is to develop young leaders and good citizens. It's basically a national urban peace corps. So I did the Servathon, and then I wanted to do more.

People have different economic situations which do or don't allow for that kind of volunteer service. I'm very privileged in that I've never had to worry about money. I did volunteer work full-time last year, hooray for me, but I was living at home. I have friends who did the same thing *and* had to support themselves. City Year gives us a living stipend, $135 a week, taxable. The minimum number of work hours to graduate is seventeen hundred. Some people had seventeen hundred and one, but a lot worked more hours than that—I had over two thousand hours, and I was by no means the only one. At the end, you get an Americorps award for school. There are eight, about to be nine, City Year sites across the country.

At City Year, you're on teams of about ten people. There's three kinds of teams. Eighty percent are human service teams, working with children or the elderly. There's teams that do physical service, which would be like building playgrounds, disaster relief. Then there's curriculum teams, which get trained in teaching—maybe about drug abuse, HIV/AIDS awareness, domestic violence . . . It can be about any issue. If there's a service partner willing to train a team, City Year can find money to sponsor the team. The types of experience you could get there were pretty much endless, it just depended on your interests. There was flexibility: you could find new projects or work on new site development. It's a public/private partnership: money comes from the federal government and from corporations in the area.

Everyone in City Year wears a uniform. I'm not really for uniforms, the idea of them is a little scary to me. But in *this* situation I'm very much for them. People have preconceptions about teenagers and about teenagers of certain races. You have kids going into all different neighborhoods. When people see you in the uniform, they know they can trust you, that you're helping. Some on my team had graduated from college, grown up in rich areas; some had dropped out of high school and were in trouble with the law. One of the incredible things about City Year is the types of friendships formed among corps members, and I think the uniforms helped break down barriers.

Any time you're in that uniform, you're working. No one can go to a bar in that uniform, you're not supposed to litter or jaywalk. We got free transportation passes, we were public transportation ambassadors. We were on call to help anybody, give up our seat any time someone needed one. You're really supposed to be a model citizen. I'd walk down the street and little kids would get so excited, or people would stop and congratulate me for what I was doing, sometimes ask for help. It's a great feeling.

The program has an identity and you become it. They tell you when you start: "City Year is bigger than you. You're not just representing yourself. When you step into that uniform, you're not just Max." Little kids call you, "Hey, City Year!" and *you're* City Year. You have to be willing to bow to that to some extent. You have to be ready to sacrifice "I" and see the bigger picture. You have to be ready to work with a diverse group of people, people who may not understand the words you use, people who may have preconceptions about you.

In a lot of ways, City Year is like the army, it's just a different kind of service. I feel that I worked hard for my country this year. I think City Year should be funded the same way as the army. If we had anywhere near that kind of money, it's amazing how much we could do for the country. And not just band-aid work. The work we do with children gives them a different outlook on the world. City Year's hope is that someday the question asked of every eighteen-year-old will be, "Where are you going to do your service year?"

We do calisthenics in the morning in public places, to build a sense of community among ourselves. We often do it where corporate people are walking by, to remind them there are young people out here who aren't selling drugs and stabbing people, young people of all races, working together. It inspired people to see it, it inspired me to watch my peers do it. Especially once I got to know them and what was going on in their lives and how much they were giving.

But it wasn't a perfect experience. A lot of things were frustrating during the year. There were times when I felt like City Year wasn't working, that it's an organization with a good idea, but . . . What kept me going was the idea that an organization is really its mission. And I love City Year's mission.

My team worked in a school. Some people teach, some help kids learn how to better interact with each other, some tutor just one kid. I was in the same first-grade classroom, all year, four days a week. I worked in Roxbury, at a bilingual school, Cape Verdean and English. It included special-needs students, and students with really serious physical or mental disabilities. I also helped in City Year's recruitment office and gave presentations to high schools, colleges, community centers, a gay and lesbian youth organization, whoever was interested in City Year. I went to Atlanta to recruit at African-American colleges, I went to a youth peace conference.

I was the project coordinator for the City Year Servathon, which meant that I went to one homeless shelter, learned all about it, talked with the volunteer coordinator there, and figured out what work could be done. I brought people from our team sponsor, an investment company, on the day of the Servathon. Had everything set up, jobs ready to assign, taught them about City Year. I was in charge and I had all these people from the investment company looking to me: "How do we do this, what do we do?"

We try to get the sponsors involved, we send them newsletters and e-mails. We try to have corps members learn about what it's like in corporate America through their corporate sponsor. But we weren't too successful with our sponsor, we had limited contact. Their community service office had good intentions, but something definitely went wrong. They said they'd have five hundred people at our Servathon, about fifty showed up. There was resentment on the team, because we were all psyched, we had these huge projects for them to do. They let us down in a major way. I wanted to say to them, "It's great you give us money, but we had a homeless shelter to paint, and you weren't there, and that's what we're about."

You're supposed to learn to work on and as a team, but my team didn't do so well. I'd expected everyone to have the same level of commitment, but people had different reasons for being there. Some were there *just* to work in the classroom, and after that they wanted to take off. Some didn't want to be at City Year, period—they were trying to stay out of jail, or had been kicked out of college. There were interesting team dynamics, and we worked through some things—we still did a lot together. But we definitely had communication and motivation problems.

We had hours and hours after our classroom work when we were supposed to do stuff as a group. I worked hard on getting the team together, but some people didn't want to hear it, they just tuned out. People were late all the time. Maybe because my team leader was new, she wasn't sure when to lay down the law. I was always saying, "We had a problem yesterday, let's talk about it." I'd be like, "Somebody, say something." I'd share with the team something I'd written the night before about how I felt. "Does anyone disagree? Agree?" Everyone would just sit there and look at me.

This went on for a while, and I felt like I was getting nowhere. No one appreciated the work I was doing on the team and some people actually resented it. To be honest, what I did was give up. With the time I wasn't in the classroom, I started doing administrative work around the City Year office, and *that* was appreciated: "Great, we never thought of doing it this way." I don't know if it's that I love praise, or that I just want to feel what I'm doing is important. I guess I need to feel that someone cares about the work I'm doing. I got a lot out of working in the office, and I gave a really hard try with the team—I put a lot into it. But I do feel bad, because I don't like to be a quitter. I don't like to fail.

One of the things I liked most was being a team leader for the Young Heroes program. This was started by City Year Corps members when an eighth grader said, "Why can't we do City Year? We want to help the community too." The Young Heroes program goes for fourteen Saturdays. Half the day is spent learning about community issues and the other half doing community service. Same thing: diverse teams, a lot of team-building, two team leaders, one male, one female, usually of different races. Taking that leadership position with younger adults was inspiring. I was a team leader with Nyari: she's African-American, about my age. We're very different: she was in the ROTC and was more disciplined; I was more nerdy and lax. But we complemented each other. We learned to adjust to each other's ideas, to accommodate our different styles, and we got along well.

I learned from watching *my* team leader that if you don't set high expectations from the get go, pretty much everything goes wrong. In some ways, the first day is the most important day of the year. If people are late and you don't say anything, they're going to be late again because it becomes acceptable in their mind. Then everyone gets the message that it's OK to be late. My team leader was into letting the team lead itself, which was good, but you also need to have expectations. She tried to establish them later on when all of a sudden the team was in a shambles. No one would show up, and it'd be, "OK, you're going to get written up for this." [Shocked.] "What?! But *he* didn't get written up!" And then it's, "Is it because of my race? Is it because you don't like me?"

From the beginning Nyari and I agreed we'd take this seriously, talk about expectations, really lay things out. I like to explain: "this is what can and can't be done," "this is how to appeal things," "this is what's going to happen if you do wrong." We gave people chances, but we set a standard to start with, and we made it clear how much of a chance anybody would get.

There was some difficult stuff. We showed up at service projects, the service partner wasn't there with equipment or something, and so you have to be creative. And the kids, they're let down. One of the best times was when we went to an elderly home . . . I was a little nervous, to be honest: ours was a small team, just six kids, all hard workers, very energetic. There were other teams, and *all* the kids have a lot of energy. I was also nervous because elderly people come from an era where things weren't so racially integrated. On one hand, we want to open their minds, but on the other hand, we want to be sensitive to them. *And* this place was run by nuns.

I kept saying, "Guys, no matter what anyone else does, I need you to be focused." They'd be, "Yeah, Max, we understand, we're cool, we get it." But I was still anxious. It can be scary for kids, even me, to see people whose bodies or minds are falling apart. We got there and the way they interacted with the elderly people was so moving. The kids weren't at all, "Oh, she's crazy." There was no horsing around, they weren't rude, they didn't make fun of people with disabilities, they were genuinely nice.

We brought all the older women in wheelchairs down in the elevator, and one of the more rambunctious kids was making conversation. He's a handsome young guy and he was giving them lots of attention, being very gentle and friendly. The girls on my team painted the older women's nails and would tell them how beautiful they looked. We had a microphone and some of the kids sang songs with the older people. There was a lot of energy, but it was so positive, the level at which it was displayed was so correct. You hear such negative things about young people, and to see these kids who have such good heads on their shoulders was really great. Afterwards they said they knew how to act from watching the way me and Nyari did things. That was so incredible to me, to be a role model.

A lot of the kids have dealt with much more difficult issues than I have. They would talk to me about all sorts of things. They respected my opinion and I respected them. At the end of the fourteen weeks, they talked about how at first they were surprised by how close Nyari and I were. We'd give each other hugs and joke around, be buddy-buddy. That we could be so different and be bound together by this commitment to service and by similar values meant a lot to them.

It's important as a high-school kid to take time to look at your life, take yourself seriously, not sell yourself short. If you're from a rich community and your parents have always expected you to be a doctor or a lawyer, don't accept that you have to do that. Sometimes people think *everyone's* ideal is to be the doctor or lawyer. Each individual has to look at what's important to them, what interests them. There are many different paths, and you need to seek them out because they're not always going to present themselves. Explore fields, investigate.

I'm lucky because, through my parents and their friends, I have a huge network. I've been able to find adults to ask about whatever I've been interested in. If you aren't so fortunate and you do a program like

City Year, hopefully you'll meet people like me—I try to share my resources, and people share with me. If not, start to build those networks. When you meet people, think about where they are in the world and what experiences they have. Think about how you can tap into that, how people can build off each other.

When people ask if they should do City Year, at first I'm always, *yeah*. But I also warn them that it's hard and sometimes it might really suck. But if you believe in it and stick with it, embrace whatever you're given to do, I don't see any way that it's not going to be educational. If you believe in the mission, you'll get something out of it no matter what. Whether you're making mistakes or doing everything right, you're *learning*.

In the future, I'd like to make a good living, so I'm a little nervous about entering the work force. Being self-employed is hard in terms of taxes and health care and everything else. But I can't imagine having one job forever. I joke about going to New York and working on Wall Street—it's really not the avenue I see myself going down. But why judge that? Why not give it a shot? You try these things. The worst that can happen is you learn it's something you *never* want to do again. To be honest, I hope to start something, to find a need and create something to meet that need.

I'm still not ready to go to college. I'm moving to New York next month and have applied for a job at a software company. I'm not particularly interested in software, but it's a small company and they're at the make-it-or-break-it stage. My dad knew somebody there. I wore khakis and tucked my dress shirt in for the interview. I used to hate doing that. I got there and they were all wearing jeans. But it was good I dressed up: it showed I took the interview seriously. I'm maturing a little in that way. In the long run, I have no idea what I'll end up doing. Maybe I'll love the software business. I'll give myself a chance to see.

JENNY PETROW

When we talk, Jenny, twenty-three, is days away from leaving her current job for Spain. A cellist since she was seven, she chose not to become a professional musician: "While I loved music, I hated practicing." Since college, she's struggled to determine a career path, connect with work she'll find meaningful. She knew she wanted to travel abroad and a temporary job with an English-language program exposed her to people from all over the world and gave her an education in office life. She dove into dealing with databases, immigration forms, immunization matters, meal plans, ordering office supplies, organizing—and the lively, sometimes aggravating task of responding to the demands, problems, and attitudes of the students. Jenny struggled through a period of feeling underpaid and undervalued. But she left the job having learned much, including, "skills you don't learn in college that you have to learn quickly when you get out." Still unclear about her ultimate career, she says, "I always tell people I know the components of my dream job—like it's a jigsaw puzzle and I just can't find the box cover."

My parents separated when I was in sixth grade and divorced around ninth. My mom worked part-time. She had a masters in music and taught eurythmics,* and also gave recorder and piano lessons. Now she's a psychologist. My dad's an inventor, a chemist, and he always had experiments going on in the house. I remember when he was working on a scent-free perming lotion. In the bathroom, you'd find swatches of hair on towel racks; you'd go into the living room,

* Body movement to music.

swatches of hair on the mantel; into the kitchen, open the toaster oven, hair drying on the rack. [Laughs.] So his work came into our daily life. And now that my mother's a psychologist, that *always* comes into our daily life. "Jenny, why do you feel you have to yell at me like that?"

My father's a genius and knew from the day he was born what he was going to do. And my mother loves being a psychologist, she's totally involved and engrossed. It's very different from my friends' parents, who work for software companies and hate it and quit. I feel I have to do something that I love, something that's me, *my* job. I plan on being successful, and I plan on being very good at whatever it is I end up doing. I don't know what that is yet, but I'll be *damn* good at it!

When I went into college I was thinking about law school, but once there I started having weird ideas that weren't very helpful. I thought that anything professional, like banking or consulting, was a real sell-out. I always mocked those people who tracked—medical school, law school, financial track, MBA. This is going to sound conservative and weird for me, but I wish I had started thinking about work sooner. I don't know whether that would have changed anything, but I wish I had. I have friends who are in the same boat as me: a lot of us are doing our search after graduating from college.

In college, I majored in the humanities and loved that. I took classes in history, art history or music, literature, philosophy. It was an interdisciplinary program which looked at how everything is interconnected. So now I know I care about these things: art, music, history. But do they have to be my job, or can I enjoy them separately from my job?

My biggest problem is that I like a lot of things, but I can't figure out what's the thing I *love*. I don't want to spend money on graduate school if I don't love what I'm going to study. I'd rather test things out making money than spending money, so working is a good way to go about it. But I don't want to waste my time at a job if it's not what I love.

I did work-study all through college, and for three years worked at the university labor relations office. I should have stayed the fourth year, because that's when everyone went on strike and it would have been an interesting time to be around the office. Senior year, I spent a lot of time looking in career services. They had all these binders for different job areas, and sometimes job postings. But I didn't want to be an investment banker. I didn't want to be a consultant, because I didn't want to spend my life firing people. And I didn't want to be a paralegal because people told me it's really boring and it sucks—if you want to learn about law, go to law school. And I didn't care about making a lot of money, except to pay off my student loans.

I had spent my junior spring term abroad in London and had the *best* time. I really wanted to go back. So, senior year, I researched connections in London: everyone's brother, sister, aunt, uncle, former employer . . . A friend gave me a book listing companies that hire abroad. Generally, the book is for the established businessperson, someone who's already in a managerial position. I have a friend who was hired to work at a record company in London. She wrote 165 cover letters and got 164 rejections. She started hanging them on her wall, which probably wasn't good for her psychological well-being. [Laughs.] I never sent out blind letters, or did the kind of search she had done. I was hoping for something to just *happen.*

After graduation, I went to Italy with a university orchestra. My best friend was dating the tour manager and she said, "Jenny, you should come along, I think they need cellists." And then later she said, "Well, actually they don't need cellists, they just need someone to carry stuff." I had to pay $500 to carry a timpani! [Laughs.] It was a very bare-bones tour, so they didn't hire a road crew. They had a truck, about four or five feet off the ground, with no ramp. We'd have to move harps and basses and timpani with this eighteen-year-old Italian hormone named Rocco. He didn't speak a word of English, so we did a *lot* of signing.

Soon after returning from Europe, I heard about a job through a friend of my mother's. It was with an English-as-a-second-language program, a residential program. The administrative assistant was leaving in a week and the company hadn't even posted a job announcement. They needed someone right away—they had new sessions every month, and it was the second busiest month of the year. They expected about eighty students to arrive two days after I started work.

The day I went in for the interview, they said, "We'll hire you. Now can you type up these labels and file these papers?" And I was like, *"Great!"* The woman whose place I was taking was whispering, "Don't work here. Why are you working here?" I said, "Well, I already took the job, so . . ." They told me it was for two months, so I was like, "OK, and by then I'll have figured out how to go abroad and I'll just go." They put out the job posting and hired someone and I trained her. Then I sort of hung around because they needed an activities coordinator, and then they hired one of those. But then the woman I'd trained went on maternity leave, so I came back and did her program-assistant job again.

Administratively, the program assistant is in charge of organizing all the files for the students. And they come from all over the world: Latin America, Europe, Southeast Asia. You get people from Argentina, Chile, Venezuela, Colombia, Turkey, Morocco, Thailand. And when they arrive, they aren't speaking very much English at all.

I loved the job, but it was very stressful. At first I was like, "I don't care if this doesn't turn out, because [she sings] I'm *l-e-a-v-i-n-g*, and I'm doing them a *f-a-v-o-r!*" This was my attitude at first: if they didn't have me, they'd have no one, and what I'm doing is better than nothing, so I'm good enough. And of course, I'm more conscientious than I let on, but people were like, "Wow, you don't seem that stressed out." Of course, once I realized what was at stake, I became *very* stressed out. [Laughs.]

A lot of the students were wonderful, but we'd get people, even ones I'd consider friends, who would say things like, "So what do you do all day? What is there to do? I mean, your job's not that hard." In fact, the woman who was leaving had made two whole binders about everything the job entailed. At the bare bones level, the job is to make sure the office runs smoothly, but you're also in charge of *everything* pertaining to the students. Their visas have to be in order; they have to have health forms. We run an immunization clinic for everyone who isn't properly immunized. You have to know who got what booster shots in the last five years, and who got a TB in the last ten, and if they need a chest

X-ray, and if they got a BCG* in France. If someone forgets to bring the proper visa material we have to get it all changed. And that's a whole other part of the job. I had to learn *all* about the immigration laws, which are changing constantly.

Even finding out who's coming is complicated. People cancel, students decide not to show up and they don't tell you; you have to fax their agent or call their families, who don't speak English, and see whether they're there. And then when the students do come, you have to make sure everything is in order. Their I-20[†] has to be signed, otherwise they're considered illegal. Their passports and visas all have to be xeroxed so you have a record of them, and a health form has to be xeroxed and sent to Health Services.

You have to make sure that everyone who lives on campus has a meal plan. But you also have to make sure that anyone who's arriving late isn't *on* the meal plan so we get credit for that, because we're a nonprofit organization and we have to scrape up every last cent. That eighteen dollars and thirty-two cents makes a *big* difference. I remember flipping out when I first started because I'd forgotten to take someone off the meal plan. I realized later, after they'd given me so much shit about it, that those kinds of things happen all the time. You get overwhelmed, you have too many things to do, you forget. It took me a month to even begin to understand the job. Luckily, the director was not the kind of person to be like, "I am director, you take care of this." I mean, she gets right in there, she gets her hands dirty. She's like a saint.

We get data from the main office and we have to enter all the student data into the main database, and I had to learn how to use the database. The woman I trained had all these computer skills, so she knew how to streamline everything. When I started, I was just out of college and had no clerical skills other than word-processing and typing. The woman who had the job before me typed every single name on little labels and stuck them on folders. When the new woman came in, she said, "This is

---

* A French vaccine for TB.
† A school form the student brings to the embassy when applying for a visa.

ridiculous. Put this on FileMaker and just print out all the labels." I had no idea about this. The job was taking five times as long as it should have. I hope I never have another job where I have to use FileMaker, but God forbid, if I do, I know how to use it.

There's all that basic stuff. And then, of course, there's the little side jobs, ordering office supplies, and drawing up staff birthday lists, that kind of stuff. I'm not very organized, but I've learned a lot from the woman I work with who is organized like you would not believe. I've learned about office supplies, like the great file holder where the files don't curl. I wouldn't even know about office equipment *catalogs* had I not worked at this job.

We have to know who is paying what and who owes what. And there's three different ways of paying: they could pay in their home country, here, or through an agent. That's just the behind-the-scenes kind of stuff. But then there's all the student services. "I don't like my roommate, I think he smells—could you put me in a different room?" And these kind of things suck up *hours* of time. There was no secretary, so we're off answering the phones in the middle of all this. The students finish class at 3:30 and their mailboxes are in the office, so you have *streams* of students coming in. "Jenny, I need this," "Jenny, I need help."

Some of the students were pretty racist. I had some tell me they didn't like their roommate's perfume when that was obviously not the problem. We had to sit them down and have a talk. One thing I *have* loved is seeing students from different cultures communicate and actually become good friends. A lot of these kids have never met anyone from another country and come here very close-minded, and usually those are the ones who stick to their own. But I've seen some wonderful friendships blossom.

I think people skills are my forte. I couldn't handle sitting in front of a computer and entering data, but I really liked the student interaction. Even though sometimes you'd just be like . . . [She tears at her hair.] We did develop a couple of lines over the year. One co-worker started it with, "God, these students, they just *suck* the life out of you." [Laughs.]

And it's totally true! And then if a student had a problem, she would say, "Suck it up." Because some, they come saying, "Jenny, I need a taxi." I'm like, "Here's the phone number, go upstairs and call them." Or, "Jennnny, would you confirm my flight?" And I'd say, "Well, you're in the highest-level English class. I'm not your secretary—why don't *you* go upstairs and call. Here's the number." They'd say, "So, you will call for me?" And I'm like, "Why don't you try first?" "No, no, Jenny, no, I can't. You know I no speak English."

When I first started, the students were generally my age, early twenties. In the summer they're younger, sixteen, seventeen, eighteen, and *very* privileged. Some of them really *think* we're their secretaries or maids. We have students who have never done laundry before. "Okay, there's the laundry room, here's some quarters. Go figure it out. . . ." We had some Peruvian kids who missed the orientation session because they got caught up in laundry. [Laughs.] We also had domestic issues. A boyfriend and girlfriend came into the program together, and he was abusive. We had a couple of students get arrested, one for marijuana. We had an Italian girl who used to bring homeless boys into her dorm and make out with them. I remember the resident assistant telling the dorm security, "Well, you'll know the guy because he has a mouse and a lot of body pierces." And the security people said, "This is unacceptable. We absolutely cannot have a mouse in a dorm." [Laughs.]

I was bombarded with proposals of love. I had this one Brazilian man who was always, "But Jenny, I *love* you." He tried to kiss me in the laundry room. He said, "I just have to try." He sent me love letters, he sent me a rose. Of course he was after every *other* woman—he was just out of control. I had one Italian who kept asking me out. My mom was like, "Oh, go out with him—it's just for fun." I said, "Mom, you don't understand *men*." One night you go out, the next night they want you in bed with them. I said to him, "Terrance, I know what you want." And he said, "No Jenny, I tell my mom I never sleep with any *American* girl." Two days later he's like, "Why don't you escape with me for the weekend? We go to the beach." [Laughs.]

The company is a big corporation with offices somewhere else, and then there's the five people I work with in the office. The women I work for never stop telling me how much they appreciate me, how good they think I am. They'll say, "You're great at that." I'm like, *"I am?"* I'm sitting here, I don't notice—I'm just doing what comes naturally. And now I'm realizing, well, I should start thinking about what I'm good at and try to market this, try to use it to my advantage. They were always telling me how much they appreciated me; but at the same time, the benefits weren't commensurate with what they were telling me. It took a while for that to sink in.

I went through a crisis when I realized that other people in the office were salaried, had benefits, and made more money, when I worked harder or just as hard as they did. I started thinking about all the strikes at my university. One was over bringing in new employees at a lower pay scale. I *really* understood why they'd been so unhappy. I was expected to do all this work, take care of projects, organize the college resource library and things like that, and I didn't have a *desk*. I didn't have a computer; I didn't have a phone.

When I started, I thought I was lucky: nine dollars an hour, a job! But after awhile you realize, "I'm indispensable and they need to pay me more." I was finally ready to bring it up, when one of the women I worked with said, "I talked to the director, because I think you need your own space, and I think she's going to give you a raise." Two days later she raised me to twelve dollars an hour, and I got a computer and a desk. It all worked out, but for a while it was definitely a *low* period.

As far as skills that may be useful in future jobs, one is the diplomacy required when dealing with the travel agents that handle these kinds of student programs. You need to be helpful and have people like you while still getting your own way. You need to be able to make your point, and compromise sometimes, but hope that it works out in your best interests without your alienating anyone. For a while I ran around thinking, "Oh, this ass-kissing is really pissing me off." I'm not as tiptoey as some are, but I still get done what needs to get done.

Communication skills are so important. For instance, another thing I do is administer the Test of English as a Foreign Language [TOEFL].

So Veronica comes in on the twelfth of August and says she wants to take the TOEFL. I take out the little form, I look at it—the deadline for her test date is August 11th. I say, "I'm sorry, you missed the deadline. The best we can do is call up and ask." She's in the advanced class, so she knows what I'm saying. Later she says, "Jenny, I just don't understand why I can't take the international TOEFL." I say, "You have to call and ask if you can send the registration in late." She says, "OK, so you will let me know." I say, "No! *You* need to call. I know you can do that. It's a 1-800 number, so it's *free!*" [Laughs.] Then I get a fax from her agent, Rita: "Veronica's father would like to know why you told her she's not allowed to take the International TOEFL."

I sit in the office and I can't scream because there are executives around. But I'm like, "I can't *stand* this!" And everyone is totally sympathetic, because we get stuff like this *all* the time. So I write back a very diplomatic letter. I love writing letters. I always read them out loud to someone else and say, "Does this sound too bitchy?" Because I am a very straightforward person, I don't beat around the bush. But I realize I have to have a bit of panache in the way I write. Like, "Dear Rita, I have explained the situation to Veronica many times and I'm very sorry that she still does not understand." I explained the problem and I said, "Could you please pass this information on to Veronica's father to make sure he fully understands the issues at hand."

I have to be diplomatic with people who don't speak much English, and sometimes you might hear me losing my patience. "Why can't I talk to them?" "Well, they don't have a phone in their room." "But I need to talk to them *now*." "Well, they're in class." "But I *need* to talk to them . . ." My favorite one was, "Hi, this is Sevalay from Turkey. I am calling because I have many allergies and I would like to have a single room." And I say, "I'm sorry, there aren't enough rooms. You can't have a single room." She says, "OK, thank you," and hangs up. I get a call the next day, "Hello, this is Sevalay from Turkey. I applied last week for this program. Did you receive my fax? I have many allergies, I need to have a single room." And I say, "It's really not possible. But we have off-campus apartments fifteen minutes away, and you can have your own apartment with your own private bath and a kitchen. Same price." And she's like, "Oh, but I really want to live on campus." I say, "You can't—not if you want a single room." So she says, "OK, I will talk to my parents." A week later she calls back. "Hello, this is——" I say, "Hi, Sevalay, how are you?" "I spoke with my parents and they do not want me to live in the apartment. So I have been thinking that maybe I could just have a single room on campus." [Shakes head, laughing.]

The students in the program were wealthy, and they often looked down on the office staff. I don't know whether it makes me disappointed in human nature, or in the way people are brought up, but the class thing bothers me. Like with those who think they're better than me. In the United States, we obviously don't have a classless society, but to a certain extent you can work, you can go to school, you can say, "I'm educated," or "I have this skill and I'm good at what I do and I earned respect for this." And for a lot of these students it doesn't work that way, you're *born* into something. That's very hard to deal with.

There was this one guy, the group leader from Barcelona, who brought fourteen students. He didn't take classes, his job was to make these likable but spoiled brats happy. There was one student who wouldn't go to class and the last day he was trying to get her a certificate anyway. Because that's what her parents wanted and his goal was to make them happy. [Genuinely outraged.] He had *no* integrity. He knew I wasn't an idiot, but he started talking to me in this certain way, and I was like, what *is* this way? The director said, "Jenny, you know what that is, it's 'I'm a chauvinist Spanish man and you're a woman and what you think doesn't mean anything.' What he's saying is, 'You don't understand.'" I was like, "Oh, my God, I can't believe this is what he *actually* thinks." If it were all men working in that office, I really wonder if the students would be asking us to do the same kinds of things—ordering taxis and whatnot. But then again, I have quite a few thank-you letters from students, and that makes up for all the assholey, obnoxious ones.

Sometimes, I can get too dramatic about things. Like, "If I don't figure out this visa issue, this woman's going to get deported!"—which is not true. But I'm someone who likes to solve problems right away, and I get *anxious* if something carries on for a week or two. My boss said to me, "The only drawback to how you do your job is that sometimes you do your job *too* well: you feel too responsible, and it comes out as stress or anxiety." And that's something I've had to learn to deal with, that any little stress attacks have to be on my own time. And to learn more constructive ways of asking for help. The people I work with are more than willing to help, but they're much more willing if you don't look like you're out of control.

In this office, I learned that the people you work with make a big difference—that it *is* important. We come from totally different backgrounds, but we get along well and *really* like each other. It doesn't matter that I went to an ivy-league school and someone else went to a state university. It does not make a difference. We all do our jobs, hopefully well, and work together. Everyone helps each other. There's no, "This is my job description—I'm really sorry, but I can't help you."

This was definitely a great job experience. As I said, I went up and down, but it wasn't totally contingent on the job. A lot of it was on me and my feelings the first year out of college. It's a tough year. It was for all of my friends, whether they were living at home or not, liked their jobs or not.

I'm leaving this job because I'm ready to do something else, and it's the perfect time to go. I have enough money and I'm ready to move on in a sane, calm way. I've learned everything I'm going to learn and it's important to *always* be learning. God forbid your brain atrophies and turns to mush. At the stage I am now, I need to learn everything I can in order to get a *better*, or higher-paying, or more appropriate job. And even just to gain life experience, experience in dealing with people. There are so many skills you need to learn to be successful in the job market. Like how to talk to different kinds of people, and how to organize, how to be clear and get your message across, how to negotiate, how to be responsible and accountable.

I gave up on the idea of working in England, 'cause I realized, if I'm going to work abroad, the one thing I have to sell *is* my English. A friend took the Certificate of English Language Teaching to Adults [CELTA] in Milan, and two days after finishing, she got a job and lived in Italy for a year. I wanted to learn Spanish, but they don't offer the course in Latin America, so I said, OK, Spain. I'm hoping the travel experience will tell me, or show me, or somehow lead me closer to what it is that I want to do.

A psychologist friend of my mother's is now taking a psychoanalysis course. I asked how it was going, and he said, "Oh, I love it! This is the thing for me." It seems right that as you get older, you enhance and better your career. As you get older and wiser, you know what it is you want, and you make it for yourself. I said to him, "People make me feel like I have to know what I'm going to be doing for the rest of my life, when I'm only twenty-three." Young people should know that's not true, that's not the way it is, there is no timetable. It might be difficult, but it's OK not to know, it's OK to try a bunch of different things. But nobody tells you that you may be clueless for a while.

People say, "Why do you want to travel? You need to get established, you need to get married." I'm like, "I'm twenty-three years old, what do you want from me?" People say, "How can you not know what you want to do?" For my own peace of mind, I wish I weren't so vague, but I'm assuming it will work out. My mom got her PhD when she was forty. In my senior year of college, I thought it just sort of happens upon you: this flow of light angel comes down and says, "You will be a . . ." I don't think that's the way it is. You have to work it out yourself.

II

"If You Knock, the Door's Open": Finding the Passion

The need to feel a passionate connection to work is not new, but the notion that you should make the search for such work a *priority* is by no means widely held. The struggle to find our way to fulfilling work often takes us through a knotty tangle of family concerns, teachers' directives, and social demands, further complicated by our own shifting priorities as we age and change.

Some parents nurture their children's interest in the arts, science, sports, or business; some parents don't care or can't afford to offer their enthusiastic support. Some schools provide opportunities for us to engage in our passions; some schools barely offer the basics. Sometimes we manage to get a foot in the door; sometimes it's the wrong door. Sometimes we find great mentors; sometimes we bumble along on our own.

For those who know their passion early on and are committed to finding its outlet, work can involve doing anything and everything in order to support time spent doing what they love. For those who aren't sure *what* their passion is but yearn to find out, the search can be sometimes daunting and often surprising.

Karen Hurley's early interest was in medicine, but the message her family gave her was to go for the money. "I thought, 'Well, work's not supposed to engage you . . .' It's not supposed to be a passion." She has jumped from job to job in an attempt to find work that will have meaning. "Sometimes you jump blind and it's a dead end. I'm getting to the point now where I can appreciate the process."

Being an actor is all Gil Santoscoy, Jr., has ever wanted. His teenage years as a children's talk-show host gave him a golden opportunity. "I learned something about work and about who I *was*, and it made me think about who I wanted to be." But when people ask him what he "does," he cites whatever job he's got at the time. For Gil, acting is something "I'm *passionate* about. If somebody's making idle conversation and asks what I do, I'm not gonna give 'em my heart."

In Ray Mancison's case, an early desire to be a doctor disappeared when college life as a working musician evolved into adult life in the music business. "I'm not someone who loves music—I'm someone who lives *inside of* music." But getting into the record business took persistence. "I printed up what I thought was the greatest hotshot résumé and couldn't find a job."

What parents do and think often has a great impact. Gabe Lyon says, "My father made a *point* of letting us know it was important to do something that made you happy." In college she discovered many interests, and the field of education seemed wide enough to envelop them all. But she has been careful about what she's chosen to do. "I said to myself, 'It's always going to be easy to find something to do, but what do you *really* want to do?'—Meaning, it's important to be conscious of your decisions. Because you turn around and ten years have gone by. And this is what you've done with your life for those ten years."

For Carl Valentin, work was what you did in order to buy time for other interests, such as serious cycling. For a time, he wanted to be a writer, but while working as a waiter he met people who were "pretty much five years down the road in their careers. I saw writers who still worked in restaurants to get by, or drove cabs or taught. I started to think that maybe at some point you decide to stay involved and interested in writing, but take it off center stage and find a career that's fulfilling in and of itself."

For all of these people, the need to care deeply about their work was or has become a priority. As Karen Hurley says, "I'm still searching. I know there's something out there I'm really going to connect with. I try to be patient."

KAREN HURLEY

Karen's strongest idea about work came from her mother: just get something that pays. Karen's first inclination was to be a doctor, but after dropping out of college, she ended up in a series of unfulfilling jobs at a restaurant, a hospital, and an office. To finance her return to college, she joined the National Guard, where she received weapons and aggression training, and lessons in discipline and endurance. About basic training, Karen says, "I don't feel fear when I try new things now, because I went through hell and survived." Less inspiring was a civil service job, which she left to become a teacher. She quickly realized that teaching high school was not for her, and took an administrative job in a university office. Longing for meaningful work at age thirty, she reflects: "I've always tried to be creative and get what I could out of every job I've had. That's important; it's what we're supposed to do: to honor the life we're given, we're supposed to be engaged."

My mother's parents were part of the black middle-class. Her father was a postal worker his whole life, and that was a *really* good job at that time; her mother worked for AT&T for many years. My dad grew up more lower-middle-class. My parents split up when my brother and I were pretty young. They were both court reporters. I learned that work was a pain in the ass from my mother. She came home tired, she came home *beat*. She was constantly up typing transcripts at three in the morning. But my dad had his own court-reporting business, so he was his own boss, and he made *bucks*.

I've been thinking a lot about work—like, "Man, what am I gonna *do?*" I'm an administrative assistant now. It was supposed to be work I could fall *back* on. My mother said, "Make sure you know how to type, you can always get a job." But it wasn't supposed to be a career. Lately I've been thinking, "How did this happen?" For a long time I thought, "Well, work's not supposed to engage you, or be something you love, something you *obsess* about because you care about it so much. It's not supposed to be a passion."

My original idea was to be a doctor. In college, I took my first pre-med course in chemistry—I got an F. As a freshman, I wasn't remotely prepared; I was living in a dorm and my mind was not on academics. [Laughs.] And sophomore year, I just could not get it together. I wasted all this money getting bad grades. I said, "Let me take a break from this," and left.

I went to the university placement center and saw a PR internship position with a summer arts camp on a farm in Southern New Jersey. I'm a city kid, and I wanted to do something really weird and different, so I took the job and stayed on that summer to be a counselor. I came back home and worked for about a year as a restaurant hostess in Water Tower Place.*

I don't like customers, I could never be a waitress. I just have too much attitude. But it was a learning experience, and I liked being exposed to older people. I was pretty shy and it forced me to come out of myself a bit. It was good to know different kinds of people. I met my first gay person. He was a caring sort of individual; he would always give me the time of day, unlike some of the other wait staff.

For a short time, I volunteered at a hospital because I wanted some exposure to hospitals and medicine. I marched a supply cart around to restock different hospital posts. I worked in the basement—there were miles and miles of tunnel. I could never find my way from building to building, I could never get to my post. I did that for a couple of months and then retired. [Laughs.] I was constantly on the phone to headquarters. "I'm in the green hallway, underneath so-and-so—please, how do I get to such-and-such pavilion?" I hate basements to this day.

---

* Downtown Chicago's well-known Michigan Avenue shopping center.

I worked for a time as a secretary in the sales department at a fancy downtown hotel. We had to wear uniforms, gray suits. Actually that was great, because I didn't have much money for clothing. But the atmosphere was very conservative, stifling and restrictive. And I was young and unsure of myself and of what I was doing. Not as far as the work, which was simple, but just in terms of who I was. I wasn't afraid, but I was reserved. I started out as a temp and then they hired me. When you're temping you sit at the desk and do what they tell you. I didn't pay attention to anything else, it was like I had a shield around me. I just didn't see. Once they hired me, I got to see the real deal.

The head honcho in sales was an asshole, and he scared everybody. When he was in a bad mood, he would just go *off* on you. I was mostly shielded from that because he didn't much bother talking to secretaries. He did go off on me once, for a simple mistake I made because I was new and didn't know any better. Whatever the mistake, it certainly wasn't worth the harangue he gave me. I'm not a crier, but I *felt* like crying. And nobody came to my rescue. Later, people said, "That wasn't called for, he shouldn't have done that . . ." The guy could say *anything* and nobody would say a word to him. I thought that was wrong. It offended me deeply that he could speak to people any old way. The majority of the staff were women, and I'm not saying it's a gender issue, but a lot of times women have a hard time speaking up. I think that was the case there.

After a while I was like, "To hell with this! I'm not staying *here*." It was hard to leave, because nobody understood—plus I didn't know what I was going to do next. I tried to explain to my relatives that the work conditions were unacceptable. I said, "I can't be someplace eight hours a day and feel like I'm suffocating." They just could not relate. "But you're making such-and-such dollars an hour." And for somebody who was twenty, I was making a decent buck. My mother was like, "Are you *crazy?*"

The job I took after that was for a children's choir. They've toured all over, they've been on TV. An old family friend was on their board and said they needed an office manager. It was actually kind of a nice job, because I didn't have anybody supervising me. I *was* the office. The work was easy: clerical, typing, filing . . . My big accomplishment was redesigning the filing system. I worked there for about six months and quit because I went into the army. [She sings.] "Be all that you can be . . ." Actually, I got suckered in by that commercial.

I wanted to get back into school, but I didn't have a plan for paying for it. It seemed like it would be hard to do. I saw this commercial on TV: student-loan repayment, GI Bill, tuition reimbursement. *Ching-ching, ching-ching* . . . I was like, "I'm in! I'm *there*." 'Cause it solved the money problem from a practical point of view. I didn't think about the time commitment, the years of having to deal with the bullshit. I joined the National Guard. I wasn't in the active army ever, but I had to do Guard service for six years.

You're tested to see what you can do in the army, you take the AS-BAT [Army Service Battery Test]. Certain positions are closed to women. My test score and my sex qualified me to be a medic, a cook, or in supplies. The army is a corporation, one of the biggest ones in the world. My way of dealing with the dilemma of joining a corporation that goes to countries and kills was to be in a job that was nurturing life: I chose to be a medic. The military, war, I'm against all that, but I didn't think about it at the time. I just had this goal. It was not really too well thought out. [Laughs.]

It took some time to get up the nerve. One day I said, "*Alright*," and went in to the recruiter. I didn't tell my mother or anybody, I just went. I took the test a week later and got the results right away. Normally it takes three months. It was just very fast, from visiting the recruiter to going to Alabama for basic training.

I have to say I was very focused. I thought, "Well, shit, I'll play this game. This is not reality. My reality is what I'm doing once this is *over* with—you know what I'm saying?" It was very, very difficult though. If you're just a file clerk, you still gotta go through basic training. Everybody, no matter what. And *man*, I swear, basic training is ten weeks of hell, *hell*, *HELL*.

You have to suspend your personality, suspend whoever it is you are, and become like a robot, a zombie. And whatever you do, *don't think*. Do not think, just *react*. Do whatever the drill sergeants tell you to do. That's how you survive. For a lot of people that's *very* hard to do. It's hard to be targeted arbitrarily. For *no reason* told to stop what you're doing and do fifty push-ups. That happened all the time. Somebody says, "Drop," you *drop*.

Here's how it's set up: you have a company of women, and companies are divided into platoons of about twenty women each. There were three platoons in our company, and I was in the first platoon. So you're standing in formation in your platoon, waiting for the drill sergeant to walk you to the mess hall for breakfast. You're doing what you're supposed to do: stand at attention. They come straight up to you, your noses touch, and they *scream* at you to drop and do fifty, for no reason. It's a constant barrage of arbitrary orders that you have to follow. And you cannot complain, you cannot be too tired. You can't say *anything*. If you do, the punishment is worse. But if you catch on too quickly, if you *understand* the mentality of "react, don't think," they're harder on you, they pick on you *more*.

I was at the top of my platoon in most of the physical stuff, I got in shape pretty quick. If I'm in a situation where a leader is needed, a lot of times I'll step in. That's what happened in basic training. I mean, it is a fucking *bitch*, so there are days when you're just so depressed, and you're so tired . . . You do a lot of road marching, and if you're not in the greatest shape you can get far behind. So sometimes I would have someone lean on me to keep them going. My superiors noticed me helping my squad-mates and asked me to be a squad leader. I liked being a squad leader, even though it had its headaches.

In basic training the drill sergeants are trying to create warlike conditions, and so they create an environment that's very, very, very stressful—that's the point. People would crack. We'd argue, sometimes people would fight. Not me, but some of the younger women. I was twenty-one, most people who join the army are maybe eighteen, nineteen. They don't have the skills to handle themselves, and they would go *off.* There was racial tension: some of the blacks would go off on the whites at a perceived insult or slight. I would try to keep the peace.

At one point, the drill sergeant asked me to be a team leader. A team leader stands in front of a platoon and acts like the drill sergeant when the drill sergeant isn't around. I declined the job. I told him I was doing badly in my weapons training and couldn't see myself improving that and being TL at the same time. I don't know if I caught him in a good mood or what, but he said, "OK, no problem girlie," and he appointed somebody else.

I was good at everything except weapons training. You have to know how to shoot an M16, which I hated, I *hated.* The drill sergeants always created competition, they made up little games and picked favorites. I think they even took bets on us. I learned how to clean and shoot, but I was always the last putting it together. Whenever I had to hold a weapon I felt physically sick. When we practiced firing I was awful. Every time, I'd imagine people's bodies getting blown apart. I couldn't think of it as a game. I understood logically that I had to *know* how to do it, that I had to *do* it. If I were ever activated and in a situation, I would have to know how to defend myself with a gun. But I couldn't get past hating to handle weapons.

Physically, the hardest part was when we had to go on road marches. Toward the end of basic, you have to do a fifty-mile and an eighty-mile march. You have all your equipment in your rucksack on your back. By then you have a hard body, and it's nothing to you. But still, they keep you up the night before, so you haven't had much sleep. That last road march I was *through*—I was so exhausted, I was sleep-walking. You learn that the body will just keep going.

We learned basic survival skills and other weird shit. You had to know how to set a land mine, how to throw a grenade a certain number of feet. I think for women it's kind of cool, in some respects, because it teaches you aggression, it teaches you how to fight. We did hand-to-hand combat, we learned how to use the knives attached to the M16, how to use your rifle as a saber. There were women smaller than me packing that big weapon.

When you're in that sort of situation, sometimes you find strength where you didn't know any existed. It can really be a building experience. It was for me, it was for a lot of the women there. It was hell—it was so hard that when you got through it, you had a sense of accomplishment. In that sense, it teaches you. I've written stories about that experience, and they have a lot of humor in them. At this point I can make fun of some of the characters who were so monstrous at the time; the military has some of the most sexist, misogynist men—and women too, most definitely. But for the most part I don't have any regrets. I learned a lot—not just then, but during the next six years with my guard unit.

Part of my ambivalence about the experience is that it tapped into this warrior, violent part of me. I don't know how I feel about that. After I finished basic training, I was teased a lot by relatives and friends because I was *aggressive*—I mean, I had this hard body, I was tough. *"You talking to me?"* I would beg people on the street to mess with me so I could go off on them. I'd been through hell and I wanted to kick some *ass*. That's what I'd been trained to do.

A friend of my parents has a son who was in the army a few years back. He was away training in artillery and he found out his brother had been hurt in a random drive-by. He and a couple of his friends came from wherever the hell they were training with all their gear on. They were on a mission to *kill* these people, they were not playing. That part, it's very easy, it doesn't take long. That's what scares me about the military. Me, I'm a peace-loving person. But you can change, that quick. I've been out since '93, but if I were in a certain situation . . . You tap into that violent streak everybody has in them, and it can be exposed—it can take over.

After basic, I tried to get back into regular civilian life. I returned to school and did my twelve weeks of medic training in the summer of '88, in Texas. I was excited about being a medic because I still had this desire to be in the health field. We didn't have any chemistry or biology, it was just basic emergency medical care, the equivalent of an EMT [emergency medical technician]. But with a twist: we simulated treatment of war wounds. If a round hits you in the chest, you have a sucking chest wound, and we had to know how to treat that and all sorts of gruesome injuries. Of course, it was make-believe—we had to pretend. We had dummy bodies and fake makeup. We'd have to react once we saw whatever the ghastly wound was. It was a lot of play, actually.

Compared to basic, it was a breeze—less stress. Nobody on you to drop for no reason. I did the National Guard from '89 to '93, one weekend a month and two weeks in the summer. For the most part, it was fun. There was no seriousness, really, until 1991 and Desert Storm. George Bush activated more National Guard and reserve units for a war effort than any other president in history. Traditionally they're not for that purpose: they're backup, last resort. He activated them as a matter of course, along with the regular army. You just don't *do* that.

So I was nervous and unhappy and anxious. Rumors were flying, and one of the companies in our battalion was mobilized. We were put on alert right after our sister company was activated: any day we'd be called and have twenty-four hours to be ready to go. We'd be shipped to a camp for more training and then flown over. I did *not* want to go. I did not want to be faced with the gloom of shooting somebody. I couldn't imagine hurting anyone, even if it was in self-defense. I could not conceive of it.

It never happened—the war ended. I had been considering reenlisting, because it had been fun, it had been just pretend. But at that point, I said, "Never will I reenlist." By this time, I was a college graduate with a job, and I remember talking to co-workers about the situation. So many of them had the attitude, "*Cool!* You get to go to Desert Storm." I thought, "You're fucking idiots." So many people think glory, guts, once-in-a-lifetime thing, war. Or people believe we need a war to stimulate the economy, or whatever other bullshit reason. To me war is a crime.

At the time, I had a job with the city of Chicago, in the Community Services Department of the Board of Elections. I trained election judges to work at the polls, I trained voter registrars. We went all over the city. I even liked going into the mostly white wards where they weren't expecting to see somebody like me—a twenty-five year old black woman—teaching. Some of these Streets and Sanitation guys would look at me like, "What are *you* gonna tell us?" But I *liked* teaching. I liked explaining, getting in front of a group and answering questions. I liked being an authority.

What I didn't like—and one thing that eventually drove me away—was the actual manager of the office. She thought of me as her secretary. Even though I was out there doing all this training, busting my ass and doing a good job, she would do very subtle things to put me in my place. She always reminded me that I was the *assistant*, even though a lot of times I was left in charge. I would *try* to be in charge, but because I was so young and most of the others had been there a long time, they'd look at me like, "Well, she ain't *really* in charge," and just go on about their business. Many days I'd come home and cry because the place was so completely frustrating and dysfunctional. There was so much dead weight and so many attitudes and nothing I could do to change that.

When there wasn't an election, we had a lot of down time, and there wasn't much to do. We had publications, pamphlets on all these election jobs. We had ten different kinds, and our department was in charge of writing them, of printing them. We had some decent desktop-publishing software, so I took it upon myself to learn the software. I took one of our pamphlets and printed it out. It looked good. I was proud of myself, 'cause I saved the department a lot of money—we didn't have to pay a typesetter. I showed it to my boss and she said, "We're going to keep going to the same company." I was *devastated*. I thought I was doing a great thing. I guess she had this relationship with the company. That was the problem there: they resisted anything new, resisted change.

I felt that if I stayed, I was going to become like the people around me. I was starting to pick up the phone on the fifth ring instead of the first. After the manager dissed my idea, I languished—I just stopped giving a damn. And I was making good money, I was making *bank*. Most of my college friends weren't making nearly what I was making. But I left, because money isn't everything. Sometimes I think, "OK, if I'd stayed, I'd be up to $40,000." But no way could I have stayed. It was killing my spirit.

There was a program called Teachers for Chicago—they recruited professionals from other fields to teach in the schools. They pay for your master's degree, and you repay it by teaching while you're getting your master's. It was a rigorous interview process, five hundred people for a hundred slots. I was surprised they picked me. That summer I took preparatory courses at a college, and in the fall I taught English to four classes of high-school freshmen and one class of sophomores. A hundred and thirty kids! I couldn't deal with it, I couldn't face them. I had *no* idea what I was doing, I had no teaching skills *whatsoever*. The summer courses were supposed to help, but nothing prepares you for the reality. I taught for three weeks and then I quit.

I felt like a failure. Before, when I'd left the high-paying city job, nobody could comprehend it. It wasn't just a generational thing—a lot of friends and relatives my own age couldn't understand. Good benefits, good money. "You giving that up?!" After I quit teaching *I* was like, "Goddamn, what did I *do*?" [Laughs.]

I looked at the job board at the college where I'd taken summer classes. I'd enjoyed the atmosphere there. A position was open, I applied and got it. I've been working there going on three years. The longest I've been anywhere. And actually, I love my job now, because of the people. I work in the academic dean's office—there's nine of us. The work is the same, typing and filing and stuff. But it makes a big difference when people recognize that without you, the office will not function. They take pains to let me know they appreciate me. I feel part of a team, like an equal.

I used to feel disdain for the work, but I'm concentrating on shifting my attitude. When you're an administrative assistant, a lot of times you're looked down upon: you have servant status, you're low on the totem pole. People assume you don't have a brain, or can't possibly have any other interests or passions in your life. If you're in a culture where people think you're like shit, it's easy to absorb that feeling: you start to think you're like shit. For me, it's all connected to feeling like you aren't *supposed* to love your work. It's just a job, you do it, you get paid, that's the end of it.

Lately I've been trying to think about this work with a more loving attitude. For example, I've been trying not to resent the filing. I hate filing and it tends to pile up. If resentment starts to build, you end up hating your work. So now I try to file regularly. I try to think of the best way to file, try to make it fun, so I don't get bored. The work feels like it's not just a job—it's something that matters, and that feels better.

Until recently, the majority of people I knew couldn't understand my longing to really connect with work. Now I have friends who do understand. My father passed away, but I think he connected with his work. My parents had such different approaches to work. My mom often said her father hated his postal job. He had been a singer. He gave up music for the nice-paying postal job which he hated, and that hate manifested in different behaviors. It was tough on my mom growing up with him—I'll just leave it at that.

Once I got him a book on black jazz by Dempsey Travis. He opened it, and the man just started talking, I mean *stories*. He went through the book, he identified people in the Chicago scene and in New Orleans—he was from New Orleans. He said, "I used to sing with this guy and this guy. . . ." It was beautiful to see his whole demeanor change. I had never seen him that excited. It was really a gift to me to see him express such joy. It was interesting to watch my grandmother while he talked. She pursed her lips.

I've been reading a book called *The Reinvention of Work*, by Matthew Fox.* That's where I got some of the ideas about how work can be a joyful thing, a passion. That's when you're really connected to your

* Matthew Fox, *The Reinvention of Work: A New Vision of Livelihood for Our Time* (San Francisco: HarperSanFrancisco, 1994).

work. I'm still searching. I know there's something out there I'm really going to connect with. I try to be patient. Journeys . . . Sometimes they take all these different curvy turns and you don't know where you're going, but you just have to go with it. Sometimes you jump blind and it's a dead end. I'm getting to the point now where I can appreciate the process. All will be revealed . . . Eventually.

GIL SANTOSCOY, JR.

As a young boy, Gil discovered acting and in high school became the host of a children's TV show. "In the three and a half years that I did the show, I learned a lot." Adults gave him too much leeway, little kids idolized him, his peers picked on him, the stress got to him, and Gil learned about office politics and the rumor mill. He left the show to go to college, where during work-study he observed how others did their jobs. "If I were a boss, I know how I'd want my employees to be, so I always try to be the employee that I would want." After graduating, he found a job as an inventory-taker. The first week was daunting. "I was thinking, 'I need a job that's easier to handle.'" Gil, twenty-three, continues auditioning and acting, and he enjoys his job as much as possible. "Inventorying a Mexican hat store, how can you go wrong?" Looking to the future, he says, "It's scary, a world of computers, a world of mass-technology. I guess it's beneficial, I don't know . . . I know I won't deposit money at the cash machine, I like going to the bank, *I like talking to the teller. Talking to another person, you gotta have that. I don't think there will ever be a replacement for the theater and humanity."*

I'm from Kentucky. My dad's Mexican, and my mom is German or something pretty white. She's been a high-school Spanish teacher for, I don't know, 150 years. The funny part is I don't speak Spanish very well. Not as well as I *should.* My dad was a manager for a sporting goods store. I remember visiting him at work and how busy he always seemed, on the phone, walking around. Then he started working for the post office. He'd come home and tell me how tired and sore his legs were. I remember thinking, "I'm *not* gonna be a mailman."

I always wanted to be an actor and I was always hyper. I remember getting in trouble a lot and being goofy and acting up. My sister says maybe I should have been put on Ritalin. [Laughs.] My parents put me into acting school when I was in sixth grade, and I also joined a theater company. I *loved* acting. It was a perfect outlet for me, for all this craziness.

In eighth grade, I auditioned for the movie *Eight Men Out*.* I was cast as a featured extra—I'm in a scene at the race track. I give this guy a tip and he gives me money and I run off. I thought, "Well hey, this is cool!" Freshman year ends and over the summer I see a television commercial about needing people to host a kids' cartoon show. So OK, that sounds fun—I want to be an actor, let's fill this out. I've been in several plays, so I'm thinking, "I've got a shot, why not?" I mean, I'd been a working actor.

I applied, not caring too much. Later, I got this call for an audition. They called six hundred out of six thousand for a screen test, narrowed it down to sixty, and then to six or seven. Oddly enough, I was very casual about it. I kept going to auditions, and finally, after five, one of the directors called. She said, "Hey, Gil, this is Nancy. Are you sitting down? You and Kelly are going to be the hosts of the *Kids Club*." *Anybody* who gets a job like that is going to be . . . [He toots a royal herald.] *Excited!*

I had that job until I graduated from high school. It was similar to being an MTV veejay. You're a *personality*, someone in the public eye. The show was on in the morning, from 6:30 to 9:00, and again in the afternoon from 2:30 to 5:30. So people are seeing my face every day. I thought, "This is gonna be *great*! I'm gonna be an actor—I'm gonna be on TV!" But in getting that part, I didn't know what was going to come *with* it.

I started when I was thirteen, and the age group I was aiming at was little kids, four- or five-year-olds. But there were also people my own age who still liked cartoons. So I'm being watched by the little kids, as

* A John Sayles film (1988) about the 1919 Chicago Black Sox scandal.

well as *my* friends in high school, *and* the people who want to tease me, and the people on the opposing *soccer* team who want to tease me. Sophomore year, high school's starting, and the first day *everybody* knows—it's announced over the intercom. And everybody wants to make fun of me 'cause I'm hosting a kiddie show. "You're a geek!" and blah blah blah—words that people use to hurt you. Then there was the other side of it, where younger kids' mothers would say, "Oh, my kids *love* your show." I'd get letters—we had fan mail. I'd like to think I never let that go to my head, because I didn't really think about it—it just came with the job.

I might go to a movie with a friend and in the lobby kids would be, "Hey, that's Gil from *Kids Club*. Mom, I want his autograph." So I'd sign a couple of autographs. That was *fun*—it was a blast! But then inside the theater there'd be people three rows back making fun of me. For a while, I concentrated on the negative part of my job, but then I thought, "How can I make it better? How can I fit in and not be an outcast? Who do I *want* to be friends with?" It's not gonna be the guy who hasn't spoken to me in two years and now wants to say he knows me.

A part of the job they didn't tell me about when I auditioned was dealing with the repercussions of playing a *character*. My character was always happy and in a good mood. I can see how that made me a target! My contract said I couldn't smoke or drink. I'd already been smoking off and on, but when I started this gig I began to smoke *more*. I was choosing a bad-guy image, not easily preyable—you understand? "I've got tattoos and I wear a motorcycle jacket." You don't look at me and think, "There's somebody I can tease."

I saw a lot of bullshit happen between co-workers, my elders. I heard them talk bad about each other. I heard about who was sleeping around. I've come to realize this *never* goes away. There's maybe twelve full-time people at the place I work now, and stuff goes on behind everybody's back. "Oh man, so-and-so can't work," blah blah blah. I guess it's everywhere. That's all I can say about that—gossip is *everywhere*. [Laughs.]

There was a time during the second year when it was all *too* much and

I had to escape. My escape was getting fucked up with my friends. A couple of times I got from my bosses, "Gil, we hear there's rumors going around . . ." There were *so* many rumors circulating. I'd go to a friend's house and we'd burn a joint with a guy, somebody I didn't know. That guy would go around saying, "Hey man, I smoked a joint with Gil." And then it would be, "Hey man, Gil sold me a bag," and then "Hey man, Gil's shooting up in my *house*." It was *ridiculous*.

I don't know what this says about the place I worked, but their attitude was, "If you smoke a joint, I don't care, that's no big deal." Like, if you want to get high after work, go ahead. Their position was, just be careful, don't do anything in front of anybody you don't know. No, "Maybe you're too young for this, Gil . . ." [Laughs.] None of that. I thought, "Oh, this is cool, I'll just keep things on the down-low."

I didn't get too much grief about anything I did. I guess it's because we had been doing the show for a while and we had a *huge* fan club. It was a good investment: sponsors paid big bucks for us to do things like appear at grand openings. I would go to McDonald's and they'd give me a free meal. It was *weird*—I was a celebrity in this little town!

When I quit, I remember thinking, "Phew, I'm glad I'm moving away." But I don't want to give the impression that I never had a good time, 'cause I had a *great* time. I learned something about work and about who I *was*, and it made me think about who I wanted to be. There was definitely some sadness when I left the show. They filmed me graduating from high school and had a big party for me. It was fun, but very emotional.

My first year of college, I was like, "OK, *Animal House*" —we're gonna party, have a great time. I was coming to a place where I had no identity: I was brand-new, I could be who I wanted, didn't have skeletons in the closet, didn't have people who hated me. [Laughs.] I came to Chicago because it had a reputation as a good theater town. I got my degree in theater and now I take inventory. Go figure. [Laughs.] But I've been auditioning, I've been hitting all the children's theaters.

After freshman year, I spent the summer being a Deadhead with a couple of friends. Following the Grateful Dead around was a great excursion. Then I realized, "I need an escape from *this*!" Fine, if you're content to sleep in your car and eat the occasional cheeseburger. You've got a bunch of people who are in the *exact* same boat who will always lend a helping hand. But sooner or later, you're going to stop being content. I came to the realization that, unfortunately, you *have* to have money to survive. To have money, you have to make money and that means having a *job*.

Sophomore year, I needed a job for work-study, so I became a secretary for one of my theater professors. She was very unorganized and I'm an organizer, as you can see. [He gestures around the tidy apartment he shares with his girlfriend.] This place may not be *clean*, but it's organized. I'm a neat-freak. So I had a great time. Well, not *literally*, but I would clean her office and organize her things. She ended up not liking me for that. She said she could never *find* anything!

I remember putting on an act for the boss. Not really an act, but just being considerate, polite—not how I would be with my drinking buddies. The next guy who took the job was different. He didn't clean up for work, and when he talked to the boss, he'd lean back and fold his arms . . . It was his manners. To do well in a job you have to be able to get along. You have to do things right, *know* what you're doing, find out how to do things so you can do them again. It's a good feeling to be trusted, to know they have faith in you.

After I graduated, I was about to take a temp job in customer service when I saw a newspaper ad for this inventory job. I figured the hours were seven in the morning till four or five in the afternoon—this is excellent. *Good pay*—this is excellent. And it's in my part of town—*excellent*. So I got out the I'm-going-to-apply-for-a-job tie and the rest of the outfit—slacks and an oxford—and applied. The people in the office were wearing shorts and T-shirts, and I'm thinking, "Not a bad deal."

I had to type up a nontheater résumé, one of the first times I had to do *that*. One *little* half-page resume. But the reason I got the job is because I had theater on my résumé. The boss thought I'd be personable, and that would make me an asset in dealing with managers and people in stores. He got twenty replies and hired three people. I'm the youngest. It ranges from people with families to men who live by themselves.

We're the guys who walk around with the little counter boxes strapped to the thigh or waist. We're sitting there typing, we count. We've counted grocery stores, a Mexican hat store. We go to liquor stores and read the count into a tape recorder: what kind of liquor, how many bottles. You get the liquor store on tape, you take it back to the office. You give the tape to somebody who sits at a transcribing machine and has a book listing all possible liquor the store could have. You write in that book how many of what they have on hand. You give that to someone else and they double-check to make sure your math is right. Then they give it to somebody to punch into the computer so they can get a printout. Then they give that to somebody else who verifies your numbers again. That's it, then you're done.

The owner is going to get a computer system that'll take care of the double-checking and the reverifying, so the job'll go a lot quicker. Of course, that'll put the guy who runs the computer system out of a job. He started out as an inventory-taker like me, and he's been working there for about thirty-five years. Now he's wondering what he's gonna do.

My first day, I come in and the owner's supposed to show me how to use the little strap-on adding machine. It's maybe eight, nine inches, and it's got a little screen and number keys. Keys four, five and six have little bumps, so you can figure out what key you're on. I was doing this for about two months [he looks back and forth frantically]—looking at the price and then typing it in. Now I can just *fly* through.

The first job I went on was to a *huge* grocery store. The boss had me do just one gondola—that's a shelving unit. I'd do it and then he would, and we'd compare. I go to the shelf and it's dusty as *hell*. I have allergies and I start sneezing. It's taking me forever just to do a top row of hairspray—there's just *so* many. I'm watching my boss and he's faster than anything—unbelievable! I'm getting annoyed at this machine: I'm not good, it's taking *way* too long. I'm thinking, "This is *not* the job for me." The next day, one of the guys said, "If you don't quit before the end of this week, you won't quit." Apparently, I started on one of the roughest weeks. And I ended up *trying* it, you know? I gave it the week. People helped me, gave me tips. I kept on, and it got easier.

You have to be able to work well with others. That's always been a prime element for me. Sometimes I've gotten teased for that. My attitude in any job is, I don't want to have an enemy. I've had enemies and it's no fun, it's wasted energy. I try to make sure there aren't any conflicts. Like I said, people talk behind people's backs about how *slow* they are, how *fast* they are, or what they *do*. I'm sitting in the van with two guys coming back from the job, and they're *talking*. I can only imagine what they say when I'm not there. It's like, don't lie to my face—don't be fake with me. If you've got a problem, let's discuss it.

I've been working there seven or eight months, long enough to say "we" now. Some stores we only do once a year. There are stores I envision I'll only see this one time—I'm not going to be back next year. The thing is, I could keep this job, start a good pension fund, get the super insurance program. I could do all that, but I don't *want* to stay that long.

It all depends on what your priorities are. If there's something you want, you have to go out and *get* it. But I come home from being an inventory taker and I'm *tired*—it's so monotonous, so tedious. It's *easy*, but draining, which is a problem with a lot of jobs, I imagine. I get home and I'm *beat*. I don't want to go out, go to an audition. It's so much easier to sit on my ass and watch *The Simpsons*. I have to force myself to take some initiative and chase after things.

We hear all about these actors who *love* acting, they've been doing it for so long and they're making millions of dollars. You know *they're* not complaining. But for us Joe Schmoes who are in the process of paying our dues, it's *hard*. It's easy to get caught up in, "Oh, my life is *so* difficult." As an actor, obviously, you don't want to be too disheartened at the turndowns. But it is disheartening.

I'll just keep doing whatever until I find an acting job. I'm willing to do almost anything. One thing that helps me keep sane in this job is that every day we go to a different store. It's better than stamping things on the assembly line. It's funny, I never thought I was going to use math and now I'm taking inventory *every* day. I suppose that keeps the brain alert. I was always bad at math too. You just never know.

Theater is what I know the most about. But when people ask me what I do, I say, "I take inventory," because that's what I'm doing. If I'm *not* acting right now, I'm not acting. Acting is something I *care* about, that I'm *passionate* about. If somebody's making idle conversation and asks what I do, I'm not gonna give 'em my heart. But if I'm at a party and someone says, "What do you do?" "I'm an inventory-taker." "Oh yeah, how's that?" "Not bad." "What else do you do?" "I act." "Oh yeah, is that what you really want to do?" Boom, there's a conversation. If you knock, the door's open. If you're just ringing the bell and running, I'm not gonna open the door.

Everything I've done has taught me a little bit, and I've gained something, even if I can't put my finger on it. That sounds pretty cheesy, but it's true that anything you do helps you understand something a little better, whether it be about yourself, or about humanity, or society.

My little brother is seven years younger and I tell him, "Have a good time before you have to pay the bills." [Laughs.] That's the trick. I tell him there's gonna come a time when somebody says, "OK, you're not a kid anymore." I remember the days when I could come home from school and play. I could *do* that verb, that word—*play*. You don't have anything in mind, go climb a tree. That's fantastic. As a kid, we think, "I can't wait to be an adult so I can do all these adult things." Shit man, you don't *know* what you're *saying*. You *don't* know what you're saying. . . .

RAY MANCISON

Although Ray's father wasn't a professional musician, music was always in their life, his trumpet practice a daily ritual. Now thirty, Ray found his instrument, the guitar, in high school. Ambitious and bright, he entered college intending to become a doctor, but after working his way through school as a rock musician, his path changed. Music—or more precisely, the music business— was it. Ray's persistence helped him land a first job at a small record label. "What I learned was to be fearless, that the worst thing anybody will say to you is no." He left that job to experience life at a large record label, where he learned about selling, business travel, corporate downsizing, negotiating, ethics, and integrity. Disgusted by corporate tactics, he quit and considered leaving the business, but was convinced to sign on with a new, small label. Upon entering his current office, I comment on his lack of windows. "I've had windows, big windows," he says. "Windows aren't everything."

The first thing I learned about work was from my father, who didn't do what he wanted to do. He was a distinguished, exquisitely well-mannered, super-intelligent person who worked in real estate. But *inside*, he was a professional trumpet player. He practiced in the basement *every* night. The basement air duct was by my head, so as a kid I always went to sleep listening to him play.

The story was that he had an offer to be the Doc Severinsen for Johnny Carson's orchestra. His parents, Ukrainian immigrants, said, "No, it's a bum's life, it's not what you should do." So here's my father practicing for the rest of his life for something he had already passed on. Maybe my father loved music too much to make it his career—I could understand that. I later learned that if you choose a career in something you love, it's possible for your career to rob you of that love. But the idea that he didn't do what he wanted to do drove me insane. My father died when I was seventeen, so he never opened up to me about any of that. I was just becoming a man and he was gone.

I play guitar now, but my father taught me to play the trumpet as soon as I could hold up a horn. He taught me music, he taught me to read notes. I got real good, real quick. Even though he didn't open up to me, he was demanding as far as my talent . . . Talent can be a difficult thing. When people say you have it, you almost don't want to do anything about it—some mechanism says, "If I already know the answer, I don't have to study." But that's not true, you have to constantly work on your fundamentals.

His discipline was an example. I learned how the smaller, more menial tasks can become your greatest sources of pleasure. I play my guitar every day. Because I want to be the greatest guitar player? Not really. Because it makes me feel good and I love the sound of what I'm creating. Playing the guitar grounds me. I'm a highly competitive and ambitious person, and without that to balance me I would probably be off the edge.

I didn't grow up as a musician, I grew up as a jock. [Laughs.] I had a reputation in my hometown as an athlete-scholar type, successful, go-getter. In my high-school yearbook it says: "Ambition, to be a doctor." But at home I was quietly learning my Kiss records.

My father was trained in jazz and classical and traditional forms, and rock and roll was not part of that. One day he came into my bedroom and said, "So, did you practice your trumpet today?" I said, "Well, I was going to get to that." He said, "I've been listening to you. What is this stuff you're playing?" He said, "Look, you cannot serve two masters—you have to choose. There's going to be ups and downs in life and you may never get what you want. But if you have your music, you'll *always* have that." I was about sixteen at the time and kind of went, "Yeah, yeah, yeah, later dad." It unsettled me a little bit, but for the next year I didn't choose because I was afraid to disappoint him. I played my trumpet when he was home, I played my guitar when he wasn't.

After he died, my mother said to my sister and me, "We didn't get a lot of money from the insurance settlement. I'm going to give each of you five hundred dollars, do whatever you want with it. This is hard enough, and you should have a little something from your father." The next day I went to the big local music store and bought the only left-handed guitar they had. I still have it. I didn't bring my trumpet to college, I brought my guitar. With that guitar, I started a band, and paid my way through school. I played in one band for six years, four nights a week.

When I started, I had no experience other than playing in my room. First semester I went to this guy who was in a pretty successful band and said, "Hey, I'm starting a band. I'm playing guitar and I have a drummer—you want to play bass?" He said, "Well, do we have a singer?" I said, "Me." The only singing I'd ever done was in the shower. He said, "OK, are you good?" "*Really* good." I'm shaking when I say it. He said, "We don't need a good singer—we need someone popular so people will come and see us." We found a popular guy who was a decent singer, and after learning a bunch of cover songs, we played at a party. Suddenly we're a rock and roll band. We called the band Rumpelstiltskin and played around campus for free.

We finally got a club date and the night before we were supposed to play, the lead singer quit! Actually, it wasn't a club, it was a biker bar. You ask for a gin and tonic, you get a Bud. The bass player says to me, "You're singing. All I'm going to tell you is, don't sing like a girl." I'm dying of anxiety, but we get through the whole set. Nobody throws anything, nobody says it's bad, and a couple of people clap. *Alright!* We're back the next night, more people. We become the house band, we're there every month. This is my first job, I'm making money. I can't believe this is happening. But I went through some of the worst fear I've ever had in my life to get to that point.

I hadn't even *been* in a bar! I was so young. These guys would be, "Don't forget to announce the shot special." You're in there, you're selling drinks, you're doing promotions, all this stuff I had no idea about. I was learning the bar business, I was learning the club business. I was learning about the people who go to those places and what they want and what they don't want and how they want to be treated. I learned about hecklers. I learned that it was a *business*. I learned that, yeah, this is tremendous fun for me, but I'm not getting paid to be good, I'm getting paid to sell drinks. I didn't figure this out all at once, I got it over time as I saw how the owner treated us after particular nights. The place held about three hundred people. When the house lights came up, if I saw empty beer bottles on top of the telephones, all over the bar, on the seats, even if we had played like crap, I knew we were going to get extra money.

We were smart enough to do anything anybody asked us to do. If somebody said, "Hey, it's my buddy's thirtieth birthday next week, will you come and play the backyard for a hundred bucks?" we'd do it, and we'd play six, eight hours. We were building loyalty because we were showing loyalty. We wanted to play other clubs, and we knew they'd come hear us any place we played.

We weren't big partiers as far as drugs—we were there to work. Playing well was so important to us that we never drank before we played, nothing. We were too busy and consumed with making up the set list, doing the sound check. It was eight hours a day on top of doing schoolwork. You'd need to get your instrument repaired, or solder cables, or take apart your amp and rebuild it to make it sound better . . . *hours* of work. When we started out, I didn't know *anything* about the electronics, the PAs, and amps.

As I went through college, all I could think of was, "I'm going to graduate and do what? *This* . . ." I gave up on being a doctor early on and went for a B.A. in communications, with a double minor in business administration and philosophy. Communications made sense because I was performing. Philosophy made sense because I wanted to understand how other people look at the world. Business made sense because by then I was dealing with agents and a manager and percentages and I had no idea how to negotiate. I was kind of yessing myself along. "OK,

I'll play wherever you want, sure, thank you." I was just happy to play.

I thought that in school I would learn how to negotiate, how to be a business person, how to understand the art of the deal. I learned *none* of that. I was a miserable failure at accounting, managerial and financial classes. Statistics, economics, couldn't care less. This business is so hard to get into, and there's no real school that's going to teach you how to do this. It's so much different when you're doing the day-to-day operational things. But I needed the paper.

I took my little diploma and went to my gigs. The band rented a house, we put a little studio in the basement, we recorded some demos, we were getting some attention. But somewhere along the line we stopped growing. I was getting bored—I was getting heartbroken, really. I wanted to continue and hit another level. Other bands were asking me to join them, but I had loyalty to these guys, my first and only band.

When I finally left the band, I left badly, but the others knew it was coming. I went back to my mom's house in New Jersey. I wanted to be a musician. But I'd seen great musicians and thought, "I don't know if I'm *that* great." And I never wanted to be a starving musician, it just wasn't in me—I liked having money. I thought, I kind of understand how this promotion thing works, and how these agents work, and how these manager people work. I thought, "I should go out and land a job in the record business. Who's got my kind of experience? I've *done* it." [Laughs.] Apparently, *everybody's* done it—or nobody cares—because I printed up what I thought was the greatest hotshot résumé and couldn't find a job.

I got a copy of some *Billboard* directory which had a million companies in it and went on a résumé binge and sent them all generic cover letters. It cost more in résumé paper than I probably made the first year I worked. I couldn't get people on the phone. I didn't know what to do. I was shocked—shocked! I'm thinking, "What is this college degree *for?*" I thought college degrees meant jobs, but they don't.

I'd been out of work for three or four months, I was on the edge of complete despair. I picked up some rock magazine and there's a two-page spread on a record company called Grudge Records. There's an interview with this guy Chuck Gregory, who'd just gotten a good distribution deal with one of the big six companies—a distributor gets your records into the stores. Gregory's label was a small, boutique label with maybe ten people working there. I read the article and this was my first real glimpse into a record company. At the end of the article, Gregory said, "This is a great place for someone to learn the business because they're hands-on from the very beginning." I called *East Coast Rocker* and said I was from the *New York Times* and wanted a contact number for Chuck Gregory. It's important to be honest—but I will say that being clever and crafty will never hurt you in business as long as you do it with the right intentions.

I had the number and address in five seconds and I started calling. I had his quote in front of me when I called at ten A.M., every morning. I'd say, "My name's Ray Mancison, I read Chuck Gregory's interview in *East Coast Rocker* and I'd like to speak to him about it." "Who are you?" "Uh, Ray . . ." This went on for almost two months. *Every day*. I got to know the receptionist's name: "Hello, Paula, how are you, it's Ray." "Oh, Chuck's in a meeting." "OK, just tell him I called." I wouldn't stop. I built up a phone relationship with her. I was extremely nice, but not kiss-assy nice, because I think people sniff that out right away. When she asked what I wanted, I said, "I want a job." The worst thing you're gonna hear is, "Sorry, we can't do anything for you."

So it's going on three months and I'm annoyed that I can't even get this guy on the phone for one second, just so he can blow me off. I need closure. [Laughs.] One day she says, "Oh, hang on." I'm expecting her to come back and we'll have our normal chitchat about what was on TV last night or whatever. Instead I hear [harsh] "Yeah." The lump in my throat is so severe I can't talk for the first second. I say, "Mr. Gregory, I'm Ray Mancison and I've been calling you for the last few months. I read your article in *East Coast Rocker* and I'm looking for a job." He says, [gruffly] "We're not hiring. If you want to come and look at the place, you can." *Click*.

I take a dry run that day and find the building. The next morning

I show up at ten. Paula says, "Ray, how are you?"—knew it was me.
I'm wearing a gray suit, very corporate. Everybody else is dressed in
shorts, dirty sneakers. It's the most laid-back mess: posters, CDs *everywhere.* They're in a marketing meeting, so I'm sitting in this little chair
talking to Paula. I wait for about two hours. I'm real nervous, and I
have *no* idea what to expect—but I don't think this guy's going to be
very nice to me.

They come out of the meeting and I spot him right away. He's a
burly guy, gray hair, beard, mustache, saying, "Alright, baby," to the
people—a real old-schooly kind of guy. He looks at me: I have my résumé in one hand, the other hand out ready to shake. He says, "You're
the kid I yelled at yesterday on the phone?" "Yes, sir." He said, "You
got a job, kid—you got balls." That's how I started in the business.

I don't recommend this to everyone. Now, what I would tell people
is, know their roster, know something about the company—do your
research. I've interviewed many job applicants in my career, and nothing makes me feel better than when they come in and know the artists
I'm working with. It shows they've gone out of their way.

So I start work that day. He says, "Jesus, kid, you've gotta relax,
we're casual in here." I take my tie off. He says, "Denny, find the kid
something to do." He doesn't even remember my name. I don't know
what I'm getting for money, no idea. It's just, "I'll sweep the floor. I'm
in a record company, this is *it!*" They bring me back to the warehouse,
which is this big room with nothing but CDs and boxes. In the record
business, we have something called cutouts. If you've seen an album
with a little razor cut in it, it means it's at a discounted price. They want
me to make cutouts; I have to cut the albums. Then we have promo-
tional CDs, and for those you actually drill the bar code, you punch out
a hole. They say, "Do the whole warehouse." It should have taken me
six months.

My first day, I do it by hand and the albums are easy. But I think, I
don't want to spend the next six months in this warehouse all by myself.
I ask Paula if I can go to the hardware store and help myself out. I say
I'll pay for what I get. She says, "Get what you need, bring me a receipt,

don't spend a lot of money." I get some pieces of wood and a drill bit, a big masonry bit. I build a little right angle with the wood. That way I can do a box at a time. I do it all in two weeks.

I come back and say, "Now what do you want me to do?" They say, "You've got to be kidding." Chuck, who I've had almost no contact with, says, "Denny, get him a chair, get him a phone. Alright, kid, you're going on the phone." So I start talking to radio stations. That's how I started in promotion. It truly was hands-on. I got to do things at that company within a very short time. If I'd been at a bigger company, I'm sure I would have been locked away in some cubbyhole as an assistant to some egomaniacal boss who was afraid to let me advance. These people were trying to break a company in, and they didn't care who did what. If you're good on the phone, get on the phone.

My job was to get records played on the air. They gave me a group of smaller stations, and I learned about the different formats: college radio, rock, top forty, adult alternative, and adult contemporary. They had everything from rap music to rock, to Jack Teagarden, André Previn piano, a complete range. I listened to the radio, but I didn't know that people had *jobs* getting this stuff on the air. I just thought whatever was good got on. I didn't realize the number of records that people put out or how much competition there was. I only knew my tiny corner of the world where I was a little rock star and local hero.

I took that job when it was a hundred and fifty a week and no benefits, no health insurance. I was working full-time and barely making enough to buy gas to get to work. I did this for three years. By the time I left, I was making three hundred bucks a week . . . [Wryly.] And I wanted to be successful . . . But what I did know was that I was on the phone talking to radio stations, and I got to visit them and give product pitches. Because Chuck liked "the kid"—and I did a good job.

One time, I went into New York, to the Bertelsmann Building, to BMG. I was freaked out, I felt too minor-league. I walked into a staff meeting of about thirty people and had to put a video in the tape player and cue up the CDs and do my presentation. But I realized I felt OK in front of a group of people, I felt OK thinking on my feet. That was my training: a lot of stage time, adrenaline, and don't screw up. *Think!*

I didn't *learn* how to sell, I think it just came out of me. Most people I know who are great salespeople just *are*. Maybe it was my salesmanship that made me a good performer. I was good at selling myself, selling the band, selling liquor, selling the evening, selling the event. I discovered that maybe the whole thing boils down to it being easy to sell something you really believe in or something you truly enjoy.

In those three years, I learned if you want something, pick up the phone and ask for it. I learned to be creative and resourceful to get what I wanted. Chuck Gregory taught me by his example as a leader to let people work, not to strangle them. If you hire people to do something, let them *do* it. If it turns out that they're better than you thought, give them more to do, let them grow. He gave me my shot, and I didn't let him down.

I know how lucky I am that it worked out well. I went on to another company, which I really loved—which, incidentally, went out of business after a year. This is a tough business, I'm telling you. After that I went to a bigger company, part of Warner Brothers, more corporate, finally making some money. Same thing: radio promotion. But now I was doing it at a different level, playing with the big boys, and that really excited me. I learned about corporate communication and how divisions have to complement each other and how to deal with people when you're talking about a lot more money.

When you deal with a big commercial radio station, you have to understand that their function is not to play your records. Their function is to get their ratings up so they can charge more for their advertising, so they can make more money. My job is judged by how many records I get on the highest-rated radio stations. How can we work together? You learn that the more you understand about the other person you're dealing with, the better off you'll be in terms of negotiating, in terms of making a business situation winning for both of you. That's what will give you a lasting relationship with your client. These radio stations are my clients. They're everybody else's clients too.

Relationship is important, but a relationship is built on what you do after the deal, not what you do to get the deal. If I say to a station, "OK, you're going to play my records three times a day for the next six weeks, thanks a lot, take it easy," and they don't hear from me again, they're not going to play more of my records. It's what I do *after* I've gotten the commitment. What do I commit to you? OK, I'm going to bring the band to your town, I'm going to give you the opportunity to co-present a show, I'm going to maybe buy some advertising on your station.

This isn't brain surgery, it's the music business—we're selling an intangible product, really—and it's a fickle business. If you put ten people in a room, you'll get ten different opinions. You educate yourself, you know who you're talking to, you do your research. When I started, it was wonderful to pick up the phone and just run at the mouth. Then I got better and better, so I could get to the point quicker, in a more businesslike manner, while at the same time maintaining the ability to talk with people in a warm way.

I was at the big Warner label for two years. Big financial commitments behind their artists. I found myself in positions I never thought "the kid" would ever be in—like being the only label representative for Steely Dan's first show in fifteen years. Walking into the Manhattan Center while they rehearsed, knowing it was my responsibility for the show to go smoothly, and that it was going to be nationally broadcast on two hundred stations. It was pretty darn cool. There's a lot of perks in the music business: tickets and front rows and things like that. But I don't get paid to do that—I get paid to break artists no one's heard of.

I was offered a substantial amount of money to go to L.A. to what people might call a dream job. People might say it was a real stupid move on my part, but I didn't go. The job was to be head of the rock department for a major label—I was offered my boss's job when he was asked to leave. The job paid a *lot* of money, but, believe it or not, I didn't have to think about it at all. I was so miserable at that company, working under the regime that had taken over during the last year.

I'd already survived complete corporate restructuring twice. For the life of me, I don't understand how people who are running companies that are complete failures wind up getting jobs at other companies for the same multimillion-dollar contracts. I should be so lucky to get fired and get twenty million in severance. I watched co-workers being let go, axed. Honestly, you feel terrible for your friends and you feel good for yourself because you feel, wow, I must be damn good—I thought *they* were good and they're gone.

The best way to keep your job is to do your job. That's the best advice I could give anybody, and that's the advice one of my mentors gave me. "Stop worrying about the politics and do your job—you'll be fine." And that's what I did. This guy said, "When it comes down to who's important to our company, who makes us money and who costs us money, be one who makes money. And it's not enough to do your job—you have to *communicate* to people that you're doing your job. You have to fax and e-mail and get on the phone and network and tell people what you're doing." It was great advice.

You might say that to be offered this big rock job was a growth potential. And if it had been at a company where I wanted to be, I probably would have packed my bags and jumped. There *is* a certain entrapment when you are used to that big paycheck. I already had a good paycheck, a big expense account, *great* benefits, and I was doing all the cool stuff. But part of my misery was that I was in a hostile environment, to the point where it was almost terrorist. When you get treated with complete disrespect for what you do, or get told, "Whatever you do, it's not good enough and you better do more . . ." There were people leading the company who were completely irrational, who would call you up on a Friday at six and bawl you out for thirty minutes, hang up on you and call back: *"Oh, I'm sorry . . ."* I hated my situation. I was empty, soulless, miserable. I let the job take my passion from me; it ruined me musically, I didn't want to play anymore. And I was sitting in the biggest, greatest office, windows all around. I had a TV, VCR, DAT player, turntable, cable. I'll be honest with you, at first I measured my success by those things too. I thought, "This must really mean something—they must really respect me." But finally I couldn't *wait* to get out of there. Those things are not what make you happy.

I was there for about a year and a half, and then business got bad, the corporate structure got bad, and it started to get to me. There was room to grow, but I was also kind of waiting for someone to get fired or die. I wasn't happy with the people I worked with or the way they ran the company. Believe me, I was very well liked, but it just didn't translate anymore. It was phony—it was fake. They try to buy you with more money and a car allowance and a cell phone and a great office. All of that comes with a price. It's like, *great*, "We gave you all those things, now I don't want to see you in that office for the next six months. Get out on the road."

I was traveling three weeks out of every month. Traveling for work is not what anybody thinks it is. I get up early in the morning, I have to work hard all day—they were an L.A.-based company, I had to be on their time *and* my time. I'd be talking business at eleven at night. You start to think, "Do I want *this*? How *bad* do I want this?" The more time you spend in a hotel, the more you realize how much better it is to be at home. It's nice to get waited on and taken care of, and probably the first fifty times I ordered room service in some awesome hotel, I felt cool. But it goes away. And when it goes away it is the *worst* reality.

The day comes when you realize that a corporation is an emotionless, unfeeling entity whose function is to make more money than it made the day before. That's when you understand that business, although it is run by humans, is not human. I realized I don't matter to these people. I matter when I do a good job, and when I don't I'm someone to yell at. It's not like that everywhere, I'm sure, but it was like that there—and it was very eye-opening.

You learn that you have to take your hurt feelings out of it when you don't get what you want. I was promised a raise and negotiated really, really hard for it with people I trusted. When the raise came into effect, I got five thousand less than what we agreed on. I didn't have it in writing, I had it in a handshake. [sarcastically] They "lost" the memo. That's what corporations do to you. I'm not saying this was something Warner Brothers did, because it wasn't, it was something the people I negotiated with did. Why? Because the company was in dire straits at the time and they wanted to keep me—I was threatening to take another job—so they promised me something they couldn't deliver. Then they put their hands up in the air and said, "What are you talking about?"

At that moment, I thought it was their fault. I was very angry, I was hurt, I was emotional: How could these people I trusted, who I worked so hard for, do this to *me?* But this is what people don't understand about a corporation. They budgeted a particular job for a particular salary and that's what I got. Whatever they said to me, the bottom line is: "We're only going to pay you what we're going to pay you. Welcome to corporate America."

I looked at what happened and thought, If I'm going to keep doing this, I better be smarter and a little less trusting. If you're going to play hardball, you better know how to play. I hadn't, because I trusted my superiors so much. And they *liked* me. But it's not about that—that's not how you make business decisions. That's the hardest thing to understand. The corporation has no feelings and I *do.* If you're going to avoid getting your feelings hurt, you better build up some armor and be ready to negotiate, know what you want and get it in *writing.*

I started to think, "Is this what I aspire to be?" These people way over my head, making anywhere from two hundred to four hundred thousand a year, are quibbling over five grand for *me,* little worker bee?! I thought, Well, if I take that promotion, am *I* going to have to do that to somebody? I mean, I've done things while trying to get what I want—I'm really not *that* self-righteous. To be honest, I'm brutally hard. There's a certain amount of harsh realism you must possess when you're running a business. But I still treat people with respect—and I believe in complete loyalty to the artist.

Integrity and ethics are more about the person than anything else. Corporations can tell you they have an ethical code, but at the end of the day, you have a bottom line, that's what you *have.* You have a financial statement every quarter and it better be what you projected or you better know how to fix it. As a person, if you're going to be in that environment, you better know who *you* are. Does it matter that you have ethics and integrity? For a lot of people it doesn't, and many are very successful: masters at running companies, using intimidation as their tool. But I don't think people who are motivated by fear will do as good a job as people who are motivated by opportunity.

When I had the chance to run the department in L.A., I knew I wouldn't get to do it my way—I was going to be a puppet for others. In high school, I had a *great* football coach. The first day of practice, he put a piece of white tape on our football helmets and had everybody write in black marker the word *character*. He said, "Character is the ability to persist against constant opposition. As long as you keep that in mind and practice that, you'll be successful." I still live by that. I realized I just didn't have any character where I was. I was playing the game of bullshit and I hated myself for it.

What it came down to was, I'd do something and think, "Did I just do something good for this artist or did I do something good for myself?" More times than not, it was for myself. I started to feel like garbage. . . . What people don't understand about the music business is that so much stuff is, if not completely charged back to the artist, at least fifty percent recoupable. So half the time, all I'm doing is running up the artist's tab: it's a loan—they *owe* that money back to the company. I don't know exactly how the accountants divvy things up, but I'm sure it's not in the artist's favor.

The five-thousand-dollar raise issue came up two years ago, January, and I was gone by June. What I learned from that experience was how to do it. I basically put the head of the company into a corner. I wanted out so bad, but even though I had another job lined up, I wanted to be "let go" so I could get the benefits—severance pay, unemployment benefits, health insurance. I thought, "I'm entitled to these things, but the only way I'm going to get them is if I force it." How do I force it? Well, I knew that my boss, the person who hired me, was being let go. It boiled down to there being two job offers for me: one in L.A. and one in Boston. I refused to move for either one. I took care of it in one conversation. The head of the company and their legal representative were on the phone with me. My experiences had toughened me up enough not to cave. They said, "There is no New York job." I said, "Well, then do what you gotta do. I decline both. I decline both." They said, "Would you *please* stay on for three months and then we'll officially lay you off? We're phasing out your position in New York." I said, "Fine"—got it in writing and that was it.

After that, I considered getting out of the business altogether, and I started working on my own business, doing internet marketing with a partner. Out of the blue, the people who now run this record label called me up—I had worked for one of them years ago—and said, "We have a new venture." I wasn't interested at first—I was still a little shell-shocked. But I said to them, "As long as I can do it my way. Because I learned how *not* to do it at the big companies." As we talked, they started describing my dream circumstance.

Right now, I'm director of radio promotion, but unofficially, I'm the general manager. It goes into effect next month. I was brought into the company as someone to build around, because I had bigger label experience and I'm an energetic bulldog. I try to train and motivate and push, the way my football coach did. I hope the people I work with will look back at me like I look back at Chuck Gregory. He said, "I'm going to teach you and train you. You ask questions and I'll spend time with you—but at the end of the day, *you* have to develop your own style." I want people to say I teach them. I've been able to move along quickly because I had people who let me fail and succeed, people who let me just *do* it.

I don't want to kid anybody and say I just *love* getting up for work every day. Some days I can't stand it, it's too much pressure, too stressful. But for the most part, the worst days I ever have are probably equal to some other people's best days. I'm not someone who loves music—I'm someone who lives *inside of* music. It is *so* emotionally powerful to me. And I love that I get to talk to people all day long about music.

GABRIELLE LYON

Gabe's high-school work experiences involved babysitting and working at retail outlets. During summers, she labored on an apple-packing line. "Assembly-line work is not personalized; it has nothing to do with you and you're replaceable." Gabe's first college work-study job led her to seriously examine her work future. A summer job at a company founded and run entirely by women provided an important business model. "I didn't realize how important until I worked other places." Her second work-study position, as a teacher's assistant at a public school, became the basis for further work in education. After earning her master's, she took a fellowship job at an education magazine. She currently works with an organization whose goal is to restructure the public school system. Her first assignment involved everything from getting teachers talking together, to helping kids raise their test scores, to quelling an out-of-control class. For Gabe, twenty-four, it is essential to care deeply about what she does for a living. "My image of work was very much shaped by my father, who was vociferous about social justice and quite articulate about why he did what he did."

I lived in New Mexico until I was five and then my parents divorced and my mother moved to New Jersey, my father to upstate New York. My mother was an artist, but after the divorce she went to work and kept working, even after she remarried. She's now gone back to art school, more to give herself a chance to paint than because she needs to go to school. I feel bad about it now, but I grew up really snotty about her nine-to-five secretarial work. I always felt like, "You could have been an artist, why are you doing this?" I don't feel that way at all now.

My dad's a pretty well-known photographer. He's always been self-employed, independent. He came from a long line of doctors and lawyers and was the black sheep of the family—this crazy person trying to make a living taking photographs. When I was growing up, he was making films too, black-and-white documentaries, all seen by just about *nobody*!

My father made a point of letting us know it was important to do something that made you happy. And for me, you can't really separate work from who you were. Now, don't get me wrong—my jobs have included selling luggage and packing apples. But those were jobs, they weren't *my* work. And I don't mean that I didn't like them—I always liked work. I love it, anything: give me a job, I'll do it.

When I was young, I often babysat for my younger siblings, but also for others. I locked myself out of my first real baby-sitting job. A six-month old, the first time the parents had left the baby. I went outside to do something they'd asked me to do and the door locked behind me. The baby was inside sleeping. My first reaction was to go to someone's house and call my mother, but I was afraid to leave the baby. I sat outside, behind the shrubs, under the baby's window. If anything happened, I was ready to go through that window. They drove up at ten o'clock. "Why are you outside?" "*Well* . . ." Trying not to cry, trying to be the grown-up I was supposed to be . . . "I got locked out of the house . . ."

I worked at a gift store during holidays, worked at a florist shop. At the gift store, I wrapped packages and made huge bows and cleaned, all that kind of stuff. I didn't like the way the owner treated customers. Any kid that came in, any teenager, she would follow around. "Are you gonna buy that?"

At the florist shop, I did everything, including opening and closing the store, running the register. I was responsible, I had keys, I could drive. I thought they were kind of a rip-off and remember always looking over my shoulder and sneaking in a couple of extra irises. [Laughs.] I loved it when no one else was in the store. It would be late at night and I'd turn up the radio and run the vacuum and clean up. There was a kind of freedom in that. I would be completely relaxed in a way that I never was at home.

All through high school I worked summers at an apple-farm stand and packing house in upstate New York. It was six miles from my dad's house and I biked to and from work. They had all cute, friendly little girls, between fourteen and sixteen, running the farm stand—but they weren't really all that friendly. I think a few were robbing the registers. Some of the girls were pretty nasty to me and I couldn't figure out why. I didn't realize it at the time, but I worked very hard and I think it made them look bad. One girl started a rumor that I was sleeping with the boss. I was fifteen and was like, "Huh?" I was *completely* naive.

I also worked on an assembly line. That's what apple-packing is about: you stand at your post. Apples ripen at different times, and it's important that, as a crop ripens, you pack and ship out those apples. You start when the bell rings and you stop at the last minute, and your breaks are exactly ten minutes.

Different kinds of people worked on the line. Some lived in the area, were lower-class, and really needed this work. They'd been doing it for anywhere from ten to forty years. There were also seasonal laborers, mostly Jamaican, who came straight up from Florida after the sugar-cane harvest. They lived in a couple of trailers behind the farm. Predominantly family men, very friendly. They worked hard but were also very laid-back; we joked around a lot. I liked them as people. I'd ask them questions about their families and what it was like in Jamaica. They loved talking about their kids and wives—they'd show me pictures. It was interesting to hear about a life and a place I hadn't lived.

The packing floor is maybe a hundred yards. At one end are crates and crates of apples—*huge* crates, stacked up, usually with one kind of apple. Someone takes a fork lift and dumps the crate of apples into a gigantic bin. There's water in the bin, and all these little cranks and things that take the leaves off the apples and then wash them. Then the apples go through a waxer and come down the line, one after another, and circle back. There are maybe ten different workstations. You have two grades: really good apples and regular.

I still know the motion. [Her hands repeatedly move in an intricate pattern as she talks.] You get a box: you make it, staple it, put the inserts in—you have a rack of inserts, purple dividers, next to you. You have to turn the apples so that the red is up—when someone opens the box they find a nice shiny apple. You have to turn it over and around with one hand, because you're packing fast. The boss walks around and points to the apples that need to be turned. When you put the apples in, you end up jamming your fingers against the dividers. Everybody has these huge bloody cuticles, except for people who have been doing it so long they have calluses. But for little babies like me, it's *really* painful. I'd come in with my fingers taped . . .

There's just the sound of the machinery chugging. You can't talk because it's fairly loud—and also you have to keep your eyes on what's happening. At the end of the line are the baby apples, which are put in bags. This is the most dangerous job: you push the apples through a funnel down into the bagger, and at a certain weight the bag drops and you have to *catch* it. You hold it, all the apples fall to the bottom. You swing the plastic through the automatic twist tie, which ties it in a snap. You have to be careful that the bag isn't too high—because you mess up the machine and everything goes haywire. And you have to be *really* careful that you aren't carrying it too low . . . If your hand gets in there, forget about it . . . You stand there for hours shoveling apples into the bag.

At night, that's what I'd dream about. The *sounds* get into your blood, you feel them in your body. I didn't have nightmares, but I never felt rested. When you dream about the work, it makes it seem neverending, all consuming. That job gave me a real sympathy for what working on an assembly line does to you as a human being, to the human spirit. That's important to know.

When I got to college, I decided to be consciously aggressive about my education. If I didn't like something, if the teacher was boring, I switched. My attitude was: I don't have time to be bored, there's no point in being bored and I want to like what I'm doing. I didn't take any loans, so I was on work-study from early on, and I also worked summers.

One summer, I worked at a postcard company started and run by women. It was important to be in an environment where all the people in positions of authority were women. It allowed me to be comfortable in work environments in a way you're generally not, as a female, when men are always in charge. The idea that I could be in charge of something isn't weird or foreign by any means. The idea that there's a glass ceiling, which is a reality for *lots* and *lots* of women, is not a factor in the way I think about things. I haven't run into one. Or I have and I didn't notice. [Laughs.]

I spent six months working in the university's undergraduate admissions office, and I liked working there—I was good at it. I left that summer having a clear picture of one possible route: to become someone who interviews college applicants, someone who goes to high schools and talks about the university. There was something appealing about that because I *loved* my experience at college. But it was also disconcerting. I said to myself, "It's always going to be easy to find something to do, but what do you *really* want to do?"—meaning, it's important to be conscious of your decisions. Because you turn around and ten years have gone by. And this is what you've done with your life for those ten years.

I spent a lot of time trying to picture the ideal work-study job and decided I wanted to tutor high-school students in writing. I'd heard about a tutoring program at my university. In the fall, I interviewed for it and was told to go to such-and-such a school. I wanted to talk about thoughts and ideas and how to articulate those and get your point across. I was put in Room 101. Now, anybody with part of a brain knows that Room 101 is on the first floor and that the *little* kids are on the first floor. I thought, "Maybe it's an eighth-grade room! No—*first* grade." I was outraged, I was depressed—but I firmly believe it was the best thing that could've happened to me.

I was essentially a teacher's assistant, and I was put in with a *great* teacher. Everything I know about the classroom I know from being

with her. She never said, "I'm doing this because . . ." she just *did it*.
She's not academic at all, and there's something wonderful about that.
She was all about helping these kids learn, about being honest with them
and setting a certain tone, a certain environment that was sincerely respectful. She paid attention to who the kids were and why they were
doing what they were doing at any given moment. She was absolutely a
mentor.

By the end of the second year, I had learned so much about social
dynamics and the way kids learn. I found, without exception, these kids
were *so* responsive. I enjoyed trying to find ways to teach a group of
kids how to read. I was often given the slower kids, ones who needed
extra help. That was really challenging . . . I'd have to come up with
games, find some way to teach them.

I found myself becoming more and more fascinated with the dynamics of a classroom. It didn't happen overnight—it took a while. What
made the difference was getting to know the kids: I started to feel welcome and appreciated. They were *so* happy to see me. I worked there
for four years while I was getting my bachelor's and my master's. The
more time I spent there, the more time I wanted to spend there. And I'm
working at the school again, six years later.

After I'd finished my master's and left the university, I substitute-
taught for six months in predominantly African-American, low-income
neighborhoods. I spent time trying to picture the next perfect job and
decided I wanted to find a way to help classroom teachers in their classrooms. The long-term question is, where do you have an impact? Is it in
a classroom where you see thirty kids a day? Is it with a whole school,
working with the teachers who are seeing thirty kids a day? Is it writing
so that perhaps lots of teachers read it? Do I work at a university and
train teachers? What's going to let me combine the things that I really
enjoy doing?

If you're a classroom teacher, you don't necessarily get to do a lot of
writing. If you work at a university, you don't get to spend time with
kids. There's all these trade-offs. I kept thinking, Why couldn't you
have a little periodical where the teachers do the writing and you have a

couple of staff writers who have their beat? A magazine that would be specifically about what teachers are doing that is working well in the classroom. So instead of *you* inventing the wheel every time *I'm* inventing the wheel—we find a way to share successes.

I picked up a friend's mail while he was out of town and noticed a copy of *Teaching Tolerance* magazine.* I was like, "Holy cow, here it is!" I thought, "Gee, wouldn't it be nice if they were offering a job." I turned to the end and there it said, "Position, one-year fellow. Must move to Alabama. Applications due in May." They were looking for someone who had classroom experience and could write and do research. I'd been in the classroom, I wrote, and I'd done research for a photographer friend of the family. I ended up getting the job.

It was a great experience and a horrible experience—in part because it was my first real job and first real experience with office politics. I was twenty, completely on my own, living in a new city, working nine to five. I had to wear work clothes. I was accountable. Now, in *my* life, my hierarchy of authority is based on whether or not I respect you. It's not based on your position, or how much money you make, or how long you've been working. That's how I was raised. I'm not a super-respectful person or someone easily intimidated. I ask a lot of questions—I really want to know *why*, I feel I have the *right* to know why. I have a sense of entitlement. I discovered that can be threatening to people. Just in terms of who's doing what when, and the things that people get uptight about. Like, I didn't care when I took my lunch hour—Sometimes I'd take it at eleven, sometimes at one, sometimes I wouldn't take it at all. Some people found that strange. When I'd tell my mother things that upset me she'd laugh and say, "*Everybody's* job is like that."

But I learned an immense amount, and it allowed me to immerse myself in literature about multiculturalism, conflict resolution, diversity, and to build up a cache of resources, books, magazines, movies. I was

* The Southern Poverty Law Center's widely distributed magazine for teachers that focuses on issues of race, gender, inequality, oppression, and social justice.

exposed to a huge amount of great material in a way I *never* would
have been had I been a graduate student working on my PhD. And
that experience gave me some very specific job skills: writing formal
letters, proofreading, knowing *how* to work in an office. But mostly,
I really liked the work—and that when I wrote something it was
published!

After the fellowship ended, I came back to Chicago and simultaneously went into a master's program in education, and I began working at the Small Schools Workshop.* And I'm going to get a teaching
certificate. I don't think I'd ever *just* teach, but there's something *really*
appealing about having a classroom, spending a concerted, consistent
time with a group of kids.

At the Small Schools Workshop, some people just work on analyzing
test scores, some are researchers, some are facilitators, some are fund-
raisers. When you get down to the specifics of who's there and what
they're doing on any given day, sometimes there's complete chaos. It
can be frustrating—especially at the beginning—because there's nobody looking over your shoulder. Some people respond well to that, but
sometimes you really don't know what you're supposed to be doing.
There is a structure, there are leaders, but it's very flexible, and the
looseness is antithetical to what most people deal with in a job. But it has
the potential to be very empowering, to give you self-confidence, to
give you room to try things and fail.

My job is as a facilitator. A group of teachers might call up and say,
"We *hate* what we're doing, we hate where we're working, but we
know we're good teachers and we want to work together." A simple
definition of the workshop would be: helping to create intimate learning
environments where teachers are professionals, where all students are
known, and where schools are connected to communities. It's more an
organizing group than a consulting group.

---

* A university-affiliated activist organization whose mission is to restructure large,
failing urban schools into smaller, more intimate, and more effective learning environments.

There's a fundamental difference between consulting and organizing. Consulting, you have a program—meaning, "let me know what your situation is and I'm gonna give you a plan: you have this problem, here's how you can fix it." Organizing, to me, is more: "*you* have the plan, you just don't *know* you have the plan. Here's some questions to help you think about what you want to have happen." Finding the right questions, asking them at the right time and in the right way of the right people is what I do. At least, that's what I think I'm doing . . . [Laughs.] Then on other days I feel like what I'm really doing is hanging out.

As a facilitator at the school, my official title is "external probation partner." This past October, 109 Chicago public schools were put on probation, based on test scores and attendance rates. Each of those schools needed a probation manager to oversee the budget, and an external partner to look at the academics. The school I'd worked at was put on probation about the time I returned from Alabama and joined the workshop. I went to the principal and kind of nosed around. "Gee, sorry you're on probation." One thing led to another and I was assigned as their probation partner.

The principal had decided the school would be restructured into three small schools. It was more or less a top-down decision, and it was good in theory. But because it was a top-down decision—meaning that people weren't really given a choice—there was resentment, resistance, and low morale. So here's me, white, in an all African-American school, age twenty-four, relatively new to Chicago. I don't really know anything about the bureaucracy of schools, I have a substitute certificate, and I've spent some time in classrooms . . . I'm kind of familiar, people remember seeing me around before, and they figure I'm on their side because I chose to be there.

The dynamics were *completely* different than when I worked there as a teacher's assistant. I spent from January to June getting to know the *whole* school and *all* of the teachers. I made it clear that I wasn't there to tell them how to do anything. I went out of my way to let them know I was learning *from* them, gave them super-respect. Every couple of weeks I'd call a meeting of each of the small schools within the larger school. I'd find different ways to get them talking about the kind of school *they* wanted to have. It was a strategy—but, the truth is, I believe that school has all the potential in the world to be an excellent academic institution.

Four days a week, eight-thirty in the morning till three o'clock in the afternoon, I'm at the school. I visit with teachers, I sit down, I talk with them about what they're doing. Sometimes I work in the classroom, sometimes I sit around in the lunchroom. I'm *absorbing*, and trying to create a presence as someone who is supportive and has a sense of what the teachers are doing. In my ideal picture, the teachers know—the way I know—what the others are doing, and they work together.

I see the real work of the Small Schools Workshop as being about changing dynamics and relationships. But the other side of the work is very much about getting the test scores up, because goal number one is to get them off probation. I consumed information about test-taking skills and category breakdowns and how tests are made. I held workout sessions, me in the classroom talking with the kids about how to take a test.

The first thing I said was, "OK, close your eyes. Imagine you're coming in, sitting down, about to take a test. Let's talk a little bit about how we take tests." In a room of thirty kids, there's always one or two who actually have a strategy: "I look at all the questions first," or "I kind of see what the story is about, I read it very fast." Thinking about how you take a test, developing a *consciousness* about it, is really important. Those are the kinds of conversations that *don't* go on at schools where the scores are really low. If they did, the scores would be higher.

We'd role-play. I'd come in and pretend to be one of them on a test day. What does it look like, what does it feel like to be focused? What *does* it feel like to be focused? One thing I did was called "secrets and suspicions." What I considered basic skills for taking a standardized test, like process of elimination. The very *first* thing you need to do is to identify the ridiculous answers—there's always one. The same with similar answers. I would say, [gently] "Here's something maybe no-body ever told you before. Sometimes they put down two answers that are kind of the same. You *know* that because you read them and see they're similar. Here's a secret: they can't be the answer." And suspicions are, for example, if you see a really weird answer, a flag should go up. This is definitely about *how* you take the test much more than what you know. You gotta demystify test-taking. The youngest grade I did this with was third, and the oldest was eighth. Those were the kids that really got into it.

I had one class, though, where a fight broke out. Pencils were thrown, marbles were hitting kids in heads, things were thrown at *me*. The fight was the *worst*. I'd never had that happen in one of my classes. I broke it up, but I was like, *kid against the wall, kid over here.* I'm like, *"You both stay RIGHT HERE."*

I was embarrassed. I was worried the teachers were going to say, "She can't handle it," or, "See, I told you so—this is why you have to be so strict." That was the one I liked the least. I felt *terrible*. I talked to a couple of teachers I was friendly with, I was just about in tears. They were great, they were supportive. They said, "Honey, it happens to everybody."

It was, in some ways, a rite of passage. Alright, this has happened, you lived through it and it's not the end of the world. I was most concerned about the principal losing faith in me. She was very matter-of-fact. She said, "Well, when a class isn't paying attention you have to stop." Later on I said to one of the kids, "I feel really bad about what happened in class the other day." He said, "Well, you shouldn't have told them they could do whatever they wanted. . . ." [Laughs.] On-the-job training!

Sometimes parents ask advice about kids and college and work. I tell them a person who can adapt, who has different skills and experiences to draw on, is the one who's gonna make it. People are interested in hiring well-rounded people, because it means they don't have to hire another person every time something new comes up. Being able to adapt is crucial.

In the classroom, I may not be able to help the kids know everything they need to know, but I want to make *damn* sure they know ways to find answers. I want them to have the skills to get to wherever it is the answers are. That's why the internet is *so* important, why familiarity with computers is important. Not because it's going to get you a good job, but because it's going to give you access: it's a *tool*.

Right now, I know much better the things I care and feel strongly about. But the more things I do, the more things I *want* to do. I feel very strongly about education. I don't know that I want to be a classroom teacher, but I think a lot about teaching and what it means, and what it's supposed to do, and what it *ought* to do. One reason for my reluctance to commit to a classroom is that once you're there, you have to *stay* there.

Right now I'm preparing to go on a dinosaur expedition with my husband [Paul Sereno, a paleontologist]. There's a big difference between going on a dinosaur dig and working in the Chicago public school system. But I like that I'm about to pack my bags and go live in the Sahara Desert for four months. It's a different life, and it gives me that much more to bring to a classroom. And I *love* doing the dinosaur work, though I never think of it as *my* work.

I feel really good about the different things that I've been able to do. I think a lot about how that happened. I'm not a self-made person—it came from parents, it came from school, it came from things I read, it came from being very conscious about trying to do things I cared about.

I fret a lot because I'm not career-based. If I were a career person, I'd get a job as a teacher, work on my administrative degree, become a principal, and then I would work with teachers to create a really terrific school. Sylvia Plath has this great, unforgettable image of sitting in the crook of a plum tree and all of the plums are possible lives, and meanwhile she's starving. I feel like that a lot. But lucky me! I mean, I'm not bitching. And I'm certainly not starving. I wake up every morning feeling very lucky and happy to be here.

CARL VALENTIN

As a teenager, Carl hated school and loved all things to do with bike racing, from training to working in a bike shop, where he did everything from selling bikes to chasing down creditors. Carl, twenty-seven, didn't take work seriously until recently. "It was always work so I could . . . do whatever, usually race." He labored in restaurants and toyed with the idea of writing as a career until he realized, "Very few writers can only write—most everyone else has to do something else to get by. I started wondering, 'What do I want the something else to be?'" Wanting to give bike racing one more try, he attempted to sell real estate and drove a cab to earn racing money. "Letting strangers into a very intimate container for hours every night is a bizarre job." Feeling on top of the world at the end of a successful racing season, he came to a sudden realization. "I was fulfilling the dream of a fourteen-year-old, and as a twenty-four-year-old I had a different agenda." Talking with various doctors convinced him that medicine was the right career for him. Once in pre-med, a cardiac monitor job in a hospital had him hooked. "I found it exciting that I was, at moments, as important as anyone there. Brief moments!"

My dad was a lithographer. He didn't go to college, he trained as a journeyman back in the early days of the profession. He was lucky enough to make the transition to laser scanning when it first came around. But any technological change serves to unemploy numbers of people, and most of my dad's co-workers lost their jobs. These highly skilled guys then had to go into usually lower-paying, labor-type work in the industry. But my dad made the transition, and it turned out to be at the highest pay scale in the union. That pretty much changed our life:

we became firmly middle-class, high-level blue-collar. My mom was a nurse, another classic middle-class job for women, although now there are more and more men. My parents both really liked their work.

There was never any pressure in our family—we were encouraged to do whatever we wanted. I'm the youngest of five. My eldest sister earned her CPA in the Marine Corps; my brother is a lithographer. Another sister is an artist and teaches the Bradley System childbirth method; another works in daycare. Then we get to me, who hopefully is about to go into medicine.

It's ironic that I'm pursuing an academic career now. I hated school and I liked to work. I had a lawn-mowing service as soon as I could push a mower. I cut lawns in the neighborhood for about fifty bucks a week, which was the big time. I was nine, tennish—at the point where your parents would trust you with a rotary-blade object.

I got into bike racing at the age of twelve. Cycling is expensive, it's all-consuming in terms of time, and it's very dangerous—three things a parent would not like their son to be involved with. My parents were supportive, but they weren't gonna buy me whatever I needed. Racing bikes are a thousand dollars and up. You crash, you need a brand-new one. I crashed one—a week before the state championships. I needed eight hundred for the frame. The guys on the team were older, and they got the money together and bought me a bike, which made me take *very* good care of it.

When they're just starting out, most racers work in a bike shop. From the time I was fifteen till I was about nineteen I worked in one as a mechanic and a salesman and an accountant—and a gardener. [Laughs.] A bike shop is a sort of organic thing; it's not any one particular kind of business. During the winter, they might rent cross-country skis, or hold clinics on training for races. During the summer they're selling, they're repairing. I didn't consider the bike shop work: it was just a way to make other things happen. Work was that way for me up until I decided to go to medical school.

I worked for a guy who extended credit to people who wanted to get into bike racing. And like in any credit program, a good percentage were reluctant to pay it back. Since I raced and knew all these guys, the owner thought it would be a good idea if I called them up: "*So-o-o,* Fred's a little low on money. Do you mind paying him what you owe?"—you know, before he called the collection agency. I was the muscle—"knuckles." I weighed about 110 pounds at the time. Knuckles were about *all* I had. [Laughs.]

I was the only midteen athlete working at Belmont Cycles. There were a couple of other teenagers who were mechanics, *real* mechanics. In the bike world, being a mechanic is more a genre than a job. They're often heavy-metal fans, smart, misunderstood. They took being mechanics very seriously and were all *very* good at it—one of them went on to become a pit mechanic for a professional automobile racing team. They didn't like the racers or the salesmen to come back and tell them what to do. But I was a pretty good mechanic just from tinkering around. You get on a bike and go forty miles an hour around a corner, you want it to work right. So they gave me a little bit of room to work on bikes.

There was a garage behind the building where the shop was, and that was the mechanics' garage—they had their own Metallica-blaring turf. Two of them were brothers and it was their lair. If it was busy, you'd go back and help. You'd have to use *their* tools, and they all had little name plates on them. If your tool bag gets messed up you can't function. With bikes, *everything's* a specialized tool—you can't just grab any wrench to work on a pedal.

Building wheels was something the mechanics trusted me to do on occasion, something they generally reserved for themselves. That was sort of a rite of passage. It's probably the highest art form in being a bicycle mechanic. You take the spokes and the rim and the hub and the nipples—the nuts that thread onto the end of the spoke—and you make a wheel. The wheel in itself . . . no single spoke could hold it up, but the total force is great from the tension of all the spokes. Yet the opposition of forces has a net force of zero. And it has to be even. There's a whole philosophy to it—it's like Zen.

It was nice to be trusted and work with the mechanics, because any job's boring if you do the same thing every day. I never like to be pigeonholed, so I made it a point to be able to do anything in the shop. There were twelve employees, and I was probably the only one that versatile. 'Cause the heavy-metal guys just didn't want to come up front and sell stuff. They were like, "*Dude*, buy it or go." [Laughs.] The shop eventually closed. Most small businesses have a certain lifespan. But it was sad for me: I raced for the team, I worked at the shop, it was my social life.

I chose to attend high school as seldom as possible. Bless them all for letting me get away with it: the school, my parents, and a few teachers that didn't think I was a bad guy and recommended I be given a diploma. Senior year, my European history teacher said, "Carl has a different agenda." [Laughs.]

My first summer out of high school I raced. I worked that winter stringing tennis rackets at a sporting goods store, selling running shoes. After Christmas, I took off for spring training in California and raced that whole season. But I wasn't winning. Artists don't get famous until after they're dead, but in bike racing you know every Saturday and Sunday and Thursday night at the track who you are and what your position is in the field. I was good, and I could've kept racing as a loser, as someone who *didn't* win. But I saw others my age who were in the career track for being pros, and it was pretty clear that I wasn't one of them. You don't want to be at the bottom of your field, no matter *what* you're doing. Since I wasn't going to become a professional, I started college that fall. It was rough. I left racing feeling, in a way, that I had completely failed.

I started college in a small town; a high unemployment, ex-coal mining town which has the university as its single business. So there were a lot of students, many of whom wanted to party—the school was mostly men who liked to drink a lot. I worked at a fifties-stylized reproduction diner, a twenty-four-hour place. On Halloween, they covered the exterior windows with chicken wire so they wouldn't be broken. We had a pretty good crew, a combination of middle-aged career waitresses who lived in the town and college students. There was camaraderie because we all had the same job. The students didn't have the attitude that, "We'll soon be professionals and *you'll* still be waitresses." There was, though, the understanding that this was the waitresses' turf and they got better shifts, which was fair.

We had to wear black pants and white shirts. I'd never been a waiter and I wanted to look professional, so I wore a tie my first night. When one is in black pants and a white shirt it is not a major leap to put on a tie. I got a few comments: "What's with the tie?" I'm still defensive about this. [Laughs.] I got nothing against ties. I grew up a generation behind hippies, and for us, a tie is not a symbol of accepting the status quo or the establishment—it's a fashion element.

The significance of this job was that I learned how to be a waiter, how to be thick-skinned. You don't want to approach a situation ready to be insulted. You go in expecting to be treated well, but the opposite will happen in any service job and you get ready for it pretty quickly.

I worked with a Palestinian guy. He's my hero of horror stories from waiting. He was wiry, he weighed about 120. He had an Arabic name that was hard to pronounce, Y-el, so we called him Wally. It was a pretty tough middle-American town, and one night three big cow-tipping type guys came in and tried to ditch on the bill. We'd get stiffed all the time, kids come in and they try and run on you. It was around midnight and these three guys took off in a car. Y-el grew up during the war in Lebanon, so he had no problem with any violent situation. He ran into the street and jumped onto the window of the moving car. He *made* them drive back to the diner, where they were quickly arrested. He demanded to get his tip before the police took them away. [Laughs.]

I always liked literature and I decided to study creative writing, but I wanted to be in a better environment. I got ten As the first year and got the *hell* out of there. I came to Chicago, back to civilization, and a job at a French restaurant where I worked off and on for five years. At the diner I'd always pretended I was working in a better restaurant, so when I got to one, I just did what I'd always been doing—it fit a little better. If the owner, Francis, reads this he'll disagree . . . [Laughs.] But I *tried* to be a good waiter.

I started out as the lunch waiter and became a bartender, and then a *night* waiter, and then a bartender again. I was a busboy, I was a gardener, I washed dishes, I worked in the kitchen, waiter, host. In small businesses, you do what needs to be done. When you're waiting tables, you're more vulnerable: you approach the table and it's easier to make a mistake, and people will really ring you on it. With bartending, you establish your own space, you have a little power—a legal responsibility to cut people off when they're too drunk. I often suggested people cut back, but that's in a sense why I was a bad bartender. When someone would get to their third martini, I'd ask if they wanted something lighter, like soda or water. People would joke that I was the worst bartender ever, but I think they liked that I was concerned about them.

Sometimes you can get cocky and not consider waiting as a profession, but there are people who make a *lot* of money doing it and are happy and fulfilled. We had one professional waiter. The others, men and women, were writers or actors or in school, or doing something else. You'd get there early and people would sit around. Maybe one of the waiters would give you his new poems, and we'd all sit there and read them, drink cappuccinos, and smoke cigarettes. Then the boss would remind us that it was time to make money in the restaurant, and we all accepted that was, in fact, part of the deal. We'd wait on people for about six madhouse hours.

The customers were often artists, writers, poets, actors, sculptors, furniture-makers. I got to see people who were pretty much five years down the road in their careers. I saw writers who still worked in restaurants to get by, or drove cabs or taught. I started to think that maybe at some point you decide to stay involved and interested in writing, but take it off center stage and find a career that's fulfilling in and of itself.

It solidified, seemingly all at once, in the fall of 1995. But I think there was a lot of process that went into it beforehand. I did my last year of college in Ireland, where as a student, you cannot get a job. There aren't enough jobs for the people there who *need* to support themselves. We're lucky in America in that, if you're trained for a particular job, you can pretty much get it. If you're a student and you want to bartend, you can bartend. That's just not the case in many European countries.

In Ireland, I wrote more than I ever had and realized I was not about to publish a first novel. After graduating, I decided to return to racing because I felt I'd left it as an unsuccessful person. In the last few years I'd matured greatly, and thought that was the element I'd been missing. So I trained for a season, worked at the restaurant a little, got a real estate license.

Real estate's *hard*. I had two nice suits and I looked pretty good. I had ties, four ties. Sold *nothing*. A friend who tried real estate at the same time had a master's from the London School of Economics. We found that a master's in economics and a bachelor's in English gave us *no* advantage over a well-connected housewife who wanted something to do while the kids were at school. The act of selling a house is not dependent on understanding the *whole* market, but on understanding each person who comes in. Anyone who's lived a life and interacted with people can do that pretty well. We found ourselves huffing around with our credentials, to no avail.

I relied on driving a cab for money. Cab driver . . . with strangers, there's a lot of individual identity, but in a way, everyone on Saturday night at six o'clock is sort of the same person. And they all change at eight, and become the next same person. Later, they become the ten o'clock variation. And by two they're all drunk—they're *all* drunk.

Cab driving is dangerous. I had to leap from the cab, calling out for police assistance to save my neck a couple times. That's *scary*. Sometimes it's someone who wants your money; often it's someone who, at three in the morning, is very drunk and pissed off and just wants a piece of someone. And if you're in the cab, it's *you*.

Sometimes the police aren't all that helpful. I was in a head-on collision with a man. I was preceding forward in my lane and he was preceding forward in the opposite direction, in *my* lane, and we hit. His fault. We clear everything up, everyone's OK. I give him a ride to the police station in my cab, which can't go in reverse because the bumper's falling off. Fortunately the station's only fifty feet away. We get there, we go in.

He has no insurance, he has *nothing*. They tell him to leave. *I* on the other hand, am written a ticket for everything conceivable. When I inform the policeman—who sports no badge, no ID, no *tie*—that, in fact, these tickets he's writing are illegal, that *none* of this is appropriate, he informs me that I can spend the night in jail. They throw it all out at the hearing, but meanwhile I lose a night's pay, I have to defend myself in court. *Lotta* stress. Bad night . . .

So now that I've slagged the police, I'd like to say that one time some guys tried to ditch a fare, and two cops helped me track them down. In about twenty minutes, the cops had them against the hood of the police car *begging* not to have their parents phoned, *pleading* to give me excessive amounts of money for my inconvenience! [Laughs.] I haven't driven in a few months. There's been a rash of cab drivers robbed and locked in their trunk. No one's locking *me* in a trunk.

I started racing again, and in about a month, I was back to Category Two. By midsummer I was racing better than ever, and had a lot more courage and determination to get through dangerous courses without slowing. It was a *blast!* I got to race with people I'd only *read* about. By the end of the summer I was racing in Ireland, had won a little money, and had this 'I-can-do-anything' feeling. But as soon as you feel that way, you start thinking, "Well, if I *can* do other things well, why would I be racing bikes?"

During that season, I'd met several doctors, all of whom said medical school was a lot of fun—which was a surprise to hear. And there's a doctor I know at my mom's emergency room. When I went in for my asthma problems, he said, "Carl, you're a nice boy, you're a nice boy, and this racing it's a good hobby, but you should go to medical school." [Laughs.] So that fall, I sold all my bikes, and begged a dean to let me in late for fall classes, and started my pre-med studies.

At the beginning it's a real shot in the dark, because *lots* of people want to be doctors. I'd never wanted to go through ten years of medical training, 'cause it seemed like a *very* long time. And if you go into academic medicine, it's a *very, very* long time before you make any money. But I was always interested in science; and because my mom worked in an emergency room, I'd grown up hearing compelling stories about emergency medicine. As a racer, I'd *been* in a few emergency rooms myself. And in terms of training, racing is a physiologically oriented sport. As a cyclist, you train with a heart monitor, you study diet.

I started pre-med, and it seemed like an incomplete proposition to go to school and not be around patients, even as a student. I got letters of recommendation from professors, and a letter of reference from a family friend, the retired head of the hospital-affiliated university where I applied. When I went for my interview, I wanted to sweep, push wheelchairs, *anything*, just to get in the hospital. They said, "Well, you've got some biology background and we'd like you to apply for a position as a cardiac monitor." I thought, "*Where do I sign?*"

You start out with a few weeks of training in basic heart anatomy, and then you study the way an EKG wave form represents the rhythm of the heart. It takes a little while to learn that. It's not real sophisticated, but you have to know it well. You learn how to look at the *bla-blip bla-blip* thing that you see on the screen and to know what the shapes mean. You have to monitor about ten heart transplant patients simultaneously, and when one of those blips looks wrong, you essentially yell *help*. It's not much more complicated than that.

But there can be all kinds of false alarms. Automatic alarms are set at parameters for each patient's condition; if someone's rate goes too high, or their pressure drops, or their respiration's wrong, the lights and buzzers go off. But not all cardiac arrhythmias will trigger the alarms. You really need someone to watch the monitor or go in the room and visually check. Some patients are asymptomatic. They'll have ventricular tachycardia—a rhythm that develops in an irritable heart, a heart that's sick. If they happen to be standing up, the biggest worry is that they'll get dizzy and fall down. If I'm watching the monitor and I see someone go into v-tach, I run and make sure I'm there to catch them. And then I yell for the nurse . . . Well, it's all simultaneous. But every patient is different. I've learned that will be a challenge. There are so many clues about what's right and wrong with a patient, but they're all *individual*.

You can't look in a textbook and say this blood pressure or that heart rate is pathological.

On a one-to-one basis, I work with the nurses more than with the doctors. The nurses essentially run the hospital and the doctors see to the medical care, but they overlap tremendously. And then you've got me in there, who every once in awhile yells, *"V-tach, room 115!"* There's a hierarchy, and everyone has their job. The chain of command is: I inform the nurse, the nurse informs the doctor, the doctor informs the fellow, the fellow informs the attending, and the attending makes a very large decision. It's like basketball in a way: whoever's holding the ball is in charge. I have a very minor job, but it's crucial: when I see an arrhythmia and call it out, *everyone* has to pay attention. They have to know what room it is, what patient it is, what the rhythm is. And then they run in there and *they* have the ball—they're in charge until it's relayed to the next level.

Patients have to go from our unit to other units and back, for X-rays, biopsies, for any number of reasons. They're all on telemetry, which is the EKG radio signal to the monitor where I'm sitting. When a patient leaves or comes back, I have to be told. There are ten rooms around me. I can visually see each room, but usually the curtains are drawn. If patients come back and I don't know they're in their rooms, I don't know to be watching their cardiac rhythm. You gotta make sure that someone's holding the ball and that everyone knows who has it. It's about communication, like any job.

In hospitals today, if you only do one job you're not carrying your weight. So they cross-train the cardiac monitors to do secretarial work. On my left are the monitors, and on my right is a computer. The medical orders written for the patients have to be entered into the computer. You can do both simultaneously, with safety as the highest priority. You look at the monitors every ten, fifteen seconds, to see that everything's OK.

The best part about that is getting to read the medical orders. I get to know their medications, what precautions are taken for those who are likely to fall, for those on a respirator, those who can't move around. I learn what precautions are being taken to keep their skin integrity, to keep it healthy. A major part of fighting infection is keeping the skin in good shape, especially in transplantation. Things quickly turn from the study of cardiology to that of infectious disease. You have to repress the immune system in order to prevent rejection, and infection is often the complication that arises. You learn a lot.

There are *thousands* of ways to put orders in. To put a medical order from a doctor's scribble into a computer, to enter the scheduling, the dosage, the routes of entry into the patient, is *so* complicated. The secretaries *fly* through these orders. When there's a code, someone in respiratory or cardiac arrest, it's very important that the secretary get the orders in immediately. Meds have to come up from the pharmacy, lab results from the labs, and the doctors need to know everything *really* quickly.

I'm also there to meet and be in relationships with doctors where I can ask for a letter of recommendation. They're taken seriously: you don't give a letter to someone you don't know. If I just sit there, I'm the secretary. I have to get up on a soapbox and say, "Hey, I'm a pre-med student, I want to learn anything anyone wants to teach me. If something's going on can I observe, can I see X-rays?" The other day I had the opportunity to take off work three hours early and watch a transplant surgery. I was standing in the room, I was there—and it was *amazing*. But to do that you have to get away from doing your job, and that's a conflict. You don't want to jump up and down and say, "I deserve to see this!" I think I handle it well by letting everyone know what I want, but also that I don't want to load my work onto anyone else. I think a lot of the nurses and secretaries want me to get into medical school, so I feel I've got this support team.

I wasn't the best at being on time in the beginning. Maybe it was after I saw my first death . . . I don't know, but I'm not late anymore. In a lot of jobs, if you're late, there's no real consequence. Part of it's showing respect to your co-workers, because if you're late, they can't leave. And this is a twenty-four-hour unit: if you're not there someone else has to be. It *is* life and death.

I've seen a few people die. Quite often, someone looks like they're dying, but the crisis is expected, the doctors are on top of it and the person's fine in a day. Other times, the doctors are convinced that death is unavoidable. As you grow older, you learn that things aren't always what they seem—but in medicine this is honed to a science. With my level of education, I can't see what the differences are, they're not yet apparent. Clinically, all their vital signs can be going down and they look really gone for, but they're brought back from the brink. And other people seem to have decent vital signs, and still it's pretty much known they're not gonna make it. I look forward to learning the difference.

I took the MCATs [Medical College Admissions Test] in April. When I got the results, I became unglued, "I got three twelve's, *oh my God!*" And then I dropped the phone, stumbled backwards, and leaned against the wall. [Laughs, blushes.] I *trained* for this for two years—I don't say "study." But to get a dream score, I really wasn't expecting it. I cried, I hyperventilated, I couldn't breathe. My mom, who was a week out of heart surgery, had to check and make sure I was OK.

My goal is to be involved in academic medicine at a large university, with all the facilities, all the students, all the gurus. I'd probably like to work in a university emergency room, with level-one trauma, for the most seriously injured people. That's the plan.

The American medical system is based on a lot of money changing hands, and I'll sign for maybe a fourth of a million dollars, and pay it back through being a doctor. But an investment in a house is a hundred grand, and that's just to move in, that's not even to keep the payments up. And being a doctor's at least as valuable as being a home-owner . . . *I* think.

I've changed a bit since deciding to become a doctor. I'm still sort of a smart-assed comedian guy, but I tend to be a *little* more serious. I'm selling my motorcycle, which I thought I'd never do. But I can't crash into the back of something now. Society is about to invest a great deal of training in me. I have a sense of responsibility.

III

"Just Fire Me": Harsh Realities

So, you've got a job, a job you think you want—maybe not for the rest of your life, but at least for now—and you think everything's going to work out just fine. But our job expectations are only that: expectations. Sometimes the job is right, but the boss is wrong. Sometimes the job's not right, the workplace unpleasant, but the boss is nice. Sometimes the job's not too bad, the boss is OK, but you make crucial mistakes. In this section, we hear some painfully honest recollections of job experiences that, while deeply instructive, were in many ways unsuccessful.

While the men I interviewed described moments of inadequacy and failure, without much prompting the women tended to delve deeper into their difficult experiences. Each of these women found herself in over her head at some point and was humbled by her own naiveté.

Mary Henderson's first "adult job" was an eye-opener. "In a way, it was a great first job because it was such a bad experience." She found her supervisor untrustworthy and incompetent, and paid attention to what she did and did not like about the overall workplace environment. "There were some things about which I specifically remember thinking, 'I do not want to work like this my whole life.'"

Isabel Lucero, frustrated by her inability to land a job in the public service sector, went to work at a bank and suffered at the hands of a tyrannical employer. "My boss was known for yelling at meetings and swearing, telling her staff, 'I can't believe you're so stupid!'" Isabel learned firsthand the toll workplace stress can take on your body: "I wasn't eating, I wasn't sleeping—I had terrible headaches." Like others in this section, she also learned the importance of documenting events when things start to go wrong.

For the young teacher, Gillian Moore, the small school where she was hired was "For me, a dream school—*perfect*." But a supervisor's sexual harassment eventually made her work life torturous. Her advice: "Find someone you can trust outside of work and admit what is going on . . . A lot of times women don't even know they're being sexually harassed; it's not always the clear-cut 'If you don't sleep with me you're not getting a promotion' version."

Overwhelmed at a Big Six accounting firm, Grace Tilsit thought, "'Alright, I have an MBA in health-care management, I know some of the words—I know what it's about . . .' I had no clue what I was doing. *No clue!* I felt so stupid, so unqualified." After she made an embarrassing mistake her status abruptly changed: "Suddenly, everything I was asked to do was secretarial . . . It was humiliating."

Through a series of internships, Julie Baxter learned as much about herself as she did about the work world. "Until your first real job, the only authoritative relationships you've had have been with your parents and teachers. The dynamic of the employee–employer relationship is completely different." About a paying internship, she says, "I thought they'd never fire me because I knew everything: their personal life, the business. I had such a distorted perception of what my role was. I didn't think it conceivable they could go on without me."

By examining what went wrong, each of these women turned a bad experience into the foundation for seeking a different and more suitable kind of work, a fairer, saner and more trustworthy employer, and a more satisfactory workplace environment.

MARY HENDERSON

Mary, twenty-five, had no career aspirations when she entered college. "It was just, you take piano lessons, you go to college." After meeting her future husband, a wildlife biologist, she took jobs in whatever part of the country he could find employment. She worked for a public research group and as a short-order cook. Her first real job was as a recruiter for a healthcare clinic, where she entered a crash course in surviving a dreadful boss. "I got a big dose of how to be politically savvy, of how to watch your back and build networks and cultivate your friendships." The working conditions gave her additional important information. "I took a lot from that job in terms of things I didn't want." After relocating to the midwest, she spent an unhappy six months looking for work. "It's so all-consuming not to have a job, and stressful because you're not making any money." But Mary eventually landed a part-time job at a social service agency which led to full-time work, and a master's degree, and a direction.

I don't have any desire to be rich. Part of that may be because when I was growing up I never wanted for anything. If you can get through that without turning into a spoiled, horrible person, it's a great experience. You get *money* out of your system. For some people it's important: they won't feel like they've made it until they've earned a lot of money. And, obviously, people who say money's not important are people who *have* money. But I'm not really into stuff. I want to have a job I enjoy and find fulfilling. I need to be in a job where I feel I'm doing something to help the greater good . . . whatever that is.

I grew up in Michigan. My dad always had his office in our home, and my mom didn't start working till a couple of years ago. I never saw anyone get up and go to work when I was a child. My dad would be in his sweat outfit and go upstairs and make phone calls. His work has always been moving paper money around, investments, that kind of deal. Now he does some sort of banking transaction job and actually goes to an office. We were pretty upper-middle-class. My father was very successful, in his sweatpants. [Laughs.]

My first job was in high school, at an amusement park. Imagine an amusement park in a town of twenty thousand people. It's the usual: old tires and go-carts. They had a little wooden maze, and bumper boats, and a water slide with a vertical drop about ten feet. I was a cashier and I ran the rides, I picked up cigarette butts—kind of did it all. Then I worked at a soap store, and in college at a pizza joint.

I never *decided* to go to college. I grew up with the conception that *of course* I would go to college, it was the thing to do. [Laughs.] In other countries, after high school people work for a few years and *then* go to college. That makes so much more sense. I had *no* idea what I wanted to do, I was a real floater. I didn't take classes with a career in mind, I took classes that sounded interesting. I fell into studying religion after dropping a calculus class three days into the term—religion was the only class available. But I loved the classes, and religion became my major. For a large segment of the world, religion is a powerful motivating force; people run their lives and make decisions with that as their orientation point. Living where I did in Michigan, everybody's white, everybody's Christian, and I was curious to know about other kinds of people.

I went to a large university, and there wasn't a whole lot of career guidance. I could've used more, 'cause I certainly didn't give it a lot of thought. I wish someone had sat down and said, "And just what are you gonna *do* with this religion degree? Have you *thought* about this?" Because it's an absolutely worthless degree for getting a job, unless you want to get a PhD and be a professor. It would have been prudent to maybe minor in religion, and I think I would have been receptive to the idea, but I had no guidance.

After graduation, I signed up for the Peace Corps. I've always been intrigued with other cultures and wanted to live somewhere else. I thought I'd do that and then go to grad school. But senior year I met the man who later became my husband, and decided to stay in the States. Of course, in the meantime, I hadn't been *looking* for a job because I was going to Africa to teach English. [Laughs.]

I graduated in '92, which was the all-time *worst* year to get a job out of college. None of the graduates I knew got a *real* job, the kind you'd want to keep. I *needed* to have a job. I had been successful at every other thing I'd done in my life and, suddenly, here I was, graduated from college and no job. I felt like I'd played by the rules, done what I was supposed to do. So where did I go wrong?

I sent out tons of résumés and went to the career-planning places. I got a job with PIRG [Public Interest Research Group]. I was supposed to run an office for them in L. A. This was *just* after the L.A. riots, so of course my parents didn't want me to do that! [Laughs.] My husband is a biologist and he had gotten a job counting spotted owls in the mountains east of the Bay Area. In June, I went to work in the Berkeley office of CALPIRG [California PIRG] to get my feet wet and canvass and do what you do when you first start.

I knew people who had done PIRG in Michigan, and they said it was OK, but oh my God—I *hated* it! PIRG mainly lobbies, and to raise money they hire people to go door-to-door. You're supposed to raise $85 a day. If you were good at it you could make a lot of money, because once you got beyond that amount, you got to keep a percentage. I was *not* good at it. We tried to find people at home, and the neighborhoods we were in . . . I couldn't *bring* myself to talk someone out of $15. They'd say, "I really can't afford it." And I'd say, "You know, that's a good call." I'd look around and think, "You should spend $15 on something else—buy some food." After about a month, I thought, "This is not me—this is *not* what I want to do."

Subsequently, we moved to Washington state. Since we didn't plan on staying long, I ended up working as a cook in a fifties diner. I know people who are like, "Oh, I just *couldn't* do that." And how *did* you expect to pay the rent? I mean, you've got to eat. I *hated* every minute of it, it made me miserable, but I did it. I'd been a vegetarian for years, and it was a hamburgers-and-liver kind of place. We used bacon fat for *everything*. It was revolting. When I had to make soup I wouldn't even taste it! [Laughs.]

The people I worked with were nice, and it was a low-pay, low-stress job, but it was so demeaning. The guy who hired me acted like he was doing me a favor to give me this $5-an-hour cooking job. It sounds terrible and really stuck-up, but I thought, "I'm *better* than this." The others didn't understand this was just an in-between thing for me. They'd say, "Well, if you stayed, you could work your way up to $6 an hour." [Laughs.] *Nooooo.*

We moved to a different town in Washington, and I saw an ad in the paper for a recruiting specialist at a migrant health clinic. My job was to recruit medical personnel—physicians and dentists and mental health providers—for six clinics, two in Oregon and four in Washington. In central Washington there are lots of orchards, and fields of hops and garlic and stuff that needs to be picked by hand. We served the migrant workers who came through. The organization had been around for about twenty years and had built a nice new clinic, but it was next to impossible to recruit physicians. I was there for six months and recruited three people, which was actually pretty good. Most recruited two or three a year.

If there was some kind of medical conference in the area, we'd set up a little booth. People mill around, and if anyone hesitates for a moment you jump in with, "Let me tell you the plight of the migrant farm worker." But primarily we got people through the Public Health Corps, because by working for the clinic they could repay some of their school loans. You have to work in an underserved area and agree to come for a certain time. For the most part, people would serve two years to get their loan repayment, and then they were *gone*. It was a constant battle to find doctors.

When I started, I'd asked what I should expect and had gotten some sense of numbers, of what was realistic. I knew you could spend six months and have nobody agree to come. I spent a fair amount of time placing advertisements, writing letters and mailing people information. (I know how to hunt-and-peck, but I've never known how to touch type. I *wish* I had taken typing . . .) I spent a lot of time on the phone, telling people about the area and the clinic. We didn't have many people who actually came to interview, because the clinic couldn't afford to bring them out unless they sounded quite serious about working there.

The woman who ran the human resources department at this place was a *horrible* person, so there was constant turnover among the staff. Everybody was new and young, and *nobody* knew what was going on. The department head was a high-school graduate who'd started as a secretary or receptionist and had just hung around for the next eighteen years. She didn't have the training or the skills to be running a human resources department, and she wasn't the kind of person to pick them up. She was unqualified, but enough aware of that to want to steal your ideas.

Another thing is she'd *lie*. I'd be on the phone trying to set things up with potential doctors. I'd say, "I'll get back to you in a couple of days." I'd talk to her and say, "Can you give me a decision?" She would say yes, the person could come, and then she would change her mind. These people were medical residents somewhere, and they would have made a space in their insane schedules to come. I would have made plane reservations and set everything up. And she would *change her mind* . . . You'd constantly be put in the position of having to backtrack. You don't want to make the boss look like an idiot to outsiders, because that's not good for the organization—that's certainly no way to *lure* people to it. So I'd make myself look like the idiot: "I'm sorry, I just got started—my mistake."

My boss was very concerned about how she came off and would *never* admit to making a mistake. She was always looking over your shoulder, wanting to know what you were doing. She wouldn't let you send a letter out without looking it over. It was insulting and demeaning. My feeling is, "If you don't think I'm qualified, why'd you hire me?" If I have a question, I'll come and ask—otherwise, just back *off*.

I shared an office with the only other person in the department who was older than me. She was very savvy and would say, "Be sure and write things down." She told me to keep track and document everything. She said, "If she agrees to something, make a note of it, and when she agreed to it, and let somebody else know. Make sure she can't back out and leave you in bad situations, that she can't lie." I got a notebook and made entries every day. I made a list of all the times she went back on what she said, or did something incredibly stupid, or claimed an idea that had been mine. I wouldn't even leave the list at work, I took it home with me. I'm sure she came in and went through our desks and computer files at night. We didn't trust her at *all*. [Laughs.]

I tried to keep my contact with her down to a minimum. My office-mate even took the extra chair away from the side of the desk because we didn't want to encourage our boss to stay—*ever*—if she came in. In a way, it was a great first job because it was such a bad experience. It was a good place to learn how to look out for yourself because the boss would say *anything* about you. If she hadn't done something she would blame it on one of us.

After six months, I quit because we moved to Chicago where my husband was attending graduate school. I would have stuck it out at the clinic for at least a year, especially since it was what I considered my first real adult job. It doesn't look good to jump from job to job. And there were things to be learned. I'd never worked in an office before—and I could see why my parents had chosen not to do that. Especially given *that* office environment. If you asked for staples, you got just enough to fill your stapler. If you lost a pen within a few days of getting it, well, "I *just* gave you a new pen." You could have one at a time. The whole place was demeaning. It was not set up to give people any responsibility, to allow people to take control of *anything*.

I didn't have a sense that this is the whole of the working world—I just thought the boss was neurotic and the place wasn't run very well. There were some things about which I specifically remember thinking, "I do *not* want to work like this my whole life." They *made* us eat our lunch between twelve and one, and you *had* to take an hour lunch break.

You had your fifteen-minute break in the morning and your fifteen-minute break in the afternoon, and God *forbid* you be five minutes late . . . They didn't treat us like adults.

I learned from that. I thought, "I don't want to have to *ask* somebody if I want to have a doctor's appointment . . ." I do my work, I get my stuff done, I shouldn't have to account for *every* minute—and I don't want someone looking over my shoulder all the time. I didn't want to work in a situation that tense and hostile. You spend too much time at work to wake up every morning and say, "Oh my God, I have to go back there again . . ."

When we moved to Chicago, I didn't have good luck finding work because I didn't know what I wanted to do. It's hard to find a job when you're all over the place. I looked for five months. I applied for anything under the sun. There would be jobs in the paper I was ludicrously unqualified for and I'd apply: I'd say, "I'm a really quick learner, I'm smart, and I'll work for half the pay of what you're advertising." *I* wouldn't hire someone who did that. But I wasn't qualified otherwise.

I probably applied for seventy-five jobs. Not having a job is, I think, just the *worst* thing. Even having a shitty job is better than having no job. And for some reason it always seems easier to *find* a job if you *have* a job. Maybe because you're not as desperate. I'd stay home two afternoons because somebody had said, "Well, I'll call you." And then nobody calls, and you're like, "*Forget it!* I'm not putting my life on hold—if I need to go to the store, I'm *going* to the store."

I spent most of my time reading through the paper, writing cover letters, trying to drum something up. It's so hard to *plan* anything. You think, "I want to take a vacation in the summer, but I don't know if I can, because if I don't get a job . . ." or, "If I do get a job, will they let me go when I've just started?" and, "Can I afford it?" And, and, and . . . I mean, you just can't get on with your life!

My husband was in school, and by February, we were so broke that I had to do *something*, so I worked as a secretary at a jewelry store for three months. I had seen a job advertised in the university newspaper and I wanted to work near campus, near where we lived. So on a day when there was a forty-below windchill, I *walked* over to drop my résumé off. A few months later, while I was doing the secretarial job, I got a call: "We have your résumé on file." This job paid less and was only part-time temporary, but I took it. The job was as a research assistant at a children's policy research center, the Chapin Hall Center for Children. I've been here three years now, and it's been a great place to work. All the things I hated about my job at the clinic, this *isn't*.

I was hired to be a research assistant for four months, to transcribe and code interviews, enter information into the database. People just expected you to be smart, expected you to catch on right away. It was, "Here's the job, let me know if you have a problem, otherwise, go do it." I liked the job, I liked the work environment, and I got the sense from talking to people that if I made an effort I could probably get more work. I went to the person who hired me and said, "Is there another project I can work on?"

I ended up working on a grant review project for a foundation. They'd given grants for staff development of youth workers, people who work in Campfires, Boy Scouts, Girl Scouts, the YWCA. I got to visit a number of states and look at various grant sites. We spent all kinds of hours on that report. The report was important to me because it was going to have *my* name on it too. I felt a real sense of responsibility. That always makes people do a much better job, because they have a reason to give a damn.

I didn't really *have* any direction when I started here, but what I've experienced has given me a direction: I'm getting a master's degree in social work. I'd never known any social workers, and it wasn't something I'd thought of doing until working here. Now I'm committing myself, and it's a relief—though I don't necessarily feel this is my life's *passion*. It's just that you have to focus in some area, and I enjoy this kind of work. But I could just as easily have fallen in somewhere else and enjoyed that just as much. Now that I'm considering this as a career and going to graduate school, I'm thinking, "OK, I need to learn new skills to further my career." I'd like to move on from the job I'm in now, to move from this place on the totem pole.

Do I have advice? Learn to type. [Laughs.] I wish when I was a freshman somebody had said, "Get to know some professors." Because, *A,* you need recommendation letters, and *B,* you need somebody who will keep an eye on you. *Especially* if you go to a big school where you're just one of thousands of people—you need somebody who's gonna say, "Now, tell me why you're taking oceanography again?" Find someone who's experienced, or at least someone you admire, or who does something you think you might like to do. Have them give you some guidance. If you don't know what you want to do? *Still* find someone. And hang in there. Don't sell yourself short, don't give up too soon. Sooner or later you'll get a real job. It *will* happen.

ISABEL LUCERO

Influenced by civic-minded parents, Isabel's attention to social and political is-sues comes naturally. In high school, a challenging job at her pediatrician's of-fice gave her a perspective on workers' rights. After college, she was awarded a fellowship at a public-policy school. She graduated during a dry spell in the not-for-profit arena and, desperate for employment, took a job at a corporate bank. Unfortunately, her boss "was on some kind of power high." Isabel's efforts to do her job went unacknowledged, she was put on probation, and finally chose to leave. Later, seeking relief from an unsatisfying real estate office job, she worked with a women's organization. "I needed to effect change, to make an impact." Through the organization, she learned of a community relations job, but after the unmotivated workplace culture wore thin, she moved on. Isabel, thirty, sees her early work experiences as humbling and instructive. Now em-ployed by a Latino organization, "I feel I'm finally doing something that uti-lizes my background and my passion."

While I was growing up, my family would sit around the TV after an election, watching to see who was going to get appointed to what cabinet position. Politics is an ongoing soap opera, and that's what I watched. I didn't really know the impact, I didn't know how important these things were, how many people they affected, or why people would care who ran for what.

My parents are from New Mexico, and I was born and lived there till I was five. My father went to refrigeration and air-conditioning school at a military base in New Mexico. Had he gone through school, he would have been an excellent engineer. The company noticed how good he was and sent him up to Minnesota for a training program, and we stayed.

We lived in a middle- to working-class suburb of Minneapolis. Racially and socio-economically it was segregated, very white. My father worked and my mother volunteered at my school. Later, she enrolled in a community college to take a couple of classes just for fun. She wound up getting a bachelor's degree in political science and went on to law school, but didn't finish because she became disenchanted with the legal process. Eventually she ran for city council and has remained in politics to this day.

My mother loved learning, and I picked up on her academic interests. She would study and my dad would take me to the park, to the zoo, to the doctor's office, to ball games, fishing—we did a father–son kind of thing every weekend. I saw the effort my father made to support my mother's interests and thought, "Oh, how cool." I thought that's what life was like. As I got older, gender differences in society just slapped me across the face.

When I was in high school, I wanted to be a corporate lawyer, counsel for a major company, for the money. I didn't fully appreciate until later what that would entail: making sure that companies kept making big dollars, often at the expense of a lot of little people. To actually like what I did for a living never occurred to me.

When I was sixteen, my parents told me I had to work. Our city had a youth employment program, and I saw a job listed at my pediatrician's office. I worked there until I graduated from high school. I answered the phones, I filed, I made appointments. The hardest thing was dealing with angry mothers. "My son came home from school sick, and I *have* to get him in." I knew my mom would be the same way, so I'd say, "Well, come in, we'll see what we can do."

I was taught to be responsible. I learned how to read the handwriting when they filled out a prescription so I could call it in. If the child had an allergy, it would be listed on the chart. If a child was allergic to penicillin, you couldn't give them *any* derivative of penicillin. You had to make sure you read the prescription right or you could be up a creek. I also had to weigh and measure the kids when they came in. I had to get *that* right because if they'd lost weight, it might be because they were sick—and, also, prescription dosage is based on weight. So I had that sense of *don't screw this up.*

That job was actually the toughest one I've ever had. I worked Saturday mornings, and the patients would all come in—*boom!*—you had to answer the phones, schedule appointments, greet people, know which rooms were empty so you could fill them, clean rooms when people left, weigh people, get prescriptions ready for when patients left, and know whether or not to set up a next appointment. You had to be careful not to get kids from the same family mixed up, like Michelle versus Michael. Or kids with the same name, but from different families. Keeping all of that straight was a nightmare. But it was also *fun.* My interpersonal skills *really* shot up, 'cause I had to be able to handle these really bitchy mothers.

That was the first time I was challenged. *Boom, boom, boom,* things came at me from all directions and I *had* to handle them. I'm very much a perfectionist, too. I never thought, "What if I fail? What if this goes wrong?" It *couldn't.* That was it, it just couldn't go wrong. It was stressful, but that's part of the fun, that's what gets my adrenaline going.

My mother and I loved the senior doctor when we were patients, but I found out that he was a *real* jerk. There were full-time people and part-time people. When it was time for the annual raise, the part-timers didn't get anything. I got upset—I got *really* pissed off. I marshaled a little attack! It was the end of the day, a few other part-timers were there, the doctor was still in the office. Everyone was saying, "Oh, he probably had a good reason." I said, "Are you *kidding?*" I laid out my argument. "This is ridiculous. There are other ways he could have handled this. He could have at least told us money was tight, but for him to say nothing . . ." So here, little old me gets the other part-timers together and I lead the revolt. I just thought, "Why not?" I'd grown up with the golden rule: Do unto others. I wasn't going to screw anybody, so why should they screw me?

We marched into his office to confront him. His face turned *red.* He said, "Yes, I have my reasons, and I'd be more than happy to talk to you about them . . . one at a time." The doctor and I didn't get along as well after that, and I don't think we wound up with a raise. But I ended up getting more respect from the other people, including the other doctors. I gave up on being a corporate lawyer around then, because I saw how that doctor was—in it for the bucks—and how we, the workers, suffered.

In college, I majored in Spanish and political science because that was familiar to me. After college, I didn't know what I wanted to do. My mom heard about a program that gave minority students fellowships to policy schools, and policy schools were pretty new at that time. I took the GRE and was awarded a fellowship. My first year, I had a *tough* time and had to retake a couple of classes. That was one of the first times something was actually difficult for me. Oh, I would cry—I *cried*.

I was also encountering big-time racism. All the students of color were basically on this same fellowship. We formed a student group, as a support system. We talked about what we were learning and how it applied to our lives and communities. The other students felt threatened. No matter what kind of protected class you are—female, minority, disabled—if you want to call for equality, the haves need to give something up and they never want to.

I ended up speaking at commencement. I talked about how people of color can influence the public-policy process, about getting equal access to process, about effecting change. About how important it is, when you reshape and rethink policy, not to just pitch everything out; if an implemented policy doesn't work, alter the parts that need changing. I talked about creating a minority presence.

My mom wanted to help me write the speech, but she got frustrated. She'd say, "That's just so idealistic, that's not practical." We got in a fight and she said, "Fine, *you* finish it," and went to bed. The next day, she was in the audience and I said, "Some say that idealism isn't practical," and my mom was just dying! I said, "But *Brown versus Board of Ed* was practical: they just wanted equal access." I said, "Rosa Parks was just being practical. All these reasons that we fight for equity, they're *practical*, not idealistic." Afterwards we had a reception, and it was *only* the families of color that came up to me and said what a good speech it was. People had tears in their eyes.

 After that, I wanted to work on something to do with advocating for equity, whether it be racial or gender-based. In graduate school I'd done two internships: one in Minnesota for the state, involving people with disabilities, and one in Chicago at a nonprofit. After graduate school, I looked in the white pages under women and called all these women's organizations, all these nonprofits, and met with people, and net-worked. My résumé was *everywhere*. I scoured the city.

 I did temp work while I looked for a job . . . for eleven months. I wanted a job in the not-for-profit arena, and this was '91, '92, and the philanthropic market was *dry*. It was so tough. I took an adult education course—I needed something in my life, the stress was just killing me. Somebody in the class worked for a large bank, in human resources, and said, "Give me a call." They were looking for somebody in their affir-mative action/equal employment opportunity section. I thought, "It's a corporation, I don't want to do corporations. But I've been out of work for close to a year . . ." I took the job.

 It was number-crunching, for twenty affirmative-action plans for over sixteen thousand employees. My job title was "employee relations specialist." Our department was the vice president, the assistant vice president, me, and some support staff. The vice president and the two support staff were black, the assistant VP was white. Whatever the vice president said went, and this woman ruled with an iron fist. She was a total bitch.

 There was no partnership, no collaboration, no communication— and nothing got done. I wasn't sent to training classes to learn how to use the computer program—my boss said, "Your predecessor did fine without them." I didn't know what I was doing, and I was doing my damnedest to try and figure it out. My boss was known for yelling at meetings and swearing, telling her staff, "I can't believe you're so stu-pid!" She was pissed off at me all the time.

 I thought maybe this was just how things went in the professional working world. I kept thinking, "Maybe I'm not working hard enough . . . maybe I'm not looking at everything . . . *maybe* if I just tried a little harder"—always thinking it's me, because that's what she was telling me. I didn't know that *everybody* hated working for her—the turnover in that department was very high. But I didn't go around talking bad about my boss, so it took a while for me to find this out.

We were supposed to have all these different reports on the work force of the bank: what it consisted of, were women increasing in proportion to men; was the average education going up? And nothing was happening, the reports weren't getting done. One time, my boss, the assistant VP, and myself had lunch with the senior VP. He asked how the reports were coming along, and those two lied and said, "Well, this is where we are, but we need more time." I wanted to say, "Excuse me, they can't manage their time, they can't make a decision, they can't go forward, they don't have access to anything—they're *incompetent!*"

The deadline for getting the affirmative-action plans in to the federal government was approaching, and the heat was *on*. If we didn't file, it would be my boss's butt on the line. But instead of saying to *her* boss, "I need more resources to get this done," she'd smile and say, "Oh, everything's fine." And then nail *me* into the ground. I'd spend the first hour of work in the bathroom because my stomach was in knots. I'd be at work until seven at night. I wasn't eating, I wasn't sleeping—I had terrible headaches. Finally, somebody said, "Document what's going on, at least the terrible treatment."

At one point my boss said, "Maybe this isn't the job for you." Her secretary had quit, and she wanted to make *me* her personal assistant. She said she'd keep paying me the same salary and bring somebody on to do my job. I told her *nooooo*. When it was time for my assessment review she put me on probation because I wasn't "performing." We outlined what I needed to do to improve and get off probation. She couldn't fire me, because she didn't have grounds.

We started work at eight-fifteen. While on probation, I was supposed to be in her office at eight-thirty to update her on my progress. After a couple of days, someone in human resources said, "Oh, so they're finally hiring somebody to help you out." I said, "What?" "I saw your job posting go up." I kept my cool—I said, "*Did* it . . . ?" The person realized this was being done behind my back. *"I can't believe she didn't tell you!"* She's having me go to her with my tail between my legs every morning! I said, "Fuck *that*. She posted my job, didn't tell me, I'm not going to give her the satisfaction of letting her know that *I* know." I kept on working . . .

After the first three months, I'd begun talking to the computer people. We'd assembled a team to solve the number-crunching problem on the computer. Two of the vice presidents in their area treated me like a normal human being—they knew I was competent. I started coming to work at eight. I'd get all my stuff, go down to the computer people and blow off my eight-thirty meeting with my boss. I'd meet with the team for that half hour and we'd work through problems. She'd look for me, the people in computers would hide me. "Well, she *was* here, but I don't know where she is now." It was comical. And then at nine, I'd come in, and *oh*, was my boss *enraged*. She'd say, "What progress have you made in the last day?" Trying to put me on the spot. The computer people would say, "Isabel met with us and had some very valuable insights."

One day I got up and thought, "I can't do this anymore." I asked the computer guys if I could use their names as references and they said yes. I figured I'd just go do temp work till I found something else. I submitted my resignation and she looked at me and said, "Good—about time." Another vice president called me into her office and said, "Off the record, why?" I said, "Because this woman's a bitch, and incompetent, and *evil*." [Laughs.] I just laid it all down—I had nothing to lose. She said, "Do you know this has happened to everyone in your position? Your job has the highest turnover." I said, "No, I hadn't a clue." If I'd known, I would have gone through proper channels and said, "Listen, I'm experiencing the same crap everybody else experienced."

So I quit and did temp work, and then *more* temp work. I felt so much better. And then I started a part-time job and they wanted to hire me. I worked with a real estate development company who funded largely commercial projects, like shopping malls, community redevelopment kind of building. I got along well with the president, and he started to treat me as his protégée. But he became CEO, and the new president wanted me to be more of a secretary. After about a year, I'm like, I'm outta here.

While I was working there, I'd hooked up with a women's organization. As I was butting heads against these unfulfilling jobs, I became involved in their advocacy committee, because that's what my background was. Since real estate wasn't my passion, being on the advocacy committee was my outlet. We wrote letters to legislatures, we addressed issues. Then they asked me to sit on their board, and I was *so* flattered to be in my twenties and on the board of something.

Through their job bank, I read about a job in the nonprofit world with a family resource organization. They had contracts with communities or state governments and did strategic planning and community assessment. For example, if a community wanted to start a family support center—a place where you could access a number of social support services, get child-care and parenting classes, or job training—they'd call and ask for a community assessment. I helped coordinate and write contracts, negotiate dollars, prepare and disseminate technical assistance materials.

I spent two years there. The first year I liked it: I enjoyed what I did, I enjoyed negotiating numbers. My boss and I had the same philosophical approach: we were hardworking and we cared. But it was an organization of about twenty people, and I began to realize our colleagues were less conscientious. If something fell through the cracks, "Oh well." *No*, it's not, "Oh, well!" We're getting paid thousands of dollars for this, and these community groups barely have any money. My boss saw the same problems and started doing everything himself. Our colleagues thought he was a control freak, that he didn't trust them. In reality, he had high standards and wasn't good at telling people they needed to improve.

The organization was very shortsighted. They wanted us to go out and do packaged presentations and bring in a few thousand dollars here and there. My boss wanted to create packages to fit what communities really needed, to expand on what we normally did. He had wonderful ideas for community involvement, and he wanted to try them out. I'm also more of a push-the-boundaries person. But the organization resisted change. They wouldn't back him up and finally he quit. I started putting out feelers for a new job.

I applied for a job at a Latino organization. I went through three rounds of interviews, and asked them about the history of the organization to find out if it was another dysfunctional place. I wanted to know the financial viability of the organization and who funded them. I asked about the tenure of the staff, I wanted to know if there was a lot of turnover. How long has my boss been there? Was she mentally stable? [Laughs.] The job involves advocacy around workforce development and building political capacity in the Latino community. I've only been there two and a half months and am already staffing a committee.

In my last job, I was basically autonomous. I always *wanted* feedback, and now I have it. I'm working on my first publication and when I get my division's feedback, I need to understand that it's constructive, not "Oh, you didn't do this well enough." Like I said, I rolled along in high school, I got the fellowship, I've been recognized for certain accomplishments. But no matter where you come from, or how easy it's been, you still have so much to learn. In order to keep your mind open and continue to grow, you *have to* have a sense of humility. No matter how confident you are, or how capable other people see you as, if you think you can just sit back on your laurels, you've got another think coming.

It's *hard* to establish the right level of self-confidence—it's easy to get cocky. "I know this, I can do it," versus always questioning yourself. You need to know the difference between somebody saying, "How stupid can you be to include that? I can't believe you would do this," versus, "OK, I understand where you could draw this conclusion, but have you considered A, B, and C?" One lays criticism on you as a person, and the other tries to make the product a better thing—that's about the work. Human interaction and interpersonal exchange is all about helping each other, and keeping your mind open, and reaching for new heights.

Then you go on to the next level, which is about the work and you. The next time you say, "Have I thought everything through? Is there a way my perspective is clouding things? Who else can I have read this?" You take yourself through that exercise, through a checklist. At first, you learn things in incremental steps—that's how you improve yourself and your product time after time. It's like a physical activity: you can't run a marathon right away, you have to work up to it.

If I could offer any advice for those going into the working world, it would be to think about what skills *you* want to get out of a job, even an entry-level job. Where do you want to be? What will it take to get there? Like, if you want to start your own marketing firm, maybe you want to spend a little time in sales, a little time in advertising, a little time as a buyer, just to get different perspectives, to get the skills you need to get where you want to go.

Definitely ask questions—not only about what's expected of you, but about what it's going to be used for. You can nip problems in the bud if you have foresight about where things are going. Ask questions of people who've been there before. Where should I go, who should I talk to, what do I need to know, where can I find this information, what did you do the first time this happened to you? What happened when you lost your first big client? What happened when you took on a great contract but found you didn't have the resources to finish it? What happened when your first staff person quit on you?"

In every other part of your life, you want to know where you're going. In interpersonal relationships, you ask, "OK, what do you want out of this, where are you coming from, what's your background?" You don't just go up to the travel agent and say, "Get me a ticket to anywhere." You find out what shots you need, what kind of clothing . . . And it's just like that in a job: you need to find out what the environment is like, what tools you need.

I grew up in such a civic-minded environment that making a difference is important to me. Since you spend more than half of your life in a job, you should care about what you're doing. There's the whole Plato outlook that there is a job for everybody. You should enjoy your job so much that you'd want to do it even if you didn't get paid. And it's everybody's own love, if you will, for what they do and how it all fits together, that makes society tick.

GILLIAN MOORE

For Gillian, school made no sense until she attended an alternative high school that nurtured her interest in visual arts. "It was like a vocational school for artists." At loose ends after college, she went on to get a teaching certificate. "I enrolled in school out of pure desperation." To her surprise, inspiration struck, and she decided she wanted to teach a particular group: troubled children. She found her dream job, working with kids involved with the juvenile justice system, and was able to create her version of a good classroom for reluctant students. "I could never teach them everything they needed to know, but I tried to teach them how to get information—how to do research; how to ask questions, where to go to look things up—to create the conditions for learning, for curiosity." There was one drawback: an increasingly complicated and destructive relationship with her supervisor. She strove to remain at the school; eventually, though, she was overwhelmed by tension, hostility, and her own failure to set boundaries, and she took a job elsewhere. "It's so ironic that I'm a teacher. I walk into schools and my palms still sweat. In a room of teachers, I do not feel one of them; in a room of kids, I feel one of them."

I was a kid who had school phobia from the earliest days. I did not take advantage of anything positive in school. I was the kid that cut class, smoked *in* school, wrote excuse notes for the other kids and signed their parents' names. I was bad, one of the worst. Everything in school seemed a series of isolated incidents, thrown one after another, that didn't hold any connection in my mind. By the time I was sixteen, I just wanted to drop out and find something work-related that I'd be interested in doing.

I'd had summer jobs from the time I was twelve on. I'd never not worked. But with each successive experience in offices, collating and copying, I realized that this was *not* what I was gonna do with my life. I found working in an office incredibly boring. Of course, I didn't really know what any of these people actually did. Maybe it wasn't boring at all.

My father is a social worker and my mother worked as an administrator at a human-rights organization. They divorced when I was in elementary school. As a teenager, I was kind of a loner and very depressed. The only thing that made me really happy was doing artwork. I ended up graduating from an alternative high school where we apprenticed with adults in the arts field. You would go work with a sculptor for a couple of months, or work in a gallery. I fell in love with art. I started *going* to school and began respecting my teachers. I connected. I started to see myself as having some kind of potential in life, whereas before I felt I had none. That art school gave me the fuel to eventually apply to college.

While I was in college, I taught art at a state-run mental hospital for schizophrenic geriatrics. I worked at the hospital maybe six months. The patients were mostly made to lay in bed and watch TV all day. These people were old, but they were still alive and they had interests, and a lot of them were interested in art. The whole institutionalization scene was appalling to me. It made me upset and angry and sad.

I was not conscious of it, but I think I was forming a whole sense of vocation or calling. I think I'd been waiting for a calling. As a kid, I never thought, "When I grow up, I'm going to be . . ." It was *unimaginable*. I did want to be good at things, because I was *never* good at school—and school was so important to everybody. My parents always encouraged my art—they didn't think it was a frivolous pursuit at all. And they had done all kinds of different jobs, so I had the sense that it was OK to change, that you didn't need to find one job and stick with it for your whole life. But most of the kids I went to college with felt an enormous amount of parental pressure to find a career, to get a "real" job.

After college, I moved back to the West Coast, lived with my mother, slept on her floor. I got a job with my old boyfriend, who was an independent filmmaker. When I'd left him and gone to college, I'd come out as a lesbian, but we were still friends. The job was with an AIDS group that produced a cable TV show. It was a lot of clerical work and "five–four–three–two, you're on!" kind of stuff. But because it was with an AIDS organization I had a sense of working for something important. My mother is a Quaker, but even before I had any concept of what that meant, I remember feeling that to help others was your duty. So I didn't go and work for Shell Oil and do their bookkeeping—I worked at the AIDS group and did *their* bookkeeping. [Laughs.]

After a while, I felt I had to get off my mother's floor, that this seven-dollar-an-hour job was not working for me, that I didn't have *any* kind of life. My father said, "Go get a teaching degree. You'll have summers off, you can be an artist." The university I attended offered a combined master's with teaching certificate and I thought, "Oh, sure, it's easy. It'll only take two years if I go full-time." I wasn't thinking, "I love kids" or "I love teaching"—it was just, "As long as I'm here and it's offered, why not?" I figured I'd make more money with a master's.

But as soon as I started the teaching program I felt that flow thing, where your skill and interest level are on par. I saw myself in the children. I was like, "Oh, *this* is why kids don't do well" and "Maybe *this* is why I didn't do well in school. Maybe it's *not* because I was stupid." In many ways, it was very therapeutic for me. I began to understand what might potentially be wrong with schools and what might be right with schools.

I hooked up with a great teacher, a real mentor, as her assistant, and that was the best part of school, because I was learning directly from one person. My job was to read everything I could on teaching urban children, to summarize it and help her write articles for journals. It brought together my interest in social and urban and child-abuse issues.

At the end of graduate school, a friend said, "Close your eyes and visualize what you want," which I had never done before. And I thought: I want to teach teenagers who have low skills, who preferably are in the juvenile justice system or dropouts, in a small school, small classes. When I graduated, I sent out all these résumés, and the only school I heard from was a branch school of the juvenile justice system. It was an alternative public school for boys sixteen to twenty-one, boys who were on probation or parole. For me, a dream school—*perfect!*

I interviewed for three days—it was *very* rigorous. The school was run by men, and the students were men, and the whole place was *men.* I come in and I'm twenty-five, twenty-six, small and white, and most of the students were black or Hispanic. There were about thirty kids in the school, five staff members, and two classrooms, one for GED [General Equivalency Diploma], one for elementary.

The director was a particular personality type: controlling, angry, bitter. Everyone was afraid of him, but I respected him because he was basically fair. The psychologist was kind of a wimpy guy. The elementary teacher lectured the kids and handed out worksheets—he believed that was the best way to teach. A very rigid, conservative man . . . The head teacher was the liaison between the home school and this branch school, and he took care of the administrative paperwork. He didn't teach.

The staff all said, "You're not going to like it . . ." The psychologist said, "I could tell you stories that would put *hair* on your chest." When the head teacher interviewed me, he talked about how rough it was, and about what you might have to deal with—like if kids start fighting, or yell at you, or refuse to do work. He told me about finding guns when they did surprise searches. He tried to scare me away. But I was convinced this was for me. I went home crying, saying, "I *know* I didn't get the job." Why they hired me, I'm not sure. I think they were desperate.

I was not at all afraid. I thought, "You're a bunch of middle-aged white guys who live in the suburbs. We have different experiences." I'd hung out with boys all through my teenage years, several were in gangs, lots were rough. I thought I could somewhat relate, and through that maybe get something done teachingwise. I think school is difficult for most kids, and for bad kids it's *unbearable*. And these kids *had* to be there—it was court-ordered. I thought, "If I can make this bearable, then I'll be doing an OK job."

The kids ran the range. The common denominator was hard-core gang involvement. There were kids who'd gotten in trouble for drug dealing, weapons charges, and violence *definitely*. Some wore the monitor, the anklet. Some were young, and this was their first conviction. Some were seasoned gangbangers and criminals who were on probation for one thing, but had done lots of other stuff no one even knew about.

I was put in a classroom and told, "You're teaching GED"—which I had *no* concept of how to teach. I wanted to teach literature, I wanted the kids to love to read like I loved to read. But teaching GED turned out to be great. I had two classes a day, no more than eight kids a class. I figured out how to make GED into anything; I took the basic goals and developed my own curriculum. I moved the desks into a circle and brought in about two hundred books, many of them by or about troubled teenagers who had survived. Books like *Down These Mean Streets, There Are No Children Here, Manchild in the Promised Land, Always Running, Monster*.

These kids admitted they never read anything, and a lot of them *couldn't* read. I required they read three books in their time there—an average stay was six to eight months. Every week we had a meeting and we'd write out a contract. They could plan their own curriculum to some degree. I said, "You tell me what you're interested in, I'll mold it if I need to, to fit in a little of what I think you need to learn." I gave them an assignment folder and it was their job, within a certain amount of time, to do what was required.

The school was very disciplined, and nobody took *any* crap. It was really necessary. These were kids that basically ran wild. They had no discipline in their lives and needed it. So they were told, "You get here on time, you take off your earring, your gang stuff, your hat." They had to sign school rules and classroom rules. I wanted no racist, sexist, culturally offending remarks in my room, unless we were having a discussion about those issues.

The class rules were: you have to agree to ask questions when you don't understand something; to try everything once; to listen to people; to constantly show communication, cooperation, respect, and responsibility. I was hoping too, that the rules would unite them a little bit. As much as possible, I tried to give every class a team atmosphere, so they felt part of something. We spent *a lot* of time in discussion. We'd check in with people, ask how they're doing: "What's going on with your case? What's going on with your family?"—personal conversation. I believe that you won't have discipline problems if you foster relationships, and I had almost no problems.

That was the classroom. The larger setting was this small-team environment that started out great and progressively disintegrated. The head teacher, Frank, had his own office; he'd sit and chat on the phone with his friends. We became work friends because he was supposed to show me everything and teach me how to work there. He gradually became like glue at my side. I'd sit in his office and we'd talk, and he'd ask me to do tons of little errands with him. There would be paperwork to fill out, but instead of showing me how to do it, he would do it. "Oh, don't worry, I've taken care of it for you . . . Oh, I signed you out . . . Oh, I picked up your paycheck . . ." Half the stuff being done for me I didn't know *existed*. I thought that was just the way he was, how the program worked.

I had to get along with Frank—he was basically my boss. Sometimes we went out after work and had a drink together. In retrospect, I should never have done that. He was married, had a few children, a house in the suburbs, hated his wife. He didn't know I was gay, and one day he said, "I want to have sex with you." I sort of flipped out and said, *"No."* After that, he pretty much left the sex thing alone. I figured it was no longer an issue.

Through a period of months, he kind of wooed me back into the friendship. I developed a genuine affection for him. We had some connection, we had things in common. It was this weird mixed-up relationship that I didn't understand. From early on I made mistakes, in that I didn't set appropriate boundaries. I continued to go out with him after work . . . I wanted to talk about teaching and the kids. This was a great program, and I felt like he knew what he was talking about, and talking about teaching was invigorating.

We kept talking and, meanwhile, he's telling me that I'm beautiful, I'm brilliant. I was in the middle of a long-term relationship that was going down the tubes; I had low self-esteem, and here was this person saying everything I wanted to hear. I never contemplated sleeping with him, but I sent him mixed messages. I said no, but I went out with him; I said no, but I flirted; I said no, but I kissed him a couple of times. I don't know what possessed me. I was never genuinely attracted to him; I guess I was just bathing in his attention.

Frank would flirt with me in front of others, touching my foot, making remarks, little jokes to me . . . intimacy things. I'd try to look the other way. He'd follow me around, constantly come into my classroom to interrupt: "Can you sign this?" And we kept going out after work. He was depressed, so I listened to him. I tried to talk about school, but he only wanted to talk about personal things. As I'm getting sucked in, he's telling me intimate things, saying, "See, if anything ever happens, you'll have this on me." He talked about how he was abused as a child—got me feeling sorry for him. He was like a classic abuser, but I didn't realize it.

I didn't know about not telling people at work personal information, and Frank was a master at, "Trust me." One of my big mistakes was telling him private information about myself: drug experience, lesbianism, tons of stuff—details. He said he didn't care that I was gay, that he was interested in the gay world and feminism . . . Just total *bullshit*. He was the most misogynist man I ever met, but I didn't have any idea I was being conned. Partly why I'm so upset about what happened is because I'm mad at *myself* for not setting boundaries, for sending mixed messages. I could say no all I wanted, but I was still *there*.

He started sending me love poetry and love letters. Finally I stopped going out after work. I'd say, "I can't today." He was hurt and upset . . . I felt sorry for him—he seemed so pathetic. He lost a lot of weight, he started to see a psychiatrist and went on antianxiety medication—because I would not return his love, was what he said. At some point during the school year he decided this was all too painful, that he could no longer talk to me. So he stopped speaking to me for days. That was hell, because it was a very close environment. If he brought me a phone message, he'd throw it at me. These things were petty. He was a baby.

One day he said, "I'd rather be colleagues as opposed to nothing, so I'll talk to you again." Then he'd say, "I give and give and give, and you don't do anything for me." The situation was disturbing, but I *couldn't* leave. I loved the kids, I loved the program, there was no other place I wanted to work. I thought, "I'm just going to have to work this out . . ."—whatever that meant.

I became close friends with a guy, and told Frank about him. I thought, "If I tell him about Marty, he'll realize I have a life, other friends—he'll *have to* come to his senses." I didn't anticipate what would happen. One day he asked what I was doing that night. I said, "I'm picking Marty up, we're going to watch a championship." He said, "But I was going to ask you out after work—I really need to talk to you." The next day he said, "So, how'd it go?" I said, "Well it was fun. Marty stayed over . . ." Which he had—he'd slept on the floor. But I didn't even get to that part. Frank went nuts, right in his office. He said, "You broke my heart and this is the *end*."

From that day forward, he never spoke another word to me. I stayed six more months, and he never said a *word*. If it had just been that, it would have been OK. But suddenly there was all this paperwork: he'd been doing it for me and I didn't know how to do *any* of it. And of course, I couldn't ask him questions. All of a sudden closed-door meetings were held, but I was left out. All of a sudden I'd be called into the office for touching a kid on the arm, for leaning over a boy. The implication being that I was coming on to the boys. The director would call me in, but Frank would be there, *oh yes* . . . I don't know *what* Frank was telling the director. Maybe he told him we'd had sex, which I think everyone assumed anyway because of the way he followed me around.

I was constantly called in: "You were five minutes late" or "You're getting out of control—I heard you yell." The environment was so stressful. I was watched: "You're having too much discussion in the classroom," "Don't talk about sex education any more in the classroom, don't talk about gangs." Suddenly they were saying, "Well, I don't know about the reading, the books you select."

I didn't tell anyone else at school what was going on because I didn't want to rock the boat or come across as a hysterical female. The age thing . . . being so much younger was a big part of it. I felt in some ways I had to be perfect because they were all men and they were older. I regret not telling the director what was going on with Frank. I guess I was so embarrassed by my behavior that I couldn't tell anybody. I felt so bad that I had gone out with him in the first place, told him anything about myself, kissed him, for God's sake. On every level I was so ashamed of myself.

I stopped staying late, I stopped doing extra things. My mental health was definitely suffering, and soon my physical health would have: I wasn't sleeping well, I was always tense. I started to think about quitting and getting another job. I wrote Frank a letter saying, "I know you hate me, I accept that. I don't understand why, but that's not the point. The point is, what's happening at work has got to stop. I'm the same teacher I was, but you guys are treating me differently. I'm being manipulated, all because I would not sleep with you. I don't care what you're telling other people, but you know the truth." I said, "I'm not going to take any action because we were friends, but you have to admit to yourself what's going on." I found it ripped up in a hundred pieces in my mailbox.

Finally, I applied for another job and was hired. I gave two weeks' notice. I told the kids. That was really hard. They said, "Oh, you must be getting more money and going on to a great job." The truth was, no—it's several thousand dollars less, and I don't *want* a new job. But I couldn't say anything.

I subsequently found out he had sexually harassed two other women at a different school. On my last day, one of them called and said, "By any chance did he harass you?" I said, "Well, by the way, yes he did."

She said, "He harassed me too, but I thought you two were friends, so I never said anything."

I didn't want to pursue it in court because I didn't want to have to tell my story over and over again. It would just prolong things, and I wanted to be free of it. I'd have had to say or hear things about myself in public that I wasn't willing to say or hear. I thought, "He's still stuck in a job he hates, with a wife he hates, with a boss he's intimidated by. He's in a horrible situation, but I'm free." At that point I felt so beat up I just wanted to protect myself. In retrospect, I'm a little sorry I didn't do anything about it, because I'm certainly not free—a kind of delayed reaction has set in. I didn't want to be vindictive at the time, but I'm telling you, now that's all I can think about. I've thought about writing his wife. I've thought about writing his boss.

To someone in that kind of circumstance, I would say: don't tell anyone anything you wouldn't want to say in court. *Really* don't. Be neutral at *all* times. Follow the rules. Because even if they say they don't care, if they can't find anything else to hate you for, they will pull that out. And definitely document everything. Then find someone you can trust outside of work and admit what is going on. Be honest about it and ask for advice. When you're in the middle of something like this, you can't see clearly. A lot of times women don't even know they're being sexually harassed; it's not always the clear-cut, "If you don't sleep with me you're not getting a promotion" version.

What makes me most upset is that this was one time when I felt I tried my absolute hardest, and loved what I was doing, and got *screwed*. I don't need *them* to say I've done a good job—*I* need to feel I've done a good job. And even though I feel like a victim, I feel like a failure too, because I did make some key mistakes. It's possible that I could have made no mistakes, done *nothing* to bring this on, and had the exact same thing happen. But I still feel like I did this to myself. For my own saving grace, I have to find a lesson in this. And the lesson is, I've learned some boundary-drawing, some self-assertiveness, some sense that this *can* happen—so that it will *never* happen again.

GRACE TILSIT

Grace's first job was at college, where she served as a resident director. "The job involved helping the kids in your building, making sure rules weren't broken." Her interest in health care made a volunteer Emergency Medical Technician job especially rewarding. "I loved, 'We have to hurry, *we're saving a life!' It was empowering." Grace applied to and was wait-listed for medical school. But when her mother was diagnosed with cancer, Grace dropped everything to care for her. Later, she opted for a master's in business with a focus on health care. "I thought, all right, two years, very practical, you can use it for anything later in life." A first internship acquainted her with the health-care field in the real world and provided leads for full-time work. After a stressful job search and difficult interview she was hired by a "big-six" consulting firm. To her surprise, she found the job overwhelming. For Grace, twenty-eight, the first year involved grasping new concepts, making a devastating mistake, and realizing the value of asking for help. She dealt with unfair treatment and a troublesome boss. "For a first real job, it was hard. I learned a lot. I'm much more humble and I will be in my next job, wherever that is."*

I was born and raised in Colombia, South America. My mom was Swiss, my father Danish. He died when I was nine months old. He had cancer, six-months kind of thing . . . After he died, my mother ran his furniture factory. There was not much time for her to learn the business because he became ill very quickly and I was still an infant. She also had a jewelry business: she dealt with and designed emeralds. Her father had been a jeweler, and she learned the business young. When I was a child, she worked to the point where I hardly saw her during the week. She had to—there was no other option. We were fortunate: we had maids and a nanny. I didn't resent it because I never knew any better; I was glad to see her when I saw her.

I wasn't quite sure what I wanted to study in college, but I wanted the experience of being in the States; I ended up attending a small East Coast university. At first I had a hard time adjusting. Drinking was never an issue in Colombia, and here, when you get to college, it's drink, drink, and every party you have to get drunk, every weekend.

My first work experience was sophomore year when I became a resident assistant for one of the dorm floors. The job paid for my room and board. It was sort of a leadership position, but I was also a counselor and mentor for freshmen. It was a great way to become part of the community, to be involved with school, to feel that I made a difference and was needed. I loved it, and really got into earning my own money: I waitressed and catered, and I was a teacher's assistant and tutor in Spanish as well.

One reason I needed to work was that while my mother was on a jewelry sales trip, she was robbed by nine men with machine guns—one of them hit her over the head. They stole everything. I didn't have the heart to ask her for spending money, for *anything*. I went from being a spoiled little girl who had everything to, *oh boy*, I need to tighten my belt. It was good for me.

My mom and I had a unique relationship, more of a friendship—she was my buddy. After the robbery, she was in pain and very depressed. She was sixty at the time. I said, "Why don't you come live with me?" That was senior year, and I'd become resident director of a dorm building. They increased my salary and gave me an apartment to live in.

To be an R.D. [Resident Director] or an R.A. [Resident Assistant], you have to be able to listen, have patience, stand your own ground, and not let your peers get to you. Part of the job is being an authority figure and dealing with problems with drinking and drugs, things of that sort. That was the bad part. We had a couple of suicide attempts. It's really difficult to send somebody to the hospital because you think they're going to hurt themselves.

There were problems—kids who hated you for shutting down the party, kids who thought you were a jerk. My car was keyed (scratched with a key) and nasty things were written on my door. Once a big fire-cracker almost blew up in my face. I walked outside the building to try and figure out where these fireworks were coming from. They were coming from a room where kids did a lot of drinking and drugging. This M-80 exploded right over the top of my head. I was appalled that anybody would do something *so* dangerous. I went straight to the dean. The boys were expelled—though, obviously, the parents didn't take it well. But it wasn't even a question in my mind that these kids should leave the school. Are you *crazy*?! Putting people in danger, playing with firecrackers in your room, doing drugs, totally disruptive to every part of living in a community . . .

Another incident involved a homosexual kid whose roommate was an absolute homophobe, big drinker, a jock kind of guy. He would come in drunk, find his roommate sleeping and pee on him, call him a "faggot." Part of being in college is learning to live with people who are different from you, so we tried to teach people to respect each other. We firmly believed that you didn't change roommates just like that. That you learned to live together, you set up rules, you made a contract. Part of our job was to help students negotiate. But it's almost impossible to change somebody who has so much hatred. This guy punched a hole in the wall, and we were afraid for the roommate's safety. Eventually we had them change rooms.

I think I made a difference, as a role model and mentor for my R.A.'s, and with the kids as well. I helped people work through certain prob-lems. Mostly I listened. I wouldn't jump in, I would rephrase: "It sounds like this is what you're saying the problem is. What do you think you should do? How can you handle this?" You bounce stuff off them, rather than saying, "Your problem is A, B, and C, and you should do 1, 2, and 3." One thing I learned was that I would be good at organizing, and at being a manager and a leader. I'd always taken that role in high school—that part came naturally—and I liked feeling respected and valued.

One of my favorite jobs was as a volunteer Emergency Medical Technician, which I did once a week for about three years. It involves knowing more than first aid, but not quite enough to be a paramedic. I joined the ambulance as a regular member. There were usually four of us: the driver, the crew chief—somebody with a lot of training—and two regular members. You're basically the gopher when you start out: "Go get this, go get that, strap this in." I took a course and became an EMT, and then was able to interact with patients: take a history, do the blood pressure, the vital signs, call into the hospital when I was in the ambulance—be a part of the team. After that, they trained me to be a driver, which was such an adrenaline high.

We had people die in the ambulance, and that's very upsetting. But then there are cases where you really help and they send you a thank-you card. It's good to feel that you made a difference, even if it was just holding their hand. "Come on, stay with me, let's talk—where does it hurt? OK, we're taking you to the hospital now . . ." That part was *great*.

It was also a way to become involved in the community, meet new people, feel good about life. Volunteer work in general, whether it's with kids, in a church, organizing meals for the homeless, can be a wonderful experience. It's very selfish in a way: it gives you a high to help someone. You get a lot more out of it than you can possibly give.

Senior year I decided to become a doctor. I stayed on after graduation to finish up pre-med requirements I needed, applied to medical school, and was wait-listed. Then my mother got cancer. When we knew something was really wrong, she went back to Colombia. We didn't have health insurance and health care is a lot cheaper there. They discovered the cancer had metastasized in the liver, and there was nothing you could do. It was a matter of months. So I put everything on hold and went to Colombia to be with her; I was with her till the end. I was twenty-three when she died.

I had to take care of all she left behind and there were tons of legal issues, the jewelry business, a lawsuit. I did that for eight months, applied to medical school, and got wait-listed *again*. But I missed my mom, and suddenly it became a priority to have my own family. I became engaged. My husband is a corporate lawyer, from the States, but he grew up in Colombia.

I continued with the jewelry business. I sell wholesale and have private clients who call me for a certain piece and I do the designing and work with a jeweler who actually makes the piece. I learned from watching my mom. I had the business and I could do it, but I didn't really want to—I wanted to have my own thing. I ended up going to business school, under an MBA program with a health-care management concentration. I thought, "I'll do that and I can still be a part of the health-care field."

I needed a summer internship in order to finish the program, so I networked with alumni of the school's health-care program. An alum with his own health-care consulting company hired me. He said, "I can't pay you much, but I can give you some exposure and you'll get to do interesting things." It was the first time somebody said, "Do this project, it's yours"—I was terrified!

I didn't know a lot about health-care at that point. You take your core requirements the first-year, accounting, basic things. I knew *nothing* about the actual terminology of hospital administration. The hospital what? A DRG? A *what*? So I learned a lot. And I learned how to write. "This sounds terrible! You can't put this in a proposal—you have to change this." Being criticized was hard, especially 'cause I felt like, "I'm in an MBA program! I'm not *stupid*—I know how to write!" But proposal writing is very different from creative or essay-writing. A proposal is to the point, it's lean, no wasted words; nothing too descriptive, just boom boom boom. A completely new way of thinking.

After that internship, I finished school, but kept in touch with my old boss. I had done well, and he'd said, "Call me next year when you're looking for a job." I was banking on getting a job there. When it was time to look, I called. He said, "Things aren't great, I can't really say we have enough work. I'd love to hire you, but I can't." That was hard, because I'd thought it was a sure bet. Not that I necessarily wanted that job, but it was nice to know there was something to fall back on. And then it wasn't there. . . . You can't count on *anything*. That's a *big* lesson.

He didn't tell me they were basically selling the company. But he did me a favor, he said, "I'm going to call my friends and see who's hiring right now." I wanted more of a hospital administration job, but they're hard to get because everybody's downsizing and the last thing people want is another administrator. But he gave me a lot of names to call: "Hi, So-and-so referred me to you. I'd like to have an informational interview." Not putting people on the spot, not saying, "I need you to give me a job." More like, "Talk to me about what you do. I want to see if I'd find it interesting and how I might go about getting into that field." That takes pressure off people; it takes pressure off you, too. I did a lot of those and got no job offers.

I was definitely nervous. You keep calling people, "No, I don't have anything . . ." No no no . . . "We got your résumé, we'll call you, we'll call you. We'll get in touch if we're interested." You *have* to do follow-up phone calls. They're horrible, because they're like cold calls. "Hi, I sent my resume and was wondering if you've received it yet, and if you have a position, if I could speak to somebody about it?" [Nasal-toned.] "We got your résumé, we'll call you." You just have to say, "OK, from eleven to twelve, I'm going to make calls." Sometimes you're lucky and get an answering machine and you're like, *phew*!

My boss referred me to someone at a "big six" consulting firm. He said, "It's completely different than the consulting you've done here. You will not be leaving at six at night—you'll be working like a *dog*. I don't know if that's what you want, but this is the company to be at if you want to do health care." I called and they needed people at that moment. It was, "Come on in—how about tomorrow?" Rushed! The next day I went in and had an hour-and-a-half interview with two senior managers. Then, "Let's schedule you for an interview with the partner." I was like, "Wow, this was easy—I can't believe it!" The timing was right. If I'd waited another week, they'd have already hired someone else.

They didn't know if I could do the work. I didn't go through the tests consultants are normally given. Usually you interview for weeks and get case studies. "Read this in half an hour, analyze it, tell me what the key issues are, how would you present it to a client?" But here, the first interview was, "Talk about yourself, what did you do? Good—this is what we do."

Then the partner interviewed me. He was a very cold interviewer, not very friendly. He attacks, rather than asks a question—very aggressive. I thought, "I'm *never* going to get this job." He said, "So what is this emerald business that you have? If I were going to buy an emerald, what would I look for?" I said, "Well, you do this, da da da, look at the color, look at the cut. . . ." I guess he wanted to see if I could sell him my product, to see if I could sell the firm to a client. But I didn't know. I thought, "This is a *horrible* interview." And he asked me technical things, like what did I think about a certain new law. I was like, "Ah . . . I just moved from to New York and I don't know." Wrong answer. You *really* need to research for these job interviews.

I should have found out a lot more about the company before the interview. I should have gone to my local library, found out what newspaper articles they'd recently been in, done a search, found out what projects they'd been working on so I could ask intelligent questions. Definitely—because you want to be knowledgeable about the company. I lucked out, but it was pure luck. Generally they hire people who are prepared, who really want to work for *their* company and know the difference between them and the other big-six firms.

I finished my MBA in May of '96 and started working in June. I jumped too soon. This was my second job offer, and I took it because I was afraid I wouldn't get another. The first was a dead-end job where I wouldn't have had room to grow. I'd suggest *not* taking the first things that come your way. You can quit, but it doesn't look good on your résumé: "Yes, I accepted a job and left after a month" is not looked well upon in any industry. You need to stick it out at least a year.

And I took the job because I was flattered. This recruiter kept calling to see if I was going to accept. You feel like, "*Wow,* they want me—how great!" It may be that the first offer is right for you, but look for other options before you take it. Because it *is* flattering when somebody's calling you every day: it's a great feeling, and it's easy to fall into that trap. You just have to think: if they want me, somebody else is going to want me too.

The first time you hear a salary with any kind of decent number you're like, "Hey—*wow!*" And then you get in there and realize you're making *nothing* compared to everyone else. That's another lesson: you need to negotiate your salary. The way I negotiated was, "Well, I think I'd like a little more . . ." "Well, we don't have more to offer, and there are five people waiting for this job." "Alright, I'll take it." I was very naive . . . But you learn from your mistakes. So next time you say, "Well, if you want me, you're going to have to give me more because I'm really good. If you don't give me more, I'm going somewhere else." It's playing hardball.

I had *no* concept of what being in a big-six firm would involve. I knew the hours would be horrible, but I had *no* idea what it would be like working with my colleagues, people very competitive, very smart. There were staff techs, consultants, senior consultants, managers, senior managers, partners. I was a consultant, basically doing strategic advising for hospital mergers. We help make their strategic plan for the next five years: how they'll merge, what the merger will involve, what fields they need to drop because they're not profitable, what their strategy to gain more patients should be, how to build market share.

I was on the low end of the totem pole. You write your own letters, you do your own thing. I got into the job and I was *miserable*. My level of ignorance was shocking. I thought, "Alright, I have an MBA in health-care management, I know some of the words—I know what it's about. . . ." I had no clue what I was doing. *No clue.* I felt so stupid, so unqualified. I felt like there was so much to learn and that I was never going to learn it.

You're working with people who have been in the industry for ten years, so of course, for them it's like talking about the weather: they're throwing out all these acronyms and abbreviations. You're like, "What is that? Can you explain?" It was hard to admit not knowing what they were talking about. They'd say, "Do you know what that is?" And you really had to be honest, because if you lied and said yes, you were eventually going to get caught.

They didn't seem annoyed at having to explain, but I was annoyed that I didn't know. Of course, neither did anybody else when they started. It's just a matter of time, it's a matter of learning. But at first, I felt like, "Oh my God, I'm an absolute doofus!" And I hadn't expected to feel that way at all. There were days I'd come home crying.

They'd ask me to run a spreadsheet, run some numbers, and I'd sit in front of the computer and think, "Oh my gosh! What did they tell me to do?" I would sit there for hours . . . Being nervous makes you nervous, it's a vicious circle. You can't think because you're nervous when they're explaining it to you. You concentrate so hard on what they're saying, listen to the words so hard, that you don't grasp the concept . . . You're like, "Days per thousand multiplied by five, divided by, OK, alright, yes . . ." I hear the words and I *kind of* understand—but then I sit down and I'm like *"What?!"* People would say, "Aren't you done with that yet? Why is it taking you so long?" "Oh, my computer crashed . . . the spreadsheet isn't working . . ." Any excuse! And then I'd admit I wasn't positive I'd done it right. "Could you check my numbers?"

You're figuring out certain formulas to get different measurements, like to count hospital utilization. And sometimes you get a measurement like two thousand, and you're thinking, "Is that good or bad?" You don't have a reference point because it's all so new. If I'd gotten two million, I'd have been like, "Oh, two million," and turned it into my manager, who would have said, "Ha—right! What did you do? Two million? Think about it." But because I didn't understand the concept, I couldn't *begin* to think about what I was doing.

I thought I knew how to use a spreadsheet, but I didn't really know how to use a spreadsheet until I started working. What I used them for in school was so basic, and the kinds of things you end up doing at work are so complicated—building models and financial feasibility studies. I was doing everything the long way. My manager, Rob, would check my work and say, "You didn't link these spreadsheets?" And I'd say, "Link it? Noooo . . ." "You input every one of these numbers?" "Yeah . . ." "No wonder it took you three hours. You should have copied them, pasted them here." The hardest thing was sucking it up and realizing I was not as overall knowledgeable as I'd thought. It's humbling. And when you're around people who know *a lot*, it's very intimidating.

Everybody said, "Oh, don't worry—come and ask me." But asking for help is a big thing, and I always felt dumb asking. Eventually you learn. I'd walk out and think, I really didn't get it. I'd walk back in and say, "You know what, you have to run that by me again . . ." I'd go to ten different people and have them explain the same thing. Eventually you get the hang of it, and then it's easy to do a spreadsheet. It took me six months to feel comfortable saying, "I don't know how to do this. Help me."

What happened was I made a big mistake. I turned in some numbers and the person who should have checked them didn't have time to check them. We turned them in to our manager, he presented them to the client, nobody checked the numbers and the numbers were *wrong*. The client caught it at a meeting. I got a call just after my boss had met with the clients. Rob said, "Grace, take your calculator out." I took my calculator out. "What's this number divided by this number?" "Five." *"Why does it say five hundred?!"* They were *so* angry. They were ready to kill me—absolutely. It happens to everyone, but normally you catch the error before it gets to the client. I made them look like idiots *in front of* the client.

They said, "We need to have a talk about this. This *whole* spreadsheet is wrong. Grace, I thought you said you looked at the numbers." I was dying. I said, "I did, but nobody checked them. I asked Marilyn to check and she didn't have time." They were double-pissed because *they* were partly at fault for not having checked. Rob got to the office, called me in and went off on me. "I looked like a total asshole with my clients. You have to be more responsible. What didn't you understand? Why are these numbers so wrong?" *Why, why, why, why?*

This was my fourth month, and I thought, "Just fire me—it'll be so much easier." Instead, he said, "I hope this doesn't happen again. We *really* need to figure this out." But Rob was angry with me for a long time, and that was hard to live with. Marilyn was one title above me, a kind of supervisor, and I'd made her look bad too. She worked in a cube right next to mine, and she'd been like my best friend before that. After, she'd barely talk to me. She'd ask me to do ridiculous things and explain them ten times. "Type the word, S-A-P, you got that? S-A-P." Very patronizing. It was the two of them ganging up on me. Suddenly, everything I was asked to do was secretarial, nothing important at all. It was humiliating.

I should have confronted them and said, "Look, I can't work like this." I should have stopped it right there and then when it was so uncomfortable. But I didn't. I didn't know how to deal with it. One thing that kept me going was that the rest of my colleagues were nice and they backed me up. They said, "They're being unfairly mean to you. We've all made mistakes." They told me their own war stories. Everybody thought Rob and Marilyn were getting too personal with me, that it was inappropriate. Some even went to Rob and said, "You're not being fair to Grace." They stood up for me.

I was ready to quit so many times. When you're not happy at work, you become a miserable person, it affects you negatively in every way. But in the meantime, I'd gotten involved in projects where I'd made a difference. Finally I felt ownership for what I was doing—satisfaction. That's empowering, and it makes you want to keep doing it. Even though you may not like it every day, it's a good feeling to do something right, to have the client call and say, "This was fantastic and we're *really* happy." So that kept me going. And I was pregnant—and, to be quite honest, I wanted to stay on and get my maternity benefits.

After the incident, I documented every demeaning comment, or anything they asked me to do that was secretarial or inappropriate. I noted everything they said, verbatim. I had a little file going in my desk so that one day, when I had to talk about how I'd been treated, I could give specific examples. Like when one of our bosses nobody liked had a birthday coming up and Rob said, "Somebody needs to organize a party for him." Making a face like, "Ugh—who's gonna do it?" And then he looks at me: "Grace, *you're* not busy—why don't *you* organize it." He made me look like an idiot in front of other people. I was so hurt. There were lots of comments like that, where it was hard for me to defend myself.

Then came evaluation time. I typed up all my comments and went to Rob. He'd started changing a little bit. I'd been working on a project with him, and he was gaining more trust in me, so I was getting back in the swing of things. The evaluation was a positive one. He had good things to say—I'd expected everything to be bad.

He was taken by surprise when I said, "Well, I have some issues of my own I'd like to bring up." I said, "I didn't do it intentionally, but yeah, I made a huge mistake, and afterward you treated me badly." He said, "You made me look terrible." I said, "Yes, I made you look terrible and you yelled at me. And then you said it was over and you weren't going to hold a grudge and yet you held a grudge for *months*. You made me look bad in front of people. These are comments you made. How would it make you feel if somebody said this to you?"

I laid it out, crying as I told him. He said, "Please don't cry—I feel terrible . . ." I said, "I'm sorry. I shouldn't be crying in a professional situation. It's just that I'm so hurt by everything that's happened." He said, "Oh, I never meant it." Which is not *true*—he *did* mean to hurt me. But he didn't realize how much it affected me. He apologized. "I'm sorry I did that, and I'm sorry you took so long to tell me about it."

It's hard to confront people, but it's a lot easier if you're prepared. So you have to write out what it is you're going to say, have your list of topics. When you're upset and emotional, it's easy to forget what you intended to say, or to say it the wrong way. You have to write things down. He was impressed with the fact that I said, "On Tuesday the thirteenth you said this to me in front of da-da-da-da . . ."

He's a real jokester: he makes fun of everybody, that's the kind of guy he is. But sometimes he would do things that could be considered sexual harassment—and he worked mostly with women. We all joked about it, nobody ever did anything, filed any complaints. He'd do things like take a phone call when you were in conference and without even thinking—it wasn't conscious—he'd put his hands in his pants to scratch. It was a terrible habit. We'd just look away. It's embarrassing . . . It would be like me in the middle of a meeting adjusting my bra straps. You just don't *do* that.

One day, I got so fed up I walked out and said to a colleague, "He's doing the hand thing. What is it with him?" She said, "Say something." I said, "He's on the phone." She said, "Write him a note." So I took a pad and wrote DO YOU HAVE AN ITCH? I put it right in front of him. He turned beet red. He was *so* embarrassed. He never did that in front of me again, *ever*.

I'm on maternity leave for twelve weeks, but I don't plan on going back. I knew this wasn't a long-term job for me—I didn't want to make this my career. It's too fast-paced—you get burnt out. I was working seventy to eighty hours a week; sometimes I'd bring work home on weekends. You get on a project and feel responsible and you do it. If it means working weekends, you work weekends. It wasn't always like this—I don't want to exaggerate. But there were weeks you'd be in the office from seven till two, three in the morning because you had a deadline.

I'd be surprised if I got back into this field. . . . In health-care administration you're completely on the outside, you're not affecting anybody's life. It's great on your résumé and it's a great experience and people respect it. But does it fill me with satisfaction? No.

I'm living one of my dreams now by having a family, and I want to have more kids. That's still my number-one priority. If later on I choose to become a doctor, great. If not, I might start my own business. I was thinking about a bilingual kindergarten. Something where I'd be directly affecting somebody's life. Some people enjoy being behind a computer and doing financial models, and that's fine. For me, that's not the thing. Health-care administration is not what makes my heart beat, what makes me say, "Yes, I'm excited about what I do." For me it's important to interact with people and have an impact and see it. That's what I loved about working on the ambulance—that passion.

JULIE BAXTER

For Julie, twenty-five, the ability to persuade comes naturally. Even as a young girl, "It wasn't enough for someone to listen, I had to convince them to my way of thinking. For a long time, I thought about becoming a lawyer." While in college, she worked as a nanny and at various office jobs and internships. At a real estate office, she gained insight into the need for good communication skills—and into the hazards of office politics. "Because someone is your work friend, doesn't mean they're your friend friend." While interning at a small, family-owned company, Julie's attitude toward her employers got her fired: "I had begun to think of them not as my bosses but as friends I happened to work for." An internship at a large public relations firm "wound up being something to put on a résumé . . . a weeding-out experience: OK, this is what I don't want to do." A law firm internship provided crucial lessons about critical thinking, organizational skills, and the importance of attention to detail, and discouraged her from becoming a lawyer. A chance meeting in New York led to a job she knew nothing about, that of literary agent. "I've been here over a year. It was the right thing for me to do."

I'm from a small town in Maryland. It's very suburban now, but at the time it was much more rural. There were still cow fields, with little pockets of houses. My parents divorced when I was three, and my dad moved to California. My mom worked as a secretary and bookkeeper. I think the work held less interest for her than did the people. She created her social life at work with the secretarial set.

My stepfather worked for Western Union. He started off as a tech and liked what he was doing. But as he went into management, his passion and love for his work lessened. The company began corporate lay-offs and downsizing. I remember the tension in the house when he had to lay off one of his oldest and dearest friends. It did a lot to shape my views on corporate America.

I don't want to work within the structure of a big corporation, to have to answer to fifty people above me. I don't want to do hypercompartmentalized work, where, even if it's not repetitious factory tasks, you're doing the same kinds of things over and over and over again. And I don't want to be managed by people whose policies are lacking in common sense.

So many times in the corporate environment I see people who don't respect their superiors. It's often because their superiors don't do anything to earn their respect, and don't feel that they have to. Working in a corporate environment gives you very little sense of accomplishment; I don't think you can take a great deal of pride in what you do. There are a few people who get credit for everything that gets done. A friend now works in corporate PR. She worked on something twenty hours a day for two weeks straight. When all was said and done, her boss took complete credit for *everything*.

I don't know how my friend does it, how she works in a structure where people go crazy over irrelevant things. But she's one of those people who likes someone to say, "Go do this." Great, she'll run and do it—whereas my feeling is, "Fine, put it on my desk." I'm much more self-motivating, I work better that way. Nobody could pressure me more than I pressure myself.

In a corporation, you wind up giving loyalty to a company that has absolutely no loyalty to you. That's what people find out when they're laid off. People a year and a half away from being fully vested in their pensions getting laid off! They've basically sold their soul to that company with nothing in return. *Nothing!* I don't want to look back and say, "Oh, I wish I hadn't worked at this job I hated for ten years of my life." That's what working in a corporation represents to me personally. Some people thrive in that kind of environment—some have it in them, and some don't.

I always wanted to work. My parents used to say that I would be a lobbyist because I constructed arguments for everything. I'd take a set of facts and manipulate them to my favor. I vaguely remember taking aptitude tests in high school; I wound up qualifying to be a social worker or something. But I wanted to make more money than that.

I was kind of troubled in high school and went from doing well in ninth grade to doing badly by eleventh. I had one guidance counselor who looked out for me. He was important, though not in a concrete way. It just really helped to know that someone cared and recognized potential, where maybe others saw none.

I left high school without finishing and later got my diploma. Eventually, I went to college in California. I was in a writing program and in film school—I thought I wanted to do entertainment law. I took out student loans and received different grants, and worked all kinds of odd jobs.

When I first started school, I worked as a live-in nanny. I was a dose of reality for the kids, but it was bizarre to be in that environment. At times my family had been really poor—but, as a nanny, I lived in a guest house in Beverly Hills 90210. I had four credit cards for two kids. There was a driver, a maid. Sometimes their parents took off for two weeks at a time. Basically, it would be me, who pretty much still needed a parent, taking care of these children. I loved the kids, but I hadn't busted my ass to put myself back in school to be a domestic—I had grander ideas than that. But the job served a purpose: I lived rent-free, I was paid well, and I was given a brand new car to drive.

My first office job was at the real estate company where my dad then worked. It was an entry-level position, and I worked there for about six months. That's really where I learned office skills: how to use a computer, type, format a business letter.

There's two skills I value now, especially in the interns that work for us. One is phone manner. It's someone's first and last impression, so it's important to be able to conduct yourself appropriately. That doesn't mean by being kiss-assy, but by being courteous and on top of it, by knowing what's going on in the office. And it's important to know how to write letters. I know from the volume of mail that I get that you have someone's attention for about ten seconds. Make your points and wrap it up, maybe throw in something to personalize it. People appreciate your saying what you have to say quickly rather than rambling on. Writing in a clear, concise way is not easy for everybody. Sometimes you have to learn through practice. I've always written well, and I worked with people who helped me polish that skill. It's been invaluable.

At the real estate office I learned a lot about office politics. The dynamic at work is *completely* different than the one at school or at home. I went into the job with the idea that everybody is your friend. You think it's the same as being with your school classmates: you talk to them every day, joke around, say whatever you want. I said things I probably shouldn't have. You can fall into the office gossip cycle, which always, *always* comes back to haunt you. You can get to know someone really well on the job, but there are still things you shouldn't say to them. You don't want to expose yourself too much at work.

A perfect example when you're young is, say, you went out the night before, you're talking with people in the office: "Oh, I'm so hung over." Even though you're at work and you're functioning, it can color someone's perception. You learn there is a distinct line between your personal and professional life, and you have to be careful about how you allow people to perceive you. Even though someone may genuinely like and be concerned about you, when it comes down to work, they can't help but incorporate that information. If they're considering you for an assignment or a higher position, they take those things into account.

My current boss has sort of befriended me, but there are some things about me she doesn't need to know. We have to somehow navigate this line between the personal and the professional—especially when it comes time to ask for a raise. I recently said, "I can't afford to live on what you're paying me." She said, "Well, I can't afford to pay you any more right now." I said, "But I know that you can." She said, "Well, then you should move to Brooklyn, because you can't afford to pay the rent you're paying in Manhattan." I said, "Well, it's none of your business how much rent I pay." She said, "Well, it's none of your business whether I can afford to pay you more." If we didn't have this personal relationship it would be much more black and white. So now I won't tell her what I went out and spent on, say, a jacket.

Another thing I learned is that if you meet somebody you instantly don't like, a lot of times it's because you have something in common. Maybe that person reflects something about you that you're uncomfortable with. Sometimes people are just assholes, that's what they are. But if you have conflicts at work, sometimes there really is something you personally have to navigate and work out. You have to recognize that's what's going on.

My next internship was at a video production company, making minimum wage. I worked there for nine months. The company was owned by a husband and a wife. The couple were great, very nice people. I had no experience, but they were willing to teach. It would have been a great job for somebody who was ready for it. But due to a lot of naiveté, I took liberties I wasn't entitled to take.

Because it was a small company, a family business, they would bring their dogs in, come in late, take vacations. I didn't recognize that despite their being casual, I wasn't part of the family, I was still an *employee*. For the first six months I was good—it takes about six months in a new job to get your bearings, know what you're doing. Then you start to become comfortable and perhaps complacent. You start taking liberties. In a corporate environment, they're *so* worried about lawsuits that they'll give you a warning about your work performance. In a small company, they can't afford to give you that extra chance.

After I'd settled in, I started to call in late and to let outside things interfere with the job. I didn't see myself as taking advantage of them, but that's what I did. I was so young and inexperienced—I was really immature. I think now about how much I involved them in my life. "My car broke down, will you come get me?"—completely inappropriate behavior! If your car breaks down on the way to work, it's *your* problem. They may have compassion for you, but basically, if you're supposed to be at work at a certain time, you're supposed to be there. They had a big investment in this company, and they needed someone they could count on. And I wasn't reliable.

They were getting ready to take a vacation. I was going to be the only person in the office. I'd been out late one night and called in—made up some lame excuse, went in a few hours late. They sat me down and said, "We're getting ready to leave for two weeks. It's really important that we have coverage of the office." Then they said, "So we're going to have to let you go."

I was *shocked*. I couldn't believe it! First of all, that I'd get fired from a job where I was making minimum wage! I'd lulled myself into a false sense of security. I thought they'd never fire me because I knew everything: their personal life, the business. I had such a distorted perception of what my role was. I didn't think it conceivable they could go on without me. And clearly—they could—because they're still in business, and they're doing *fine*.

Once my anger and self-righteousness subsided, I felt *terrible*. In thinking it over, I had to take responsibility. I liked them and I had let them down. I recognize now how really vulnerable they were to whoever it was they hired.

Getting fired was a big lesson. If you learn from it, it's probably one of the best things that could happen to you when you're young. It's humbling. It shakes you up. When you start building your self-worth around your job and you're fired, it rattles your sense of who you are, of your worth in the workplace. And financially it rocks your world—especially when you're living paycheck to paycheck.

After being let go, I did a public relations internship for six months. The entertainment industry in L.A. is so competitive and backbiting—there's no such thing as loyalty. People were constantly on the defensive, everybody talked behind everybody else's back. Definitely not my favorite job. I *dreaded* going to work. At the real estate and production companies the atmosphere was laid back, everybody wore jeans. This place was not corporate in that we had to wear suits, but everybody was so *stylish*. As a starving college student, I'd sweat: "Oh my God, what am I going to wear to work today?" Because if you didn't look the part, you *really* got treated like shit.

The boss, who also owned the firm, came in at eleven, went to lunch at twelve-thirty, came back at three, left at five. She had a fantastic job, an exciting, glamorous job. The firm specialized in music. Every day she had lunch with *somebody*, she went out on tour with clients. But it's a really insecure industry. There were so many other PR people clamoring for her clients that if she wasn't on top of it at all times, they'd be snatched away. I realized I would never want to feel that constantly insecure.

I felt uneasy the *whole* time I was there. I didn't trust anybody; I felt people constantly looked down on me. No one had any genuine interest in teaching, they just needed the labor. I did learn about the process of public relations, about the industry. But mostly, our jobs were shit—just scrambling to get press releases out. I realized it was a superficial job, and that I would rather *be* Billy Idol than Billy Idol's publicist. It wound up being something to put on a résumé. And it was a weeding-out experience: OK, this is what I *don't* want to do.

I clerked for close to two years at a law firm. I liked the idea of litigation, of being in a courtroom and arguing and formulating strategies. This firm did some entertainment law, but much of their work involved contractual disputes. Someone wouldn't get proper billing on a film and would say, "You ruined my career," and sue for ten times the movie's budget. The firm also did personal injury medical malpractice—someone slips and falls crossing a driveway and then sues the property owner. Those were my boss's bread and butter.

I'd be assigned and work just one case. I'd pore over all the documents, affidavits, and depositions. I'd say to the lawyer, "Well, how are you going to get past *this*?" He had all the case law in his head. Really, I learned a lot of critical-thinking skills working with him. Everybody says, "Oh, an English degree—what's *that* worth?" But it forces you to read critically and to analyze. In law, I found that method really interesting. You learn to look for the subtleties and the subtext and the motivation. So I really learned analytical and critical-thinking skills. Those are invaluable.

The whole law industry is built around interpretation: you have to carefully word what you say and how you say it. I would look at the fine points, at what was going on, at how an argument was presented, at how it was broken down. I would think about how to anticipate people's responses and reactions. You sit back and listen, you rely on your instincts and intuition. A client will say, "I was walking through the grocery store and slipped and fell and banged my head on the floor." "Well, did you trip over something?" ". . . No . . ." And you *know* that pause means something. You ask questions and try to figure out what happened. I learned a lot about the nature of deceit.

I'm not very organized by nature, and it was vital I learn organizational skills. We had rooms full of documentation. My boss would say, "Will you pull that geological survey from October 1984?" Not the one from '92 or '96, and October not December. You had to be able to find this particular record in a room full of documents. When you're working on something, you get a sense of where things are. But I had to learn *exactly* where everything was. They counted on me to know.

Most companies, you have a filing cabinet, you slip the page into a file. It's not exactly in chronological order, sometimes it's in the back, sometimes it's in the front. But at the law firm, every time I added a document to the file, I had to go to the computer and add it to the index, assign it a tab, make a new tab. It's cumbersome. I used to get so frustrated. You had to go through that *each* time—you *had to* renumber. You kept things in chronological order, and when the defense counsel said, "Oh, we forgot to give you this one report," you had to make new tabs for the *entire* file—redo the whole index! Organizational paperwork was the worst part of the job.

Until your first real job, the only authoritative relationships you've had have been with your parents and teachers. The dynamic of the employee–employer relationship is completely different. Like the first time you really screw up, it's difficult to know what to do. This is not your mom. Your boss doesn't have to forgive you. How do you deal with that? Paperwork formatted for filing in court had to be perfect. In the legal profession, if there's a comma out of place in a document, you could lose a case, you could cost someone dearly.

My brain works faster than I can type and I have a terrible habit of dropping words. There were times where my attention was not that exact. I'd take something in for a signature and my boss would say, "Look at this! You dropped out the 'not.' You *completely* changed the meaning of this document." You apologize. Then you start to question yourself. I became nervous, I'd read things fifty times before I took them in. I was friendly with my boss, but if I'd kept screwing up he would have let me go. There was too much at stake.

Even as an intern, you have to be accountable. Especially if you're working in a small company—people depend on you. I'm in the position of supervising interns now, and one thing I impress on them is not to think of this as a hobby. Even if you're working for free, not getting paid a *dime*, you have to come in with the same attitude as if you were on salary. Otherwise you won't *learn* anything because you won't be invested in being there. In a small company you really can gain valuable experience. I don't think it's the same in a corporate company. They'll have you filing and copying—you're not going to learn anything anyway.

I remember specifically when I stopped wanting to be a lawyer. We were defense counsel. The plaintiff was an actor who sued our client for not giving him proper billing. The dynamic between the two lead counsels was vicious, they were directly attacking each other. It was no longer about law—it was *personal*. That happened a lot. This guy's claim was fraudulent, it was a bullshit case, but just the level of animosity . . . I didn't meet one lawyer while I was there who really *loved* what they did. And never for one *second* did I want to have my boss's job.

What initially appealed to me about entertainment law was that I thought it would be fun to represent the rich and famous, or to be in-house counsel at a network. But in the end, it isn't. You're not the rich and famous, you're the poor and overworked. My boss made a decent living, but he was never going to make a million dollars. And ninety-five percent of what he did was really dull. He spent a lot of time on the phone arguing with people. It wasn't intellectual argument, arguing in principle—that would have appealed to me. It was just emotional arguing. But it was great I took the job, because otherwise I'd probably have wound up going to law school, and I'm *so* glad I didn't.

My last two years of college, I worked twenty hours a week at the law firm and bartended at night and went to school full-time. How I did it all, I have no idea. When I graduated, I came to New York to visit a friend. Two of my college professors suggested I meet with their book editors for informational interviews. Both editors suggested I meet with a literary agent whose assistant was leaving.

I don't remember the interview going that well, but I guess the chemistry was right. I had the confidence of not needing a job, I didn't even think of it as a job interview. I was relaxed and very calm. I've always been a big reader, and we talked about books I was reading. I said, "New York is so exciting" and "What do you do?"—I had *no* idea what a literary agent did

The agent said, "I would love for you to work with me, but you have to start in a week." I was still at the law firm and bartending. I had a boyfriend and a car and an apartment I'd lived in for three years . . . but I didn't want to stay in L.A. It's a beautiful city, but I never felt comfortable, it wasn't for me. And in New York, I was amazed by the pulse, the energy.

I thought about it. I didn't want to say two years down the road, as I'm working some shit job in L.A., "I really *should* have taken that job." When my mom graduated from high school, she was offered an art scholarship. Her mother discouraged her from accepting it—she's *always* regretted that. The truth is, every decision you make affects every other decision.

Since I've always been a book person, I had thought abstractly of maybe trying to get into publishing, but I thought I would be an editor because of my education, my degree. I think I'm a better editor than I am a writer, and a better agent than I am an editor. I love working with books, and I have a profound respect for writers and what they do, so it just sort of fit.

I've learned so much at this job, though the foundation was laid through my other work experiences. Work really can be a catalyst for personal exploration. I never thought I would be in a business sales job, but here I am. I never thought of being an agent but, as it turns out, I'm pretty good at it.

The role of literary agent has changed dramatically over the past five years. The relationship with the client is close. At this point, book agents are probably much more editors than editors are. Editors change jobs so quickly, by the time your book gets published you could have had five. My clients get to be friends, they call me at home and cry on my shoulder when their book gets rejected. I have to be a calming presence in their life.

People who go into business for themselves or work for small companies have to be disciplined, they have to be motivated. If I leave to go on vacation, I can't take off two weeks in a row. I have too many obligations and responsibilities. There's no one to hand off to. It's a responsibility. Someone who needs a lot of structure wouldn't do as well in this environment.

I've always had a sense that I needed to find passion in my work, not just get a paycheck, come home, and have a full life *outside* of work. You know, you try on many different hats and one day you'll try on one that fits. Now, all the things I was looking for in a job, I get to do. I get to take a project and put a new spin on it. I get to talk about why someone should publish a certain book, about who the audience for the book is. I love the deal-making stuff, the contracts and negotiations. And then, to watch something become a book is really amazing. You bring this work to a really big audience and let other people learn what *you've* learned. It really is amazing.

IV

"A Foot in the Door": Making Their Way

No life is without hardship, but some people meet with it at an earlier age than others. The type of family you have, what they do with their time, and how they treat you are all factors in your developing ideas about the kind of person you want to be and the way you want to live your life. By setting good or bad examples—more often both—parents provide you with strong first reference points. What you do with that information depends on the intensity of your dreams, the force of your need to know more, the luck of the draw, and the different people you meet or are exposed to, especially early on.

The people in this section share one thing in common: however far they've come, it hasn't been easy. Throughout these interviews range stories of good and harmful behaviors, parents absent or present, blessedly helpful adults, neglect, poverty, financial assistance, encouragement, and the power of chance connections.

For Mick Betancourt, who has been scrambling to earn money since he was very young, "your work ethic, your work habits, directly relate to and are formed by your family." He pays no mind to America's "anyone can be president" myth. "In school they'll say it's up to you. But there's luck involved, there's lessons involved, there's requirements involved, there's skills involved, there's connections involved."

Chino Pinex benefited from a combination of determination and fortunate timing. The last time he found himself in jail he thought, "I can't

keep coming back here. I can't carry my life like that no more. . . ."
Soon after his release, someone gave him a steady job. "I had to work
my way in, just like everybody else work their way in . . . get to
know what to do, what not to do."

Credell Walls, a former co-worker of Pinex's, and from the same
economic background, is constantly looking for ways to expand his ho-
rizons, through school and work. "Learning, not just from the job itself,
but from meeting all these different people, can make your job wonderful, make you want to go to work each day." But he's learned that relating to others in the workplace is a complex experience. "With the
people I work with, I immediately tell myself they're human, they will
say things about you behind your back . . . It's going to happen, expect it."

Cesar Rivera went from the South Bronx to Wall Street with the help
of a prep-school scholarship, hard work, and a series of internships. He
sees Wall Street as a good place for minorities because, "You never have
to worry about hidden agendas or what you're being measured by.
You're measured by dollars." In order to fit into the culture at one investment firm, Rivera had to teach himself to behave in new ways. "If
you kept *acting* the way you were supposed to, you could sort of become that role. That was a big learning experience for me, and it
strengthened my confidence."

Iliana Roman's father set an example as a good provider, but the father of her three young children did not do the same. Leaving him made
it that much harder for her to finish school, earn a living, and care for
her children. "I want my children to see what I saw in my father: work,
work, work." A positive attitude helps propel her forward. "Always
think you can do it, determine what you want out of life. "

As those in this section illustrate, success in any complex endeavor—staying out of jail, avoiding abuse, ignoring negative messages—requires intense personal effort . . . *and* as much outside
help as you can find.

MICK BETANCOURT

For Mick, twenty-three, work involves struggling against the family history of alcoholism as well as uninspired and uninspiring work habits and jobs. He sees his low economic status as a major obstacle to success. "People don't think class is a really big thing. I think it is." He's already held a number of jobs: "I've delivered newspapers, worked in a sign shop, worked for Kentucky Fried Chicken, Giovanni's pizzeria, worked at my high school, at a pool hall, as a short-order cook, as a waiter, a truck driver, a telemarketer. What else . . . Valet parked cars, was a doorman at a club. I'll tell ya, I'm hungrier than most." Home Depot is his first long-term job, complete with a prolonged period of hazing which he struggled to bring to an end. "As the new guy, you have to bite the bullet and do the shit work—that's just par for the course." At the heart of his conflict: he doesn't want a job. "I want to be in comedy, I want to be an entertainer. I don't want to be blue collar—I don't want to be any collar. I don't want to go to the company-funded dinner . . . I want to be the guy at the function making everybody laugh!"

When I was a kid, I was a goof, I always made people laugh. I wanted to know where funny was—and where it was, that's where I wanted to be. Because *nothing* was better. Everything was *so* bad at home, and to laugh felt so *great*.

I grew up in Chicago. My dad was Puerto Rican and my mother Irish. I lived in Humboldt Park.* My dad's sisters and mother lived with us. One sister's a junkie; the other is getting her nursing degree and dating a police officer—she made it out of the neighborhood. I mean,

---

* An ethnically diverse working-class neighborhood five miles northwest of downtown Chicago.

you'll have your scars, but unscathed physically. And then my grand-mother was there, and she was just a *raging* alcoholic. She would drink those huge oil cans of Schlitz and talk till four o'clock in the morning.

I think my parents got divorced when I was four. When I was born, my dad was sixteen, my mom was seventeen. It's hard on *anybody* to have kids, but when you're that young I imagine it's gotta be unreal. For me, twenty-two was the hardest birthday. My dad died when he was twenty-two. He was electrocuted on the El.* He was under the influ-ence. No one has ever been straight with me on the story, but I saw the newspaper articles. It was maybe a paragraph, page-twenty "Man Dies on El" kind of thing. He was in the morgue for three days before any-one knew he was gone.

After the divorce, my mom and I moved into her father's two-flat building—nice backyard, two-car garage, in a better but pretty racist neighborhood. My grandfather lived on the top floor, with one of my uncles staying in the living room. My mom lived downstairs.

I think that your work ethic, your work habits, directly relate to and are formed by your family. My dad started out as a motorcycle me-chanic, but later worked in a tool-and-die factory. I always knew him as someone who was filthy when he came home. My mom didn't work much. She'd get social security, for me, then she wouldn't. If she made a certain amount of money, she couldn't get the government checks. Ei-ther she could sit back and get those checks or go out and work like a dog and maybe make a hundred dollars more. I guess to her, working didn't make too much sense.

When she did work, she'd love her job for a week or two. Then somebody in the office would say something to her, or she'd hear them saying something . . . She would pick someone out, make enemies with them, get in a real torrid battle and quit or get fired . . . *guaranteed.* When my mom complained about people at work, I'd say, "Well, maybe you're taking it the wrong way. Everybody has a bad day."

---

* Elevated and subway rapid transit system.

Sometimes she'd work *too* hard, not understand the work schedule. You can come in an hour early, stay three hours late, but if you work a twenty-four-hour day and don't show up the next, that's bad. My mom would be like, "Screw those people if they think I'm coming in today"—then she'd say, "Pay attention in school!" [Laughs.] But if she was lonely, she'd want me to stay home with her, and I'd stay home. I got a lot of polar . . . "Don't drink!" [mimes guzzling] "Work hard" [mimes a phone call] "I'm not coming in today, I'm sick" [a whispered aside] "Don't ever do this . . ." Everything was a contradiction in my house.

My mother's an alcoholic and totally abusive, so I pretty much stayed upstairs with my grandfather. My grandfather is the reason I stand today on two feet. He was my rock and he'll be my rock, till the day I die. My grandfather could do anything. You would say to him, "Gramp, my bicycle's broken," and he'd fix it. Or, "Gramp, there's a hole in the garage," and he'd fix it. He'd say, "I have this picture in my head," and he'd paint it, and it would be a gorgeous painting. He could do anything. He could do *anything*.

My grandfather worked at Sears, but he was always looking to make the quick million dollars. He invented the gun lock. Back in the fifties people used to go into Sears and say, "Let me see that thirty-eight." "Sure." *Boom!* Shoot themselves in the head, right there in the store! So the guys in the marketing department said, "Tom, can you come up with something? Just fool around with an idea." So he comes up with a gun lock that's still used today. My grandfather draws it up, goes to a lawyer, the patent lawyer steals it . . .

My grandfather worked for Sears for thirty-two years. I know he didn't really want to—and that, to me, is true-fire all-out courage. He was an alcoholic for many, many years, but did not miss a day of work. But the reason I think he was a real man is because he finally stopped drinking. In the long run, his building was paid for, he had money in the bank, he had stock in the company; he had his daughter below him and his son to the right of him. I don't know if he died a happy man. I hope he did . . . I loved him more than anything I'll ever love again.

I've worked my whole entire life, really. Maybe it was instinct, maybe it came from my dad's side, his trait of being a hard worker. When I was nine or ten I had a paper route. I saw other people delivering papers and thought, "Well, I have a bicycle. I'm not doing anything while I'm watching them work. Why don't I do that?" The papers came early in the evening, and you'd roll them and put the rubber band on them. You'd wrap 'em and stick 'em in your bag, and deliver them the next morning. The Thursday paper came at three o'clock in the morning. My grandfather would wait up and he'd wake me. "Let's roll the papers." We'd roll the papers and go back to sleep, and then he'd wake me up again to go deliver them. I was fourteen when he died. The day of the funeral the papers came. I had to wait up all alone and go deliver them. That was it, though—I didn't want to do the paper route *any* more.

My uncle had already moved out by the time my grandfather died, and I didn't have much contact with my mother. I lived upstairs in the apartment by myself. I remember one time I had a Wheaties-and-mayonnaise sandwich. That was bad. On stale bread. I lived off a box of rice for a week and a half, those big white Minute Maid things. There were mice all over, and I had *no* money—I was stealing food. The only time my mother would come up and talk to me—this was right when my grandfather died, before she completely stopped talking to me— was when I would turn the air conditioner on and it would blow her fuse. She'd come up and tell me if I turned the air conditioner on that would be *it* for me.

I just remember going to school one day and walking down the halls. My clothes were dirty and I hadn't eaten. I walked into the counselor's office and said, "I have to talk to someone right now." I said, "I don't have any parents, I'm living by myself, there's mice all over the place." I was pretty much against asking for help then, and I'm the same way now. But I guess I didn't know what else to do. I knew something was wrong. I was hoping that everybody else wasn't in the same boat and just playing it out better than me; I was hoping I could find a remedy and make it all better. That's when I moved in with my uncle and his wife and kids.

After elementary school, I'd gone to a private school, a great school. My grandmother was their registrar for years, and they found grants for me. I worked there to pay off half my tuition. I answered phones and did clerical work in the office before and after school, and sometimes at lunch. I knew all the faculty, everybody. In school, my attitude was like this: "If I get one A, that shows I can get an A. If I'm on the B line, I'll get rewarded for the As. But if I'm on the A line, I get a B, I've failed." *Failed.* That was always my mentality.

After high school, I got a scholarship to go to college, but I wasn't mature enough to handle school. I lasted a year. I didn't treat it as a school, I treated it as a place to drink and scam women. No matter what, there was always a party to go to, and that's what I did instead of going to class. After I lost the scholarship, I just floated and partied my ass off for about two years. That was probably the lowest part of my life.

Ya know, I feel like I should be able to walk into an advertising firm and say, "Look—here's my book, I wrote these ads. I can do this for *you*." But in the real world, why are they gonna take me over a guy that put in four years at college? "Yes, you're talented, *but* . . ." My friend Mike and I are the same age and have the same background—I've known him since grade school. He's an underwriter now, he's making thirty thousand a year. Just took the bull by the balls. He said, "*They*"—you know, *they*, the word that means those other people— "They are *not* gonna give *you* the job, they're gonna give it to the college kid." And they're not, they're just not. Ninety-nine point nine percent of the time, the money's goin' to the guy with the degree. And I don't know if I want to go back to college.

I went to a Catholic elementary school, and it was all working-class kids. You just knew that none of their parents were doing great. When I got to the private school, some rich guy came and made a speech. He talked about how when he was in high school he started a lawn-mowing service and hired other kids to come and do the work while he collected the checks. I went from working-class to: "You can do something, there's opportunity for you out there." You had to wear a sportcoat, tie, dress shoes. Dress for success. In class, they constantly told you, "You're the men that are going to lead the world." But I'm a firm believer that where you live is gonna influence you a lot more than school.

What it boils down to is connections and people you know. You're brought up a certain way and you're told certain things and you wind up going to certain schools. The rich man's son, or uncle, you do *them* a favor, then *he* owes *you* a favor, and that's where *your* son or nephew comes in, it's like a network. That's a force in the work world, definitely. For the *real* jobs. The jobs that don't involve you talking to an assistant manager or a shift boss.

My college scholarship involved me in teaching, which I did the summer between high school and college. I taught sixth through eighth grade, English and math, in the housing projects in Chicago. The Robert Taylor Homes ended, and about forty feet away was a grade school. I was white as a nun's ass down there, I'll tell ya. But the look on my face said, "You don't have to fuck with me. I'm not coming in here patronizing you. I know what it's like to *starve*." That's about class. Take one look and you'll know.

I had this huge argument with the scholarship people, because they're like, "School is . . ." and I said, "It's *not* school." In the real world everything is *so much more* complicated than just making simple statements. I said, "No matter what you teach these kids at school, no matter how great the school, they have to go home. And roundabout lunch they start to think about the ass-beating they're gonna get when they get home, or about how their ma's gonna be on the floor with a needle sticking out of her arm." That's what they see. In the morning they get it before school, and maybe by eleven, they forget. Then they eat and start thinking about it again. And that's what happens with *all* these kids: they share the same problems, and that energy fills the entire room. And you can't see it because you live in Lake Forest.* I'm not saying anything bad about Lake Forest, because if *I* could live in Lake

---

* A wealthy North Shore suburb thirty-two miles north of downtown Chicago.

Forest I'd be moving right next door to ya and we'd toast every night over a big dead calf sitting right there on the table!

I learned there's working-class and there's upper-class. Where do you want to be? In school they'll say it's up to you. But there's luck involved, there's lessons involved, there's requirements involved, there's skills involved, there's connections involved.

After I lost the scholarship, I worked at a quick-grill and pool hall. You could smoke and drink beer while you worked. [Laughs.] Work and vice at the same time. I wanted to remain beaten and just lowing it. It's hard to get interviewed after a fight—when you lost, when you're out. Why do you need to talk to anybody? Your face is *beaten*, everyone has seen you go down.

When I started looking for different work, I went to Blockbuster. It was all younger kids. "How you doing? Where's the manager? I'm looking for a job. Can I fill out an application? Just wanted to know if you guys were hiring." It's hard to suck it up and do something like that, but you have to. I was a waiter at Bennigan's, and I killed at that—I made *great* money. Other waiters would say, "Oh, I made twenty bucks on this lunch," and I'd have made seventy! I'd make it a good time for the customers. I'd be a nut, bring them outta their day.

Now I work at Home Depot, which is just your average company started up by two guys, entrepreneurs, grown into a multibillion-dollar business—American dream kind of thing. Home Depot is like a huge warehouse of construction goods, anything you want: plumbing, electrical, doors, windows, bags of cement, any kind of wood . . . I'd been working as a delivery driver for a travel agency where my fiancée, Kate, works. Her boss told me about a newspaper ad he'd seen.

Great—hired me on. I'd never driven a real truck before in my life. The truck with the forklift is a ten-speed, about twenty-five feet long. I'd watch the guys drive it and when they'd go home, I'd take the truck around back and practice, so it seemed like I knew what I was doing! I'm making $11.70 now, driving two different types of truck. When they hired me, I had a CDL [commercial driver's license], I had a year of college, management experience. They just hired this new guy a week and a half ago. He's never driven a truck in his life, no college, his last job was seven bucks an hour, doesn't have a CDL. They hired him at $11.50. So I'm making twenty cents more than he is; he's got no experience, I've worked there two years. To me, it's reason without rhyme.

This job is not me, it's not what I *want* to do, but at the time, I saw it as my step into the real working world. I'm gonna be making an OK paycheck, I'm gonna have benefits, I can have stock. Home Depot really likes their employees, and there's a chance I could become an in-store manager. Which is *so* unappealing to me. It'd be a cage: "This is your area, keep it clean."

I come in, my orders are there: a piece of paper naming the type of merchandise and the quality. Say someone wants four hundred 2x4x8 wood studs. You pull those, you band 'em up, you throw 'em on the truck with a forklift—you have to operate all kinds of fork-lift machinery. You unchain it, drop it, pick up the load, deliver it, put it where the customer wants, reattach the forklift, go on to the next stop. . . . With the box truck it's pretty much the same thing. Pull up, jump off the truck, climb up back, grab what you got, throw it in the garage and leave. That's about it. Mindless drudge. That took sixty seconds to describe and I had to do a week of training.

The store was open for a year and a half before I was hired, and there were already three other drivers. One of the three got promoted above us. That left Kenny, who had worked there since the store opened, and Ray, who'd been hired a week before me but acted like he'd been there the whole time. He's two years older than me; Kenny's about forty. Kenny's got one tooth and been written up by the bosses for personal hygiene problems. I'm thinking, "Look at you and look at me. I can work harder than you, I can work longer than you, I'm smarter than you, and I'm *not* gonna have you boss me around." But he had tenure. Tenure is something you learn about when you start to work. Tenure still doesn't make any sense to me, but it's like breathing: you might not understand the whole mechanical process, but you've got to accept it.

When I started, *everyone* was trying to be the boss to me. But sometimes the things they did made no sense, plus they were busy milking the clock. My very first day, Ray was telling me how great he is and how long he's been driving a truck. But, really, he's a lazy guy. Every morning he comes in, you say, "How you doing?" He puts his head down and rolls it back and forth—like he just worked thirteen hours. And he *just* walked in the door. The first thing he says is, "I'd like to get out of here early today." Every day! And if it looks like a full eight-hour day, he starts swearing and throwing stuff around. And then he complains that his knee hurts, or his foot hurts, or his arm hurts.

And Kenny, he's a real Mr. Know-it-all; a pathological liar, too. We're driving down the expressway and see a Hooters sign*— "Yeah, I dated her." I'm like, *"What?!"* "Yeah, I dated her about seven years ago." Which would have put her at the ripe old age of thirteen. And he's telling me how he's a lieutenant colonel, but that he shouldn't talk about it because he was in a part of the military that's so special forces it's ridiculous. He tells me he knows kung fu and that special forces used to fly him into designated areas in a plane with a glass roof!

He'd get in my face and tell me all the things I was doing wrong. It got to the point where I'd be lifting something or I'd be writing something: "Oh, you can correct your handwriting this way"—just like I was a kid. It really lowered me down. One day I snapped. We were driving and I said, "Stop the car." He'd been egging me on all day. I said, "Kenny, in case I don't see you over the weekend, I want to make sure you know that I think you're a motherfucker. Just in case I don't see ya." I started to walk away. He's like, *"What?!"* I ran back, I lost my temper—I said, "We're gonna *go*. You're Mr. Lieutenant Colonel in the special forces and I'm gonna kick your ass." Which has *no* business in the workplace, it really doesn't. He jumped down, I grabbed him . . . and we just stopped, we didn't fight. Later, I said to one of the managers, "We gotta take care of this."

We had a meeting: an assistant manager, all the drivers and me. It was like I was on trial. The assistant manager said, "Did you do this?

* A restaurant chain reputed for its large-breasted waitresses.

Did you do that?" I said, "Wait a second, *I'm* not the one who should be defending myself." The other two were saying, "Well, he drives like a maniac." But *they* were the ones who'd had accidents. I'm like, "I've never had an accident in my *life*." All the things they accused me of, I defended myself against, I proved moot. It was basically that they didn't like me.

I started the meeting out by saying, "I don't come here to make friends. I have my friends—I spend time with them off the job. I'm here to work and get along with people. If you don't like me, get that out *now*, but don't say I'm a bad worker or I'm lazy." It resolved nothing, just everyone clearing their chest. That's the work environment, though. If there's friction, they want it ironed out. They don't really care what the employees think or feel, just as long as the work gets done.

Ray and I, it's been bitter . . . I'm upset that everyone tolerates his lethargic behavior. But I came to realize it's none of my business. He doesn't sign my checks, he's got nothing to do with me—except for when I'm working with him, which I don't anymore.

Kenny and I wound up getting along pretty well. Later I said, "Kenny, let's iron this out. We're gonna be in the truck all day, just shoot out what's on your mind." He said, "Well, I like to haze the new guy." I realized, that's the kind of guy he is. He's balding, he's forty, he's unhappy, and he's working on a truck, with me—and I'm maybe twenty-one. "Well, you hazed me," I said, "and we're done. I'm not gonna hold it against you, but we're gonna go on to the next step, we're gonna be co-workers. We'll bullshit, we'll make fun of each other, but your hazing is over, agreed?" "Yeah." So I gave him his day. We resolved it.

To me, the "real" job is the job that makes you happy. Not everybody finds that. I'm not happy working for Home Depot, but I have to go in and work. As long as I show up, I'm gonna work hard. It's practice for any other job—you know, for *my* job: entertainer.

I've done stand-up comedy and split my vision right down the middle: my left eye looking at the crowd, my right eye looking at myself, my left ear listening to the crowd, my right ear listening to my words. A hundred percent commitment makes the joke. You can say, "I was walking down the street yesterday and this tree was in *full* bloom." If you *believe* it and at that moment you're walking down the street and the tree's in full bloom, then people will see—they'll be with you. My problem now is, am I going to commit myself one hundred percent to my true passion and my goals, or am I gonna be faded and flubbed by driving a truck? It's a lot harder to do something creative after you've worked ten hours.

I don't want to be thirty, a Teamster, living in an A-frame bungalow. I don't want to hear somebody saying, "He thought he was such a hot shit, look at him now." I don't want to hear, "He was so talented—it's such a waste." I have dreams and I want to *act* on them. But maybe I'm afraid of success. I'm not afraid of failure. Failure's all I've got—*tons* of failure.

I was talking to Kate's dad. Police officer, thirty-two years. He and I have almost the identical past. He becomes a police officer because he's got nothing else, he's got no family. He likes taking pictures, he starts working for a wedding photographer. Worked two jobs for twenty-five years. He's creative, but he put a lot of that behind him because he wanted security. Four years ago, I told him I wanted to go to Second City.* He said, "Maybe you're afraid to find out that might not be your dream. You get there, find out. Now you're twenty and you got no dreams—then what?"

It's very scary to me that this is what I want to do. I can live on a box of rice for a week and a half—I've done that, it doesn't matter to me. But am I gonna be a good provider for Kate? I don't want her to see what I've seen, *ever*. When I have a family, I want to have money in the bank, I want security. Instead of driving a truck, I want you to tell me what you want, or we'll work together on something, on an ad idea, on *anything* to use my mind.

Maybe being an entertainer is a utopian job that millions of people

* A decades-old comedy group known for spawning famous comedians.

want—which I imagine it probably is, 'cause it sounds like a dream to me—and only certain people can do. Whether I'm one of those people or not, I don't know. I feel that I am, but I just haven't gotten the chance. But even saying that makes me mad, because what am I doing wrong? Where am I *not* right now? I know schoolwise, handshaking wise, where I'm not . . .

I've lived like a junkie since I was born. I've got two hundred dollars in the bank. It kills me. I make $11.70 an hour, I get good checks. I still owe for college, I *still* live like a junkie. I live in a one-room apartment that's this big . . . The walls close in on me. And it's worse because at work I'm doing something that I don't like, so when I come home . . . I'll tell ya, sometimes I feel defeated. And to be an entertainer . . . Not only do I not have a foot in the door, I don't know what the door *looks* like. I wouldn't know the first step. Who am I going to ask? Who do I talk with? The bathroom mirror and truck drivers!

A while ago, I was living with a guy who had moved to Chicago to study acting. He said, "You're hilarious—why don't you come down to Second City with me?" He was in his third week of class. Since I was a little kid, I've always wanted to be on *Saturday Night Live*, and Second City is where *SNL* looks to find new people. On *SNL*, they used to show black-and-white photos of New York and then the guy would come on, "*Live* from New York . . ." I thought, "*Man*—that's what I want to do." I want to stand on that platform at the end of the show and clap with the audience. I knew there was a party afterwards, too, and I wanted to be at the party—I wanted to be talking to everybody.

I visited New York once, and I fell in love in a *second*. I said, "These streets are *bubbling*!" The air, the way it smells—and the people, and everybody's going, going and you can't stand still. I *love* that. I want to come from the cast party, have a few in me, and we're all great and funny, we just made everybody *laugh*, and we're gonna go into the New York City night and make *more* people laugh. That's what I want. So I said, "Yeah, I'll go."

So we go to Second City and classes are full. Out front, we ran into a man by the name of Martin, who is like the third guy in charge over there. I didn't know who he was, but my friend did and he said, "Martin, Mick wants to get into one of your classes." Martin said, "Come here, let me talk to you for a second." I went with him and he said, "You have the gift, you have to start taking classes." He said, "Go over to"—I can't think of the name, some hole in the wall place—"and start learning the skills, the craft."

I went there till they asked me for money. I didn't have any. I went for four weeks, they're like, "Pay," and I'm like, "I'm gonna go feed the meter . . . Be right back, two seconds." Never went back. That was depressing, and I let it get to me for a while.

Finally I said, "I can't *not* be that person. That's who I am." So I went back to Second City and applied for the next class. They said it was two hundred bucks. I drained my bank account . . . "Here you go." I've been taking class five, six weeks. In another year I'll audition for the conservatory program. They said *Saturday Night Live* will usually come out and take a look at the main stage cast after three years. I say fine to that.

I don't think I'll ever know all of the things I need to know about work. All I really want to do is to be good at something, be recognized as someone who's good, and enjoy doing it. That way I'll have lived a complete life. But every day that I work at something I don't like, I lose something of myself.

I have to work tomorrow. I'm gonna hate every second of it—it's almost like torture for me to go in. But I'll bring a tape recorder with me and I'll set it in the truck and work on all my different voices and characters. Then I'll go home and write them down. We'll see what happens.

CHICO PINEX

We meet at his job site at the Overton Building, on Chicago's south side. The building is in the process of being gutted in anticipation of rehabilitation. A community group has hired Neighborhood Conservation Corps, the small company Chico works for, to do this job. It is a blistering hot day.

Directly across the wide, two-way street stands Stateway Gardens, a massive Chicago Housing Authority project. Several yards down, volunteers and various Chicago Housing Authority (CHA) residents lay out railway ties to create garden plots in front of a couple of heartbroken structures. Directly across from us, finished plots with flowers spruce up an otherwise-blighted building. A woman sitting by a large cooler sells snowcones to heat-stricken neighbors. Chico, twenty-six, puts his yellow hard hat on the sidewalk and we talk. He smiles frequently at passers-by—he is known. For years, he alternated between dealing drugs and serving time. Then he got a job. "I don't miss my wrong life because it was leading to me getting locked up. I would say now I'm doing very well. You gotta look at it like this: it ain't what you're making, it's how you're making it. And I feel much, much better than I used to feel."

I've made it to twenty-six as of this month. I was raised over here in Stateway Gardens. My father, he used to drive tractor-trailer trucks for a moving company. He used to take me on his jobs, in and out of town. I wanted to be a truck driver throughout the years I was growing up. I like driving stickshift—I'm one of those *fast* drivers. Right now, today, I still want to be that truck driver, but basically I ain't found no good job I can drive a truck for.

I've been liking to work since I was a kid. I learned that through my dad, by him telling me, showing me what to do, what not to do. 'Cause working's gonna keep you surviving. My mom used to work at a music lounge. She couldn't work too much because she was busy taking care of the kids. My father and my mother taught me a lot.

I got my first job when I was in seventh grade, helping to deliver milk. Five brothers owned the company, and they all liked me 'cause I'd always be there early, always stay late when there was work to be done. I'm a good worker: anywhere I go, anybody'll tell you that. I try to impress everybody, show them I'm a qualified man, whatever kind of work I'm doing. My next job, I was about sixteen. I worked for this guy, he sold and delivered paint; sometimes we'd do paint jobs. I was his right-hand guy.

In high school, I had an afterschool guidance class about work. They gave us information about all type of jobs, what we can do if we want jobs. I got one job through them, at UPS—that was my third job. It was right before Christmas, and I wasn't there but maybe seven weeks. When I started, I didn't know all the new faces and all, I didn't know what to do. Once I got my uniform, they told me what to do. I made sure I was there on time, made sure my hours were straight, did what I was supposed to do and I was gone. Lifting a whole bunch of boxes all day every day with a few breaks, it wasn't fun at all. And these wasn't no light boxes—they was *heavy*.

They let me know off the top there wasn't gonna be no regular job, it was just temporary. It was better than nothing. I wanted a regular job, but I couldn't get hired on that easy. I wouldn't say there wasn't a *chance*—it's just there were so many people on the list, my name was under a lot of other names. They knew I knew how to work, they knew I *will* work. But the fact is, they're going by the list, it's the list they're going by, and there's nothing I can do about that.

After that job, I started hanging around in the hood and slinging, selling drugs. I wouldn't say I was running with a gang. Everybody always think everything is a gang. Everything is *not* a gang— everybody has different names for themselves and how they carry themselves. Gangbangers do crazy things, that's what gangbangers do.

But other people like me—*me*, I'm a businessman. I'm talking about taking care of my kids,* my family, and myself. Selling drugs is the second-best thing you can do if you don't have a job—that's how I see it. A lot of people don't see it that way, they think it's a bad thing. I *know* it's a bad thing, but I got to put food on the table just like everybody else.

I was just standing around outside, watching people make money. One day this customer asked me, do I have product? Once I got the product, I was right off the top getting people to buy it. My last UPS check, instead of me just spending it, I invested in drugs. First of all, the money was looking *good*. I was making it as fast as I could get the product. *Big* money. It happened so quick, and I just . . . wow. Before I knew it, I had cars after cars after cars, females . . .

I could have got a regular job instead. I signed up for truck-driving training school the year before I got out of high school. I didn't go 'cause I got locked up for slinging drugs. Thrown in jail—seven months. Got back out, did it again; locked right back up six months later. I was in and out of jail. I've been locked up seven times, I've been to the penitentiary twice; the first time for three years, the second time for a year. Every time I got out, I started selling again. See, it was the money, the money was carrying me along. It was just so good, the money was so good, and it was coming so fast . . .

At first I didn't feel bad about what I was doing, I didn't really care. If I'm not selling it, somebody else will. But when I'd be in jail, I'd lay on my bunk thinking, "I should have just gone to truck-driving school. I could have done anything with my life but sit here." I was thinking all kinds of things I should've thought *before* I was slinging. It was upsetting to me that I'd wasted my life on these drugs. I sat there, day by day—I just couldn't believe it. But it was basically too late for all that: I did the crime, I had to serve the time.

When I went to court, the judge let me know he was going to release

* At the time, Chico had fathered seven children. Two more have been born as of this writing.

me, but that I had to do 175 hours of community service. I came down to Stateway, to the CHA office and talked to the manager, and he gave me community service around here. I cleaned vacant apartments, did janitorial work, threw refrigerators out of old apartments, stuff like that. I liked it. It was better than sitting at the Cook County Jail.

Everybody around here was shocked when they seen me. They were like, "Wow, how did you get that job?" If I hadn't gotten community service, I wouldn't ever have got that job because people in the office knew I sling—I knew there was some people suspicious about me. See, what I did, I proved them *wrong*. I showed them I'm a good guy more than I'm a bad guy. I figured I can prove my point, show them how reliable I am, how good a worker I am. And they liked the way I worked. I impressed them one day when a guy had a truckload of new refrigerators and stoves. I had to take them to the peoples' houses and bring the old ones back out. So I take one, I bring one back. I delivered basically a whole truckload. And I didn't use no truck, I used a two-wheeler. [He points.] I walked from that end to this end, just doing it.

I finished my community service and I was trying to figure out the next step to bring me some money. Well, once again, I got to selling drugs. I got caught and sent back to jail for nine months. On my way to the penitentiary, I'm thinking, "I know what to do when I get out and what not to do. I've been on and off parole. I can't keep coming back here. I can't carry my life like that no more . . ." Them hard times make you do hard *time*, and I've had enough of that. That's the whole point of me getting a job. With that three-strikes-you're-out law, they'll lose you in the system.

While I was in jail, the housing people contacted my mother. They needed extra help, they knew right off the top I was the guy for it. They didn't know I was locked up. My mama told them I was out of town and I'd be back at a certain time. At that certain time, I got out of jail. I went down to the CHA office and I told them the truth. There was no use in me lying; once they go through the computer, it's going to pop up anyway. They let me know I couldn't get the job back too soon. But the guy I'm working for now, Jamie, was in the office. They introduced us and told him what a dependable guy I was, how hard I worked. He told me to check with him the next Monday, that they was doing a little demolition right around here.

When I started out, I let them know right off the top I'm dependable. When they pulled up in the morning, I was already sitting there waiting. My first day on the job, well, first of all, I didn't have no boots. I just put on anything and went to work. I *had* to get some boots. We knocked down a few walls, cut holes in walls for windows, cleaned it out. There was lots of debris in there. This was a place they were rehabbing, turning it into a shelter for people who don't got homes.

I didn't know nobody on the crew at all. I had to work my way in, just like everybody else work their way in: get to know people, get to know how to do the work; get to know what to do, what not to do. The usual. I wasn't nervous, but I wanted to get into it so I could keep myself a slot on the job. Jamie told me if I work well, in about a month the pay will go up.

We made a four-man crew: me, Alvin Palmer, Cre Walls, and Jamie. [With pride.] Us four, we all made this business what it is today. I didn't think I could do something like that! [His smile widens.] It makes me feel good just thinking about it. Basically, we do all kinds of things: interior demolition, landscaping, clean up big buildings like this one. We do vacant lots, we do a lot of good things for the neighborhood. We try to keep the neighborhood looking nice, keep it from looking destroyed and torn-down. Keep it in order—we like to keep things in order.

I learned about landscaping and interior demolition. I didn't know the first thing about nothing to do with interior demolition—I didn't know what it *was*. But I found out what it was and how to go about it. Say, for instance, we had to take this wall down to the brick. We got wood, wood lath in front of it, and round top of the wood lath we've got sheets of plaster—no telling how many sheets. In order to get to the brick, we gotta take this plaster down first, take it off the whole wall, the ceiling, take it all the way down, all the plaster. Dump that and then come back and get the wood. At first, we took down the wood and the plaster together, but we found out it makes the job harder, you have to pick through that stuff. What we did is just do things one step at a time, one thing at a time.

Any job we go to, like if we're going to take tar off a roof, we try to go about it not just the best way but the *cleanest* way—because that shows the person how good we are, and they'll recommend us to the next person, and we can keep on getting good jobs. Any job: I like to make myself a good reputation. You need that wherever you go, that's number one. There's my reputation and also the company's. I got to think about something bigger than me. I'm *part* of it, see, I'm part of the crew. Without the crew, it wouldn't be what it is.

When we get new guys on the crew, I wouldn't say that's no bad thing. There's a lot of things they don't know that I could teach them, and it ain't just me, other guys could teach them too. If you want to work hard, you want to impress somebody, you got to *show* them, you got to give them a good example. I had to teach a couple of the new guys how to work hard. Some days they'd come late, they'd take their own breaks. Well you can't do that. Before they take a break, they have to ask me or Alvin—we're the ones that call it. Being respectful is the most important thing, period. Be respectful to everybody you work with, because you have to work *with* them.

Contributing to the community, it's OK. I'm staying in the neighborhood, and I'm doing stuff to better it. I have loyalty and respect for the hood and everybody down here trusts me. A lot of people, they look at me like, "Yeah, I see you've found something better to do than just selling drugs." It was time for me to get my life together, because my life was going down the drain. Before, I was in and out of jail, and out here killing my own black people. I'm thinking if I just leave the slinging alone, I'll live longer and find a better life.

My son, little Chico, he stay over here, and the other kids know me through him. They're like, "Yeah, that's little Chico's father—well, we gonna go see what he's doing. OK, we'll learn something from him. He's gonna show us how to do this, he's gonna show us how to do that." I like to show the kids what I'm capable of doing. But at the same time, when the kids try to show me what they can do, they just make a big mess. Like I can be digging a hole, I turn my back, they could be filling the hole. They just trying to help. They don't know what they're doing or how to do it. They need somebody to *teach* 'em.

Young people should strive for something good in life. Don't let the older guys influence them by selling drugs, beating people up, shooting people. I want them to find their life out there working. See, *us*, we're out here *doing* things. I like the kids to see something positive, like planting flowers, building things.

Could I work in an office? Like a secretary or something? Well, I'd say I could sit in the office maybe two days out of a week—*if* I could sit that long. I find it better being outdoors. I like doing the *work*. I figure I'll just keep on living my life, and sooner or later, something'll come good to me. I really want to get to the eighteen-wheeler. I know I will get there somehow.

This job has changed my life. It surprised me, because I didn't think I would be doing nothing like this right now today. I thought I'd probably be in one of these buildings over there trying to sell a bag. I've been working here almost three years now, I've got some years under my belt. It supports me, it helps support my kids, it puts food on our table. I ain't making the money like I used to, but I don't think that really matters because slow money is the best money.

And I learn a lot. I learned a lot from wrong, and now I learned a lot from right. My wrong life was always in a mess. I got this job, my wrong life changed to right. It's a very big difference.

CREDELL WALLS

Cre got his first job when he was a child, working at an outdoor flea market: "It was great being in that carnival atmosphere." After high school, a grocery store job was distinctly less enjoyable. Work with a community group exposed him to manual labor and new people. "I hadn't known any white people, not outside of teachers—and with teachers there are no colors, I loved all my teachers. But with strangers, that was different." Working with the Neighborhood Conservation Corps demolition crew increased his skills in group dynamics and staying true to himself. For Cre, learning new things is crucial. A Parks District summer job confirmed his interest in working with children. At a university bookstore, Cre, twenty-four, refined his ability to deal with the public, co-workers, and complex situations. "I'm excited about work, and I'll never not like working. No matter what your job, there's going to be some kind of difficulty. If you go in knowing you'll learn, that'll help you out a lot."

I grew up in the Robert Taylor Homes in Chicago.* I think the majority of people there had a job, whether it was paid or not paid. By job I mean work. If you're talking about somebody like my mother, or any housewife, they'd say "This is a job, this is hard work." Running a household *is* hard work.

My father worked for this guy, Jerry, who sold socks and T-shirts, pants, whatever would sell, on Maxwell Street. Maxwell Street is a huge outside flea market that's open on Sundays. You can get anything you

---

* A South Side Chicago Housing Authority project which was in the process of being demolished at the time of the interview. At one time, it was the largest housing project in the city of Chicago, if not the nation.

want—used, new, stolen. And you did have some thieves running around there. That was *their* job. Other days, Jerry sold this and that in front of a currency exchange. When I was eleven my father said, "I want you to go to work with me." I was excited. "OK, what time?" "Four o'clock in the morning!"

We drove to this storage place where Jerry kept all his boxes of merchandise, loaded up his red truck, went to Maxwell Street, and set up our tables. I was excited from the beginning of the day to the end of the day. Jerry was a heavy-set guy and he seemed mean, but he was pretty nice. They told me what to do, like if a customer comes up, what you say to them. One thing they stressed was to watch people, because they tend to grab and not pay for things.

Around nine, when it gets crowded, you hear Mexican music, smell all sorts of things and see a diverse group of people. To me it was weird and it was fun and it was cool. Jerry gave me eight bucks just for being there. I wasn't expecting anything. So here I'm sitting on eight bucks— I'm a rich man now! When I had a chance to walk around with my father, I spent it all. It was the first time I'd ever been to a place like that. They decided to bring me out every Sunday, and I didn't mind getting up at four in the morning after that.

After a while my father stopped, but I kept working for Jerry, every Sunday for seven years, and sometimes on weekdays. The worst part was when people actually did steal. Once when I was younger, on Maxwell Street, Jerry said he'd be right back and left. There I was at this twelve-foot table. This big guy came from behind and his hand was trying to grab a sock. I grabbed the socks from *him*. I was nervous, but I said, "You can't take this." He said, "You must not know how hard it is out here, do you?" I'm thinking, [small voiced] "no . . ."

At the end, I was making thirty dollars a week, which taught me how to manage my money—I didn't have much to go on. I stopped working for Jerry when I graduated from high school. I said, "OK, now I need a real job." My sister worked at a grocery store, and they hired me. Every job I've gotten has been through somebody I knew or luck.

I was working full-time and taking classes at a business college. The store owners paid me under the table, didn't pay taxes. I made four dollars an hour, and when they paid me they'd try and cheat me out of some of the money. If I was supposed to get ninety-six bucks, they'd pay me eighty-four. It was up to me to step up and say, "This is how much I'm *supposed* to have." If I don't say that, I'm not going to get my right amount. In a way, they were teaching me to stand up for myself— but that's not what they meant to do.

I did everything: I was the janitor, I cleaned up the bathrooms. I stocked, I helped the produce guy put ice on the vegetables and keep them fresh, water them down. I took out the garbage. I never worked the cash register—and that was good, because they would go in your register and take money out. At the end of the day, they'd say you were short. After a while, I asked for a raise, but they said no. I said, "Why not?" They said I wasn't doing a good job. I said, "I'm doing *five* jobs!" After that I slacked off, I started doing what everybody else did. I wasn't as bad as the rest, but I felt like, "You're screwing me, so I'm going to screw you."

Working there developed a bad habit in me, which is if I'm unhappy, my work slacks off. If I'm in a good mood, I work better. But it's a habit, it doesn't have to happen. I'm aware of it and I'm trying to break that habit. I've known people who, when they're in bad moods, they work harder, just for the distraction. In the beginning, I worked hard, but I started to think, "Is this worth it?" After working with people who treat you better, I realize it *is* worth it. Do everything to your fullest regard. Whether you get treated well or not, you should work hard till the day you leave, because at least you go out on top—leave with people saying, "*Wow*, what a good job."

A guy I knew since I was a kid told me his uncle got him a job doing landscaping with a community organization called Turn A Lot Around. They claimed vacant lots and turned them into gardens, or at least made them look better than before. I asked if he could get me a job. They told me to come down Saturday.

I had never done any kind of landscaping. How I said it at that age was, "I'd never messed with the dirt." That day I was moving rocks, I was digging dirt, moving it from this part of the land to that part of the land, picking up paper, cutting grass. I thought, "Am I going to do this every single day?! I can't do this *every* day!"—because the first day was so hard. It was *so hard*—real physical labor. The work was new, and it was painful. [Laughs.] I didn't like it at first. I had to get used to it, build up my strength. Now, to this day, my body aches for physical work. When I'm working at the bookstore, doing all this typing in the computer, I'm like, "Y'all got some boxes you want moved?" [Laughs.]

People from Hyde Park* started coming out to help, and what I've learned is, people is where my knack is. When I'm around people, that's when I'm happy—that's when my work is good.

When those people started working on the vacant lots with us, it was like black meeting white. I was around nineteen, but I felt very young. I hadn't seen much outside of my neighborhood. I liked talking with the people, seeing that quote-unquote white people weren't bad people. I was like, "wow! These are actually nice people!"

Talking to them did a lot for me. The majority had graduated from college or had some kind of educational background, and that helped me decide to go back to school. And I got my first bank account. Talking to them opened my eyes to a lot of things. Some of them took me to their houses, spent time with me. I assume part of the reason was because I was a poor black kid—like, "Well, hey, but he's a good kid." But I always felt we learned from each other. I didn't fit their stereotype and they didn't fit mine. Learning, not just from the job itself, but from meeting all these different people—that can make your job wonderful, make you want to go to work each day. What makes work hard is if your job is repetitive and you're not getting anything out of it. That's when you need to move on to something bigger and better, or at least different, so you can learn something new.

I worked there for about two and a half years, and then it became the Neighborhood Conservation Corps and concentrated more on interior

---

* An integrated neighborhood on Chicago's South Side.

demolition. Then I worked with guys from a different housing project, Stateway Gardens. That was a challenge in itself: they were a *lot* more aggressive and rougher, they had the attitude of guys I avoided. I didn't want to *be* or be *with* those guys. But just like the guys I grew up with, they all have a sense of humanity, they all have good sides to them. I shouldn't have gone into that situation saying I wasn't going to give them a chance. All of them were cool and good, and it was fun working with them. The only fear I had was that I would change—that they'd rub off on me. I wanted to stay Cre.

Some people go to work and make friends of their co-workers: they hang out, party. Some people leave work there and go back to their second life. I wanted to leave work there. There were things the guys did that I didn't want to do, and so I just wouldn't do those things. I'm a grown man, and it's up to me to decide what I'm going to do.

I've learned how to get along with my co-workers. Even if they tell offensive jokes, rude or crude, you can still manage to get along. One of the challenging things is to think about whether you want to confront these jokes at work. How do you deal with things that offend you on the job site? Do you say, "Can we talk outside of work?" Do you do it right then and there? You have to worry about it stopping the flow of work or affecting other people. You can blow off steam, but it can be the wrong time—the job still has to get done. Sometimes we'd argue while we worked. That can make you work harder . . . especially if you have a sledgehammer in your hand and you're doing demolition!

After a while, I needed a job switch. I didn't feel I was getting a lot out of it and I didn't feel marketable enough. I wanted more on my résumé. If NCC exploded, I wanted to feel there was another place for me to go. This woman once gave me some advice: she said, "If to grow means you have to move on, that's what you have to do." But not to leave just because you're upset or mad at people. You're always going to get mad at people. You have to work out the conflicts, deal with the situation. Leave on a good note.

I knew some people who worked at the Chicago Park District, and they needed counselors for summer camps. I wanted to work with kids.

I have a lot of nephews, but working with kids in your family is different from working with kids outside it. One, you're a lot nicer to kids outside! I applied to be a camp counselor. There were at least thirty kids in a camp, and I had to teach them how to set up a tent, take them fishing, kayaking, and teach them nature games. I had no experience with *any* of those things. I had *never* been camping. The only thing I had done was work with inner-city kids, but that was good, 'cause half of these kids were from the inner city.

They hired me, even though I didn't have any of the camp stuff. When I applied I said, "Your model is, let's have fun." I said, "But I already have my personal agenda," which is what they really liked. I said, "Outside of the whole camping thing, I want them to learn some things about life." My dream was to, at night, when we're in the tent with the kids, sit down and talk to them about things that aren't related to camping. Like, "What do you do when you're afraid?" Or "What are your alternatives when you confront a bully?"—little things like that. To me, it was a big-brother kind of thing. When I was young, I wanted somebody to run to and ask for that kind of information. Someone to teach me other ways of dealing with things, to present me with options. So if I had the answers, I wanted to share them.

The only thing that worried me was actually doing the activities. I had to memorize and explain them to the kids. I wasn't a good explainer if I wasn't in a certain mode. I would have to warm up, get into a groove. Other people didn't have to read the book like I did: [pretending to read aloud] "Step one says to . . ." [Laughs.] "Y'all get it?" So I took the easy exercises.

I learned a lot about myself. After the first week, the introduction phase, it was so much fun *because* I took the fun approach. The first week was all about me trying to have the kids respect and listen to me. It didn't work that way. I said, "Well, the kids are here to have fun. They can respect me while we're having fun." So I made it fun, I played with them.

The rule is, you can't touch a child in any way. I understand why they say that, but I'm going on record to say I touched them—I patted them on the head. I might give them a little noogie. The kids loved that. A touch is more than just saying verbal things, it *helps*. A lot of kids run up behind you, "Could you hold my hand while we walk? I'm scared." But you're not allowed to hold their hand.

In each camp, the kids voted me the best counselor. They all wanted to know, "Are you coming back next summer?" I said, "I don't know, I don't know . . ." And I'm back. I'm going to do it again. I'd overhear them talking about me. It was so nice. I was totally glowing. This one kid—and this was a white kid, which made it a bigger thing for me—said, "I like Cre, he makes learning fun." This was a kid who wasn't team-oriented. One time, I said, "We need two people to carry this tent because it's very heavy." He said, "I can carry this tent that way and this way ten times." I said, "OK, show me." He said, "Alright, fine." I said to everyone, "Let me predict what's going to happen. He's going to stop the second time because he's tired. And he's going to learn that it takes two to carry that thing." He carried it once and was panting. I said, "Can you do it again?" He said, "No, I need some help." I said, "I'm sorry, it'll take him *one* time." The kids started laughing, and he was alright with that.

I'm working at a bookstore now, and I like it—but I don't love it. It's a steady income, forty hours a week. I've been reading more since I started there, and I'm learning about how retail works. At first I was overwhelmed by all the new things I had to learn. I knew how to use a computer, but this computer is not like Windows 95: you have to type in codes and key words, F1, F5 . . . you have to memorize all this stuff. I know they can't show you every little detail, but they should have the codes on a piece of paper, have everything written out. "What is F3 for, if I don't do F3 what will happen?"—a little training manual. And I had no idea about publishers. I didn't even know what an ISBN was.* But they have employees coming and going all the time, so they're used to people taking a while to learn.

* The International Standard Book Number, a Library of Congress identification number system for books.

There's supposed to be one person training you to work the cash register, but that person was occupied. Instead, I had six people training me and giving me six different shortcuts. Each one is telling me the other's shortcut is wrong. After all that training, I said, "Why don't you just show me the basic way." At this point, I don't even listen to them when they give me certain tips. You have to develop your *own* shortcuts.

One of the first things they told me was that when you answer the telephone sometimes you encounter rude people, people with serious attitude problems—you have to be a diplomat. Some people are nice, and some people are a pain and will sit on the phone for a half an hour until you find the book they want. When I'm dealing with customers, I put myself in their shoes. How would they want me to talk to them? If they're upset, how can I change their mood through conversation? Maybe it's through a series of apologies, or by helping them understand why things are a certain way.

If someone's rude, I tend to see it as they've come in with a problem. I'm not going to ask what's wrong, but I treat them with sympathy. Sometimes it works. I've learned a lot about controlling myself, and about how to deal with people with attitude problems. And I've learned a lot about co-workers.

With the people I work with, I immediately tell myself they're human, they will say things about you behind your back. Everybody will, your best friends will. It's going to happen—expect it. When I leave a room full of people, I might say, "I'm going, now y'all can talk about me." [Laughs.] Sometimes it's nice to know what people say. It could be good or it could be bad. If you take it as something to learn from, that's good. If you hear somebody say something negative, you can still talk to them the next day: "Hey, how's it going?"

But sometimes people cross a line. I heard someone say, "Somebody misfiled this paper"—it was a little thing. Someone else said, "Oh, well maybe Cre put it there. He's always doing things like that." I'm thinking, "Well, maybe if y'all would tell me *exactly* what to do, or where to put things like that, I would *know*." I interpreted it as them saying, "Cre will always screw up." I said to myself, "In order for that not to grow on me, in order for me not to think I'm always going to screw up, I have to let it go." It's important not to let things build up.

Sometimes when I'd answer the phones, I'd get questions I couldn't answer. "Do you have the 1987 version of the Oxford Dictionary in Latin?" What? In Latin? I'm like, "Hold on." I'd ask the person next to me, "Could you deal with this?" At first, it was hard for me to say, "Hey, I need help," or "Do you understand how this works?" People are busy, and if I have to constantly ask for this and that they tend to get frustrated— "What do you want *now?*" I've seen them do that to other people. Turn and make faces to me, you know, and I'd think, "I thought that was your *friend*." Now I think, "OK, well, they're human."

When I started, I didn't tell the manager I wanted to work for the Park District this summer. I was afraid they wouldn't want to hire me if they knew. There was somebody in the bookstore I thought I could trust, and I told her a lot about myself and she went and told other people. So I said, "OK, if I know this person is going to tell everybody this and that . . ." I told her about wanting to quit and work with the Park District *before* I talked to the manager. When I finally asked the manager, it was no problem. I asked two months in advance if I could cut my hours back a little, and they were just happy to hear I wanted to keep working part-time.

I'm taking college classes now, majoring in child psychology. A lot of kids come from a hard childhood, and some kids get scarred. I want to somehow help, or learn more about it. Who knows where I'll go with that? At least I'll have grabbed a certain amount of knowledge I need to go to the next level. All my life, I've just been grabbing for things I need.

CESAR RIVERA

With the help of a guidance counselor and a scholarship, Cesar, now twenty-eight, went from a public school in a tough New York neighborhood to a high-priced boarding school in the country. After exposure to classmates and their well-off parents, Cesar decided to aim for Wall Street. During college he interned at various brokerage firms and investment banks. "As an intern, I did a lot of lunch runs, a lot of running for drinks after hours, learned all those sorts of rituals." He learned about supervising older workers, ingratiating himself, and the hazards of having a big mouth. He learned the lingo, and how different firms have distinct environments. He survived a pressure interview and learned to adjust his behavior to the demands of the job. With other minorities, he shared feelings of "We're here!" And he discovered an affinity for the wild world of trading. "It's akin to playing lotto. It's a dollar—[he claps] but you think it could be so much more."

I grew up in the South Bronx, Fort Apache basically. While I was away at boarding school, the *L.A. Times* came out with an article about the twenty most dangerous intersections, and we were number six. There was a big party. I remember my mom going, "Next year we'll be number one!" [Laughs.]

I was born in Brooklyn, but my family moved back to Puerto Rico till I was five, and then we returned to the States. My dad left when I was six. My mom was on welfare. I was always a bit of a weenie, and when I turned twelve my mother gave me a model rocketry set and a knife. She explained why she preferred fighting with short, fat knives over long skinny ones. The Bronx is sort of weird. There are people you can mess with and people you can't. We were among the people you can't: we weren't completely logical and rational at all times. You sort of develop a rep.

My mom wasn't kidding about being prepared to fight. I remember once when my older brother came home to visit. Someone stole his radio and my mother was *incensed*. He had come back without a scratch, and she didn't want the word getting out that he was soft. That would have been dangerous. She made him find the guys who did it and fight them. He lost the fight, but at least he got some licks in. He didn't visit as often after that. It was that kind of neighborhood.

I always liked school. I was good at it, and anything you're good at is usually fun. I had a really cool guidance counselor and I used to cut classes and help her. I had a crush on a girl who applied to boarding school, and she and the guidance counselor convinced me to apply, too. I did a lot of the paperwork in the house and I got my mother to sign all these forms, but she wasn't *exactly* aware of what they were for. Eventually I received a scholarship and told her I was going away to boarding school. The scholarship paid for me to go and gave me an allowance. While I was there, I hustled a little, sold newspapers, things like that. So I went from the South Bronx to one of the most expensive boarding schools in the country.

This boarding school was a completely new world. Since I was so good at school, I went thinking I'd eventually become a professor at a college, a research chemist or a physicist, something along those lines. I took my first lab class and the reading was exciting because you were learning, but I had to bend over a test tube for hours at a time. I realized *that* was not for me. After the Bronx, the pace of it was just so slow and dull.

I was the minority male in my class. I got in through Better Chance, a program that sends mostly inner-city kids to prestigious public or prep schools. There were "names" in my class—the children of famous people; but aside from those, most people's parents were corporate lawyers or bankers and so on. By the time I left school, my goal was to try all those jobs in college, as a summer intern. That, and I wanted to be like Mr. Lançen, my roommate's father. He was the general partner for a law firm that represented a big investment company. I remember once the Lançens came to pick me up at home—they were going to Yankee Stadium and decided to bring me along. They showed up in a Mercedes Benz station wagon. I guess they didn't *quite* realize where I lived. The car did not stop, I had to run to catch it . . .

Junior year, I did the LEAD [Leadership, Education, and Development] program in business. Graduate schools grab minority juniors in high school and ship them around the country. You stay in a dorm and take intro-to-business-type classes. Different professionals come in and talk about what accounting's like and so forth. I'd started reading the *Wall Street Journal*, and I really wanted a Wall Street job. Mr. Lançen drafted my first résumé and sent it to a friend at a brokerage and investment firm, and then it got to Credit Suisse. I had a phone call and a job within twenty-four hours of finishing the résumé. I was quite impressed.

The job was as an accounts-payable clerk. This was the summer between prep school and college. I had my first Wall Street job, and I had *really* high expectations. I got there and I was very, very disappointed. It was strange in different ways. It was my first office job, and my first contact with the middle class—I'd been hanging out with the upper class and was lower class by birth.

I was put into an accounting group, to replace people when they went on summer vacation. It was accounts payable, which isn't the most dramatic part of accounting to begin with. You're not analyzing anything, you're just putting numbers to numbers. It wasn't what I expected out of Wall Street. You read the front page of the *Journal* and see that some company loses a billion dollars. I had no concept of what that meant. "Uh, where did it go?" My image of Wall Street was big numbers and bla bla—not, "OK, we bought a bunch of file folders, that's paper and so X department gets charged." The job itself . . . Accounting, accounts, it was *quiet*. Literally quiet. Everyone had routine tasks. Meticulous. Details were very important, but routine. It required no thought.

I was only seventeen, and most of the people I worked with already had twenty years on the job. The people I was to replace included the supervisor of the group. That meant that people *much* senior to me in time and experience were supposedly reporting to me. When I was in charge, while people liked and respected me to a certain extent, it was clear I wasn't really legitimate.

This group had five distinct tasks, and the one *everyone* hated was filing. The firm literally had people doing the exact same job for twenty years. Let's just say that those in the group were a little bored, and it added excitement to their lives to do someone else's job. I had to learn everyone's job, so I was sort of cross-functional. I offered to teach people the other jobs, which they really enjoyed. It was something different, and to some extent it helped them do their own job better. The problem was, it slowed efficiency, you know, in quite a big way. Because any guy who's doing something for twenty years, he never needs to look up a number. After all that time, well, he just has it *down*.

When the work backed up, we switched back to people doing their normal jobs. It didn't occur to me until just now that I was shaking things up. I was giving people what they wanted. I've tried to do stuff like that elsewhere and gotten slapped for it. We were responsible for getting the job done, but at the same time, if we could switch things around and still get the work done, I was very pro that. And I needed to ingratiate myself with them. I learned about that in boarding school.

At school there was an official cool candy, Nerds, and you could buy them in town for about thirty-five cents—but town was a mile or so away. We were required to go to church and since I wasn't Episcopalian, I had to go to church in town, for Mass. I started buying this candy by the carton and selling it at a small uptick. And even after eating some of my inventory, I was making money! But what became apparent was that while I was making cash, I was losing friendship points. There was a lot of tit for tat in the Bronx, and at boarding school I became aware that my tat was dollars and the tat I really wanted was more along the lines of friendship. I wasn't getting there being a vendor, so I gave up that business.

The good thing about that accounting job was that if you got your work done early, there was free time. One afternoon I gave myself a tour of the place, just walked around. I followed a red carpet and after circumventing a couple of security doors, I walked into their FX [foreign exchange] trading room. It was filled with people in white shirts, men and women, standing up. Some of them had two or three phones up to their heads and were yelling and screaming. I was like, *"What* are these guys doing?! That's what *I* want to do!"

The following summer, I did my second internship at one of the smaller investment banks. I was told I would be in fixed-income strategies, which is bonds. I was horrified! I thought I'd be selling penny stocks to people on welfare and social security. I couldn't imagine it being a very large market. [Laughs.] I had a very boring job, but I was in a cool place. Once a month we did reports on what people were making and on how much people had sold. But the bulk of the job was getting prospectuses—legal documents that are prepared whenever a company does a deal. I got to learn a good part of the lingo and what the terms were for a large host of bonds—callable, puttable, dozens of different phrases.

This particular firm had a big mix of people on the trading floor. Traditionally, the firm was sort of disdained by the white-shoe firms on Wall Street. A lot of the people hadn't gone to college, some hadn't even finished high school, and they were making millions of dollars a year buying and selling and trading. It was humorous. There was everything from a Playboy bunny, who was one of their better salespeople, to the cigar-smoking gruff types.

They had a big open bay, no one really had offices, so you might be sitting right next to your boss. There was a sense of hierarchy, but it was all dependent on how much you made. If you ever see a Wall Street guy with long hair, you know he's good at what he does and incredibly wealthy. The more senior you are, the more you can deviate from the rules. You learned such things as that only managing directors can wear suspenders, which is not something you *ever* see printed. But one day you wear suspenders, you get laughed at, and you learn . . . Some stuff was kind of funny. The first time you did a trade there, they cut off your tie. Even female junior traders would wear ties until their first trade. You walk onto the trading floor and there are pillars *covered* with ties.

So, on the floor was this mass of people, everyone having at least one conversation. They were always on the phone. People yelling and screaming—it's not considered unusual to stand up and bust your phone. It was very dynamic, it was very exciting, and it was *loud*. There was a certain amount of danger, there was a lot of profit—and it was *fun*. It was definitely the kind of place where you could forget to eat lunch and suddenly the day's over, and it's *over*.

I got to see what some of the other groups were doing. I went down to the investment banking area, the corporate finance area, which is the kind of stuff that makes the *Journal*. These guys have *awful* lives: they work 150 hours a week, and *never* know if they're going to be in this city, or even in this country. Someone comes up to you with business at six o'clock, and the next thing you know you're in the office for three days straight. A lot of these places have showers and beds. The guy talking to the interns said, "This is a great job if you want your wife to cheat on you." He was never home—he even got called back from his honeymoon.

A lot of people are more comfortable with investment banking be-cause the pace is slower. You might be working incredible hours, but in general it's for something that's due at the end of the month. Whereas in sales and trading, when someone calls you and they want to bid, you just need to *deal*. If you have to do a twenty-page paper for school and you're the kind who starts a month before, then you should probably do corporate finance. If you're the kind who does it the day before, you're more fit for sales and trading. I kind of like living on a rollercoaster. It's definitely not boring and you're never sure what's going to happen. You know, fifty thousand Danes in Denmark vote the wrong way and financial markets all over the world react. Some of the stuff is com-pletely random. It felt a little like home in a strange sort of way, and I liked it.

I did go on and try other jobs because it didn't make sense not to—
with internships, that's what you're supposed to be doing. One of the
guys on the high-yield desk explained to me that this firm was one
thing, but that I should really try the bigger ones. I learned a little about
the Wall Street hierarchy. The culture of different firms may vary, but
the trading floor is the trading floor. Sort of like most locker rooms, I'd
imagine: the coach may be a little different, but a locker room's a locker
room.

My college was weird in that you had to take one winter off and go to
school one summer. So the next winter I interned at a very prestigious
law firm. It was a pretty easy job to get because everybody else—all the
partners' kids, for example—was in school. Corporate law is like banking in terms of the hours you put in. It was broken up into two divisions: litigation, which I didn't want to do because I thought it was kind
of slimy, and corporate law, which I figured would be better.

I was amazed by how clerical the corporate work was. They have
these indentures, which are like prospectuses, but they're longer—
literally 500-page documents. It's not like they're being *written* by these
law firms, they're already in the computer and you just call them up. A
secretary puts in the name of your company so it changes all the way
through. And then they change, OK, this is a retailer, so we add the
retailer paragraph. And okay, this bond is puttable, so here's the puttable section. And once that's done, generally by the secretary, the lawyers read it and make sure everything is covered. That was a big part of
the job.

There was some thought involved, because every once in a while a
client would ask, "Can we do this?" And you had to put out the firm's
opinion, which means there's a lot of prestige on the line. You come up
with a form and you send it to the SEC,* and the SEC says, "Well, I
don't like this statement, it sounds too much like a guarantee!"—so
they send back a version and you rewrite those sections. It seemed like a
very high-powered and intellectual clerical job. They weren't making

---

* The Securities Exchange Commission, a federal regulatory group.

any decisions, they weren't doing grand strategy. That's not true of M&A [Mergers and Acquisitions], or at least some M&A, which involves buying and selling companies. But corporate law in general, contracts and that kind of stuff, was very cookie-cutter.

And it's a weird industry in that of eight people hired, only one makes partner. They work an incredible number of hours. Your salary is pretty much capped at like two or three hundred thousand, which is a lot of money. But your odds in getting there are one in eight, you're working hundred-hour weeks, and you generally need to have the same kind of qualifications as the people in investment banking, some of whom are making *millions*. And the atmosphere was really different. It was slow. *Sl-o-o-w.*

In investment banking, the people even tend to move slow. They don't get a lot of sleep, so they literally sort of shamble. No one's hair and clothes are quite right, this might be their second day wearing them. You'll see people walking around with buttons buttoned in the wrong hole . . . It's just amazing. People really give up a lot, like family lives. It was clear to me, quite soon, that this wasn't something for me. I could see it if you had security, but you don't. So, OK, let me get this straight: I can work longer hours, make less money maybe, if I'm good, and I do this *because* . . . ?" I just didn't get it. So what I got out of that job was, *why*?

For my final internship, I tried to get a job at a consulting firm but I couldn't get into one based in New York. I tried to get into SEO [Sponsors for Educational Opportunity], another minority business program—which was a back-door way of getting into a consulting firm. I got into SEO the second time I applied, and ended up getting a consulting job at Salomon Brothers. It was kind of funny, because I had the worst interview at SEO. I told them I wanted to be a consultant. They ran me through a very high-stakes interview and at the end of the day decided it would make more sense for me to do the yelling-and-screaming thing.

SEO has a reputation of giving pressure interviews, and I knew that going in—but this was *ridiculous*. I get there, a woman offers me coffee, takes my coat, and offers to make copies of my résumé. I had copies on nice paper because I was very proud of my résumé by then. I come upstairs and there are five people set up in a semicircle—some of them behind me! Test number one was that the woman who offered me coffee was actually the committee chair. So the first test was how you treated her. And now she's one of the people sitting behind me. Each has their own little agenda of questions, and they're literally hitting me with these different agendas.

The idea was to put you through Wall Street stress to see how you react. It's Wall Street, once in a while something random happens. Someone throws something at you, or a managing director yells and screams at you—they're not exactly swinging, but it's everything but that. And basically you have to eat it. That's the exact term they use: *eat it*. They don't want anyone who's going to react.

So I hand over my precious résumé. The guy crumples it into a little ball, throws it over his shoulder. And here's a trash can full of these little balls, and balls all around it. And he says, "Cesar, I'll put it to you straight, you've given me a headache. This C you got your freshman year in Spanish is horrible. Do you have any excuse for yourself?" This was the opening question. I was floored. I was shocked. I was *annoyed*. They had my transcript, so if this was an issue, why make me pay money to come all the way into the city for the interview?

I thought, "OK, what's the appropriate answer?" I could say something like, "That grade wasn't reflective . . ." I could whine. I decided I wasn't going to give them the satisfaction of groveling. I said, "Well, I tried hard in that class but I wasn't very good at it, and I got the grade I deserved." His jaw dropped. He picked up a piece of paper and said, "So far I've gotten two divorces," bla bla bla, and he went through this list of excuses people had given. And the last one was, "and someone's dog died." He said, "The only thing I know for sure is that you're the only honest guy here."

It's not unusual for a pressure interview to be done this way. This is one of the standard ways of interviewing, even for an internship. I was sure I wouldn't get in, that Salomon Brothers wouldn't hire me. I left and I was literally *kicking* things—cans, rocks. "There's *no way* . . ." Some months later they call and tell me I'm hired, and I'm like, *"Really?!"* Not only that, but one of the guys was so impressed that he specifically wanted me to work for him. A friend gave me a copy of *Liar's Poker*, which is about the horrors of working for Salomon Brothers.* That book is required reading in certain organizational behavior classes in business school. I read it and was horrified, but I figured I'd given my word and had to go. I went in with low expectations, but enjoyed it and went through a lot of personal growth.

There was no structure to this training program. I get there and they say, "Go find a place to sit." I say, "What do you mean?" "Just go out to the trading floor and find someone who will let you sit and listen to their conversations." They leave me there with no guidance. And you have to understand the scene—it's ten-thirty, everyone's talking into a phone, people are yelling and screaming, telling what happened to the market. Generally, a loud environment. People are running back and forth, everyone is busy. Every once in a while a couple of people huddle together and have this whispered, impromptu meeting, and then sit back down.

It's a large bay, basically the size of a basketball court, and it's all desks. People are arranged by products: you'll have government sales, insurance company sales, mortgages, and so on. There's a desk of six to eight people, arranged so they can all talk and yell to each other. Mostly, everyone spends their day talking into one phone or another. In front of them is a list of phones with fifty or sixty different autodial numbers. There are five or six computer screens, some of them piled on top of each other. A lot of papers everywhere. Then they have this intercom thing called the "hoot and holler," or squawkbox. So everyone's yelling, everyone's busy, and I'm just there by myself . . .

I figured I might as well start with the simplest product, government bonds. I figured I'd go to sales people rather than traders, because

* Michael Lewis, *Liar's Poker: Rising Through the Wreckage on Wall Street* (New York: Penguin, 1990).

professionally sales people *have to* be nicer. [Laughs.] I found an empty seat at the government sales desk, waited till someone got off the phone, and asked if I could sit. I sat there for a while and then asked if I could listen to their phone calls. That phone had *so many* buttons—it doesn't ring either, it just flashes light, and you have to know what the lights mean. Eventually I learned the phone system, at which point I had a marketable skill: I could answer and direct calls. And in between people doing things, I would ask questions until I'd figured out what that market was doing. After a week or so, when I sort of knew the stuff, I'd find a new desk with an empty seat and offer to help with their phones. I'd learn what their product was and how they sold it, and then move on.

I felt shy at first, because it was *so* intimidating. There was a culture of risk-taking: if you weren't taking risks, you had no worth. It was the kind of place where they questioned your ability and maturity, and there was a lot of attack in the attitude. Yelling back was rewarded and expected. They had a certain amount of disdain for people who didn't react that way.

It came down to this: if I wanted to do it, there was a certain way I had to behave. I had this image of myself, of what I wanted to do and be. I wanted to be a trader. I was at the right place and this was what I wanted to be, so it was either give up that image and find something else, or—goddamn it—just *do it*. But it was quite a chore at first. For instance, someone much senior to you, making X millions of dollars, is calling you, and I don't mean like, "Hey, Cesar," it's more like, "Hey, you *dumbshit, how could you* . . ." They're *yelling* at you. One of the things you learned was that the right response was to yell right back. The first time, it's like . . . [He lets out a tortured yell.] It felt *really* awkward at first. I didn't think I could get there, I angsted over it. But I forced myself, and after a while it became second nature. If you kept *acting* the way you were supposed to, you could sort of become that role. That was a big learning experience for me, and it strengthened my confidence. I became a louder, more outgoing person after that, and I actually started enjoying the place.

It's kind of funny being a minority because there are parts of it that white people can't share. You never pass a minority without saying hi and smiling, even if you've never seen them before, because they're so rare. "Hey, you made it! I made it, too. Great, cool. *We're here!*" There's a level of casual bonding. But I can see it hurting on the client side, because the clients are almost always old, white males. I can see it being a hard sell. I'm also one of the few Democrats, and I actually think that's looked at more than the color of my skin.

There are a lot of jobs where it's hard to tell how much someone is contributing, and if they're really good or not. There you generally had, "I made this amount of money today." You know *exactly* how much someone's worth—it's very clear and distinct. That's one reason Wall Street is a good place for minorities. You never have to worry about hidden agendas or what you're being measured by. You're measured by dollars.

After that internship, I decided I wanted to work for Salomon, but what happened was the wrong group was interested in me—there was some talk about putting me in investment banking. I didn't *want* to be a banker. And it came as a complete surprise that I didn't get an offer on the sales and trading side. I thought I'd left the firm on good footing; my review seemed to go that way. It could've been that I pissed someone off. Maybe once I got back to college I took it too much for granted that I was going to get hired. I was slow to send back thank you letters and things like that. I was cocky.

Graduation day was probably the worst day of my life. I graduated without a job. Like I said, I had this big image of myself and I didn't get there. It was awful, it was depressing . . . The problem was, I knew what I wanted to do and I couldn't seem to get a job in that area. I've had this happen to me a lot. You go for a couple of rounds and at the very end are told "there's no fit." If there's anywhere you worry about being a minority, that's where it comes up because you get this vague "no fit" thing. You try to get people to give you some reason, in case it's something you can fix. But thanks to the legal system and fear of lawsuits, no one will ever explain to you exactly *why* there's no fit.

I was living at home and very depressed. Originally I'd interviewed on campus, I'd sent out résumés. That wasn't working, so I started going to headhunters. I had bad experiences—they do the bait-and-switch a lot. They tell you it's a job at one salary, but then show you this *other* job because the job you came in about has been filled, sometime between when they sent out the ad and when you showed up. And generally the jobs they *have* are at places you don't really want to work, and they aren't jobs you really want to get. But at that point I wasn't choosy.

I took a temp job at the bond mart and eventually got an offer from Nomura to be on the sell side, selling their CDs [Certificates of Deposit]. I wasn't too excited but I was going to take the job when suddenly Lehman Brothers became interested in me. There's sort of a rule on the street that once there's a bid for you, somebody else will want you. Lehman Brothers offered to put me in operations in mortgage allocations. The idea is, you're there for a year and then you get a spot in sales and trading. It was kind of a fast-track area. This one interview question was, "You went to an ivy-league school, and most of the people in this group don't have ivy-league degrees—how will you react to that?" I thought, they're asking me if I'm a snob. I said, "You don't understand, I'm from the Bronx: I drink beer—from the *bottle*." [Laughs.]

I was excited to join, but I never did get to be a trader. One problem was my concept of professionalism. I don't know what TV show I got it from, or how it came, but I did the exact wrong thing. There was a lot of drinking after work, and for some reason getting drunk in front of co-workers or my boss seemed unprofessional to me. I didn't do it, I begged off. If I showed, I made a cameo, did my duty and ran. And this is completely *not* what you're supposed to do. When there's a chance to get drunk with your boss and meet other senior people, you're supposed to be one of the guys. That was a *major* screw-up. I never really became part of the team.

After a while, I said to my boss, "Listen, I'm not learning anymore. Can I move to some other part of mortgages?" He didn't know anyone in the emerging markets area,* so he said, "Why don't you go there and be my man." It made sense to me. Emerging markets were new, there was a lot of money being made; it was hot, it was sexy, and it was growing quite quickly. I figured if there was any place I could get a job, that had to be it. So I was pretty confident. And he told me the next time a job came up, I'd be considered. I screwed that up *completely* within two weeks of starting. I got there and joined the group as "Larry's boy." I didn't really anticipate what would happen, but a lot of people were gunning for me to lose just because I'd been foisted on them—they thought I was some sort of spy.

I did my job, I did it well, but I spent a lot of time upstairs with the traders, getting myself seen. At some point, I was introduced to this accountant and he gave me a big speech, laid down the law. It was along the lines of: "I'm a very important person in a very important division and unless you hop when I say hop, I'll make sure you get nowhere." To me, he was an important person in an *unimportant* division that made no money. I wasn't exactly impressed, and I said so to the guy taking me around. He immediately went back and told the accountant. A half hour later, I'm called into a little meeting and my *butt is* handed to me. It turns out the accountant was a senior guy, even if he wasn't in the right department.

So that set me back a year. They put out a memo saying I was spending too much time upstairs with the traders, that I wasn't focusing on my work. I was like, "Wait a minute—have I had a problem?" They said, "No, but you *might* have a problem." I'm like, "Have I been *close* to having a problem?" "No." "Has there been anything that hasn't been done *perfectly*?" "No." I got them to put *that* in the memo too. But basically, they were out to get me to a certain extent, and I walked right into it.

A lot depends on the quality of the firm you work for. Picking your boss carefully is *very* important. I've had bosses where anyone says something bad about me, my boss was up in front, setting the record

---

* Emerging markets sections invest in developing countries.

straight. And I've had bosses who've basically licked their finger, held it up, and blown whichever way the wind was blowing. You just have to know what you're walking into. I didn't and got hosed for it. I did my job well, got good recommendations and commendations from my boss later on—but I had already been put in my place. People treated me in a certain way after that. How can I describe it? I was looked at as a "new guy," and even if I had X years of experience elsewhere, it wasn't going to count. They made sure I spent a lot less time trying to get promoted onto the trading floor. The work didn't change, but the attitude about me changed.

I'd been at the firm close to two years, and I still wanted to trade. I went to my original boss and he set up an interview for a trading job upstairs, but I didn't get it. They gave it to a guy twice my age, who had a family and a house and a dog. I said to my boss, "Listen, I want to trade and it's not happening—what do you suggest?" He said, "I can make a call and probably get you into a third-tier shop, if that's what you want to do." I didn't want to do that.

What made sense was to apply to business school. I thought getting an MBA would get me on the trading floor. It was the current background for traders, and it was a piece I was missing. So I applied, I got in, and I went off to school.

It had become clear that, at the end of the day, doing the job right has very little to do with being successful—especially with getting promoted. There are people out there with knives for your back. In trying to get ahead they'll push you down. There are people with separate agendas. People will try to take credit for work you've done or else they'll slander it. The worse a firm is doing, the pettier people are. And the farther you are from doing something that's easily quantifiable, the worse you'll be treated. You start work with a school background: if you did really well on the SATs, you got patted on the head, you got a prize. It's not at all like that in the workplace.

ILIANA ROMAN

Iliana became pregnant as a teenager and dropped out of high school. At her first job, an entry-level position at a sporting goods store, she discovered her best asset: "something I was taught at home—don't talk back, good manners." Reliable and capable, she advanced to a managerial position. After leaving her boyfriend, Iliana and her children lived with her parents. She sold cars, took business classes and entered cosmetology school. For Iliana, thirty, her hardworking father has been a role model as well as a rock of stability. With her family's assistance she recently opened her own hair salon. Past work experience helps her to negotiate the strains of getting the bills paid and dealing with customers. But new problems arise, such as employee friends who don't take their work seriously. Her next ambition is to sell real estate. "I'm doing this for my children, so they can say, 'My mom did it. She did not sit on her butt and let life pass her by.'"

My parents have property in Puerto Rico, but I was raised here in the States. They took me back and forth so I know both languages. When she was younger, my mom worked, but once she had children she became a homemaker. My dad's worked for the Park District for years, he's a head attendant for the parks now. He also works on cars—that's his hobby. He loves work, he *has* to work, he's not a person to sit at home and let life waste.

In high school, I got pregnant. I wish I'd have finished school before having kids. I was seventeen when I had my first boy, nineteen the second, and twenty-one my daughter. I lived with my boyfriend—we weren't legally married, but we were like married. I had everything you could want: a house, everything brand-new. I wanted to go back to school, but my boyfriend stopped working so I had to work and take care of the kids.

I was about to get married, but when I saw that my boyfriend was changing, I broke the engagement. He started drinking. I didn't want the children to see that. My father raised me with good values, so I said to my boyfriend, "You gotta go your way, I gotta go my way." My dad said, "Come back home." Thank God for him! It was the best thing I ever did, because it helped me accomplish everything I wanted to accomplish.

I was twenty-five when I left my boyfriend. I finally got my GED and went to community college to study business. My children motivate me. You can always do better in life, and I'm always one to do better, better, better.

I started working at Sportmart when I was eighteen, and I worked there for eight years. I started as a regular cashier and was promoted to an assistant, and then from there I took off. They gave me decent raises, too. I worked with the computers, I did payroll, and I took care of customer complaints. When I left, I was a cash-control manager. I did finances, daily cash, balanced their books. I'm good at numbers.

They hesitated with me, because I was so young. But I always wanted to learn more and more and more. I talked them into teaching me things, I proved myself. I showed them I was serious, convinced them to give me more responsibility. I was motivated, and my work performance was excellent. I've always been dedicated to my work, whatever it is. I've always loved coming in early. I've always been cool and calm, and known what to say and what not to say.

It was a good company to work for because I learned a skill, and they encouraged me. Payroll, computers—I did not know anything about either of those. I didn't know how to balance books. I learned all of that on the job. I think if you set your mind to learn something you'll learn it, there's no stopping you. Basically, I knew how to treat people, I knew how to relate to people. That's something I was taught at home, how to consider people. That was what I had when I started.

I loved that job so much—I loved the people I worked with, I loved the company. I quit because I wanted to go back to school, and I also had to take care of my kids. The manager was a total jerk about it, he was like an obstacle. I wanted to work fewer hours, but I could have still done the job. All I was asking was to leave work early. He didn't want that, he was mad about that. I think he liked me but I didn't like him in the same way, so he was punishing me. As much as I loved working there, I wanted the education *more*. I didn't want to stay there forever, there's more in the world than just one place.

But it was a big decision to leave that job. I cried. But we all have to do what we have to do in life. I got another job at an electronics store, at Circuit City, doing basically the same thing as at the sporting goods store. They knew my skills and they wanted me to work, work, work. I was working full-time, long hours, and I started slacking off in school. I had to drop out. It was like the end of the world, like I was incomplete.

After that, I worked at a car dealership to get the experience. It was like a little challenge for me. I didn't see women selling cars and I thought a woman *could* do it—and sure enough, I did it! They had fantastic sales managers at the dealership and they taught me. It was interesting. Consumers aren't educated, they have no knowledge of the car industry. People are indecisive about what they want. They have an idea, but you have to convince them of what is right for them. OK, they want a Caravan, they don't know which one to get, the Chevy or the Dodge. You have to sell *yourself* a little bit, in order for them to believe you. And you have to know the differences between cars, between competitors.

It worked out. But when they saw I was getting good at it, they wanted more hours from me. And at the time I'd started cosmetology school. I quit in order to finish my cosmetology certificate—you have to put in hundreds of hours. I got my license last March. Since I was twelve years old, I've loved that beauty, glamor-girl stuff, and I wanted to learn about it. We learned on mannequins and then on clients.

When we do chemicals, like for coloring hair, I'm very careful about what I'm doing because it's a big responsibility. We learned a lot of

science. We deal with strong chemicals, so we had to study anatomy—
you can actually damage someone's scalp if you don't follow instructions. We had to learn about the functioning of the body, circulation,
and the muscles in the face.

I grew up watching my aunts—they're cosmetologists. One of them
started in cosmetology school, but she never finished. I said, "If I'm
going to do that, I'm going to *finish*." So that's something I was proud
of, because I *did* it, thanks to my father and mother, of course, because
they helped so much. Sometimes we don't appreciate the kind of support we have and that's wrong. If I'd listened to them about school in
the first place, I could have done this years ago. I could have done who
knows what!

When I finished cosmetology school, I didn't want to work for anybody. I felt in my heart that I was ready to have my own business. I was
always one to have my hair and nails nice, so that part's easy. And I also
have this knowledge from the sporting goods store about managing
money. My dad was there for me, he helped me. He told me, "If you
take it seriously and finish cosmetology school, I will buy you your own
salon."

There was a hair salon a few blocks from where we lived, and the
owner was ill and needed to sell the business. I was born and raised in
this neighborhood, and I know the area's getting better. I thought it
would be a good place to be, a good investment. We bought it and
remodeled—my father did a lot of the work. The remodeling wasn't
very expensive at all, because my family helped. They broke down
walls, they painted. So *much* was given to me. It was an old-fashioned
salon. We went from Pepto-Bismol pink to a more art-deco look. It was
slow, but I got things how I wanted.

The clients from before were older. Some still come, but not as many.
I don't know if they feel they've been pushed out, but to me they are
always welcome—I don't neglect anybody. But I have a bigger clien-
tele now, I made it more profitable. People saw the salon looking more
modern, so now there are younger people, more my age. I see people

with money coming to the neighborhood. You'd think they would change the environment, be all mean, but I don't notice anything like that—they're easy to get along with. I have lawyers, doctors, police officers, business people, professional people.

When I was ready to hire a staff, I got in touch with friends from the cosmetology school. I've learned that sometimes friends and business don't mix. I hired two friends, and they took advantage of me—they thought they could get away with things. They would smoke and not clean up after themselves. They tried to make their *own* schedule, they'd be on the phone all the time. To them it was like I was not a boss, I was their friend. Like this is easy money. It is *not* easy money, it's a responsibility.

They would come in an hour or two late and I'd say, "You can't do that. This is a job. In order to have this place run, you have to be on time." I had several appointments for one girl and she called me ten minutes from her starting time and said, "I'm going to be late." I said, "What do you mean? I have clients waiting for you and I'm supposed to be doing other things. How can you do this to me?!" There are times I've run the whole place by myself because people didn't show up. So those two don't work for me anymore.

The one quit because I was so upset with her. I said, "Fine. I'm still your friend. But remember, I have to run a business." Maybe she took it the wrong way, but I feel I'm still being a friend. It's just that I have to do my job and run this business right. The place doesn't run itself—I run the place.

The other one, she was just terrible. She'd gone to the cosmetology school, but her skills weren't good. I look at it this way: being young, being pretty, being skillful is good in this business. I looked back and thought, "Was it just because she was beautiful that I thought she'd be good?" You have to *be* good, not just *look* good. If someone's not real pretty but knows how to look her best and has skills, I will hire her in a heartbeat. I learned from experience.

It's not easy running your own business. I have to budget myself. I think when you first start out, you should be careful and not spend too much money, just work with what you have. If I have extra money, I buy more shampoos and extra chemicals. I'm not one to think let's buy more until the bills are paid, until the rent is paid. It's something we all have to do: make sure the bills are paid.

I've taken all my other work experiences and brought them to this shop. I already knew how to do books and how to present myself and how to treat people. In the sporting goods store, I dealt with people's emotions, their complaints. This is different, but in a way it's the same. I love dealing with clients and customers. Of course, people always have their problems, and sometimes they don't even know why they're arguing or mad, but you do not go at their level. You compromise—you let them speak their mind.

People's appearance means a lot to them, and also, they're coming to me to relax. A stylist and a psychologist are a little alike. People come to you about their problems too, so you're doing two things at once. Some clients treat you like family. I take care of the client just as well as if I were taking care of myself, that's how I feel. With customers and clients, you're trying to satisfy them in what they want. To me it's easy, 'cause I'm a good listener. Sometimes they just want to let you know how they feel and how stressed out they are. You've got to really observe the person, don't have assumptions about what they might want. I like to study people, watch and understand their reactions.

Like Saturday, one of my clients, she just moved to Chicago from Idaho. She needed her hair fixed, she had a bad haircut. She told my stylist she wanted a certain look, but with the haircut she had, it was impossible. My stylist was confused about how to satisfy her. There was a way to create the *illusion* of what she wanted, but the client didn't understand that. I had to jump in and make her feel comfortable. My stylist is Colombian, so I don't know if the client felt she wasn't skillful because of her accent or what. But I stepped in and calmed the client down. It worked out. When I started explaining what we could do, she felt at ease and let her hair be cut so she could get what she wanted. *And* she ended up getting a manicure and a pedicure.

I have my hair salon, but I want to do something more. I want my salon to run itself so I can study real estate. I want to earn more money. And being a real estate agent, you can work at home, arrange your own time. I know I'm a good salesperson, so if I set my mind to it I think I can do it. People always want to buy homes, but they just don't know which one.

You have to have a positive attitude. Always think you can do it, determine what you want out of life. I've never been afraid to ask questions because I've always wanted to *know*—I've always wanted to learn. Education is the best. Even when you're old and gray, keep learning. Learning does *good* for you. That's something no one can take away from you—no one.

These little girls from the neighborhood come up to me, they think I'm a teenager, they're amazed that I'm a mom. I tell them not to drop out of school. I say, "Yeah, I started young. But if I could do it again, I'd have finished school before becoming a mom." They say, "You went back to school?!" I say, "Yes, and I'm thinking about going back again." They look up to me—I try to set a good example.

I *have* to work. No way could I be a housewife and not work, ever. Women do not have to be at home and just the husband works. If I get married, the man has to accept that I am a businesswoman. But I'm not thinking about marriage. My priorities are my business and my children.

I want my children to see what I saw in my father: work, work, work. I want to be my kids' idol, to take those values from home, like I took them from my dad. I don't want my sons to be deadbeats or to be in gangs—that's a waste in society. So I show them a different way. One of my boys wants to become a veterinarian, the other wants to join the FBI—he wants to do good for society. My daughter wants to become a police officer. My family, we're a minority and we've proved many people wrong—we don't fit their stereotype.

When I first opened I knew this was a serious job, something that I had to devote myself to 100 percent, *110* percent. It's going on five months since I opened, and we're doing real well. I'm still scared, of course, but I don't think you should worry as long as you've done your very best. It takes a lot of energy, but hey . . . my family gives me the energy! I made a promise to my dad that I would do this right. When I was younger and left school, that was very irresponsible of me. But I wised up, I don't want to mess up in life again. He did so much for me. I do not want to let him down.

V

"Real as It Gets": Creating Careers

Figuring out what kind of work you'd *like* to do is hard enough. Finding a job where you get to do it is a different story. In this section, people describe their efforts to find long-term work that suits them. For all, self-awareness, persistence, anxiety, and a willingness to consider the advice of parents as well as mentors played a role. Emily Hanford remembers her father's advice, "Take the time to figure out what you want to do." Looking back, she realizes, "I actually *did* take time to figure out what I wanted to do, and that means the world."

An exciting class can spark interest in different kinds of work, as can conversations with adults who hold jobs that may sound appealing. One way to investigate the work world is through internships, which can provide everything from familiarity with the rhythm of the workday to practice in phone- and letter-writing skills. Hanford says, "internships taught me real skills . . . vague things. Good writing skills, good communication skills. . . . In my job now, the vague skills are the *only* things I do." Those communication skills came into play when she called people in the broadcast industry, hoping to find a job. But she cautions, "It's rare that you'll *immediately* get anything concrete from connections. What you get in the moment may be knowledge or enthusiasm or support or one more sense of what direction to go in."

An internship can offer young people exposure to careers they've never heard or thought of, as well as provide a more realistic view of careers to consider. Jeff Marcus's unpaid museum internship "led to my first paying job." And it started him thinking about different careers in education: "The supervisors were good role models because they were very energetic, very involved . . . I'd never been exposed to that type of job before."

Interns are exposed to a variety of workplace styles and cultures, allowing them to discover what they find comfortable and what they cannot bear. Of internships at two different banks, Kate McFadyen says, "I learned there are *huge* differences between organizations, between corporate cultures. It was an eye-opener in terms of, well, they're both banks. A bank's a bank, right? [Laughs.] But nooo . . ." Internships can also clue you in to a basic truth about work. As McFadyen says of a paying job, "I worked there for two years and it was *great*. I mean, it was lousy in some ways, as any job is, really—and I think you have to realize that: there are lousy parts to any job."

Especially important, workplace internships give young people opportunities to hear about adults' actual experiences; about how they got to where they are, and how they feel about those journeys and their jobs. Robert Richman's volunteer internship evolved into a paying job and a career in politics, and his boss's advice proved crucial to Richman's developing political consciousness. His boss said, " 'You understand the technology, you understand *how*.' By which he meant . . . how a campaign is run, how money is raised—the nuts and bolts, the tools . . . But you have no clue why you're doing it and what you're doing it for . . . You need to figure out why, you need to find some center, some values and beliefs and reasons to do it."

At one time Marc Spiegler considered political work, but instead became a freelance writer and eventually a columnist. He urges those dissatisfied in their jobs to pay attention to exactly what they're reacting to: "If you don't like the job but there's something you like *about* it, try to make sure the next job has more of that and less of what you don't like." He strongly suggests regularly taking stock: "People think if they're busy, their career is moving forward. That's not necessarily true . . . You also have to put time aside to meet the people who can make things happen for you three years down the road, to develop other contacts within your industry. You have to take the time to dream a bit, to think about what it is you want to do."

Figuring out where your interests and abilities lie, and how you can earn a living doing something involving those interests and abilities, is no easy task. But, as the people in this section know, it can be a fascinating road to self-discovery.

EMILY HANFORD

Emily's most valuable career guidance came from her father, who urged her not to rush into a career. Her first significant job experience was as an intern in a press office, where one of her assignments was to record press conferences. In college, she briefly entertained the notion of becoming a lawyer, but an unsuccessful internship at a public-policy organization changed her mind. Later, a summer job teaching English in Poland offered her a concrete idea about the value of work: what she did could make a difference in someone's life. Even more pivotal was a waitress job, where she developed a sense of what she wanted to do: tell stories about real people. After college, her part-time job at a small public radio station offered her an opportunity to tell those kinds of stories. While trying to find radio work in a new city, she took a job teaching reading and learned what makes a team player and how it feels to be laid off. Only twenty-seven, Emily assumes that her work future may involve more than radio. What matters is that she has found the thing she loves to do, and that is to keep telling real stories. "You gather all this information; you're the sifter the sand goes through."

My father was a banker. I think he liked his work but never loved it. But it was the kind of job where if he needed to leave at two o'clock to come see my brother's baseball game or to see me play field hockey, he did. He was really interested in being a good dad. My mother was a teacher and guidance counselor before she got pregnant, and now she's a psychotherapist. She's from a more working-class background than my father. Her mother was a teacher and an actress and had a radio variety show every morning. In the thirties she was invited to do summer stock with Henry Fonda, but her father wouldn't let her. Radio was her second choice to being a real artist, a real actress. It was a little bit radical that my grandmother was not a stay-at-home mom.

I remember my first women's studies class in college. We debated maternal instinct. All the other students shot it down as a cultural construction. I've always had a maternal instinct that was very real to *me*. I got emotional about it in class, and the professor asked me to write a paper. I thought about my own mother and how important it was to me that she didn't work for the first five or six years of my life. I thought, "If I have children, what kind of choice would I make?" Because work is incredibly important in my life, and I don't know how I could survive without it.

In high school I was *very* focused on college. I went to a big school, and not many people seemed concerned with helping you find your own way. I don't have anything to compare that to, so I may have gotten lots of help that I don't recognize as help! I certainly got a lot of good context and a lot of good content. I had good teachers, but I don't remember a lot about guidance counseling. One thing that my father always said was, "Take the time to figure out what you want to do." That was *very* important. Though it's been stressful, I realize now that I actually *did* take time to figure out what I wanted to do, and that means the world.

My very first job was when I was fourteen and worked as a bagger at a supermarket. I didn't come from the kind of family where you *had* to work as a teenager, but I really *wanted* to work—I wanted a job. Some of the cashiers were seventeen and they were kind of tough and real—and there were women who had been working there *forever*, I thought they were cool. It was this new world and though I felt young, working there made me feel adult.

I had another job the next year, at a pizza chain. I worked there for six months, and I didn't work again until I was a senior in high school. A friend of my mother's got me an internship working for then-Governor Dukakis of Massachusetts, in his press office. I did that for the school

year, three days a week, two-thirty to six. Didn't get paid a dime, but it
was great. I loved the job so much I gave up sports for it.

It was, again, work as an entrance into the adult world, and this was a
serious world. This was senators and representatives and stuff that matters, and I felt like my job mattered. The press office was on the first
floor, and you had to go upstairs to get to the governor's office. It was in
a beautiful stone building, and I remember walking down this long dark
hallway feeling really cozy. There was something comfortable about
being in this place and having this job.

I recorded press conferences and cut out small soundbites to put in
radio feeds. I used little Marantz tape recorders, like I do now . . . I
just recently identified that as being an early radio experience! I clipped
newspapers and typed up news summaries and delivered them around. I
worked there again the following summer, when Dukakis was running
for president. I got one of the *real* internships along with college students hired for the summer. They paid me, and I felt like I had something to teach the others—that was validating.

I was very concerned with doing a good job and not screwing anything up. The most nerve-wracking work was when I had to record
things. I was intimidated by the technical stuff, but also empowered that
I could *master* it, actually get back and have something on tape. It
seemed like a real triumph. I remember being nervous when I had to
choose something that the governor said. I felt like they were giving me
a little *too* much responsibility, because I didn't necessarily understand
what was going on. I would go to press conferences and, on one level, I
couldn't quite listen to what the governor was *really* talking about because I was too *stressed*! But there were very concrete things I could do
every day, ways to contribute, and I felt of value. It was a great internship for that reason.

Work was a relief from school. I liked school—I *was* school, it was
an important part of my identity. For kids that don't like or do well in
school, the lack of connection between school and work can be a serious
problem. In the school world I was one kind of person: tied up in it,
intent on doing well. But for me there was a freedom in the work world,

which was task-oriented, engaging in an entirely different way. I didn't necessarily understand everything, or the larger connections to the world, but I was *part* of something. I realized that people thought I was good at something. I still felt like a little kid, but a kid whom they could trust to draft press releases, to *do* things.

In college, I took a lot of political science classes because I thought about becoming a lawyer. The summer after sophomore year I did an internship at a public-policy place in Washington, D.C. It was a bad internship because there wasn't anything concrete for me to do. I would show up and pick at my fingers. I barely breathed that summer because I was *so* anxious. I was supposed to do this nebulous project about youth voting. I didn't know *what* the purpose was, I didn't know *how* to do it, and I needed more guidance. My anxiety prevented me from being a good observer, which it's really important to take the time to be. I wasted time being nervous, and in the end felt that I'd failed. I thought that maybe that was the way the work world was going to be—a lot of people not really doing anything.

I started to realize that, in order for me to find work that was fulfilling, I needed to figure out how the thinking and reflecting aspects of school connected to doing concrete tasks in the work world, to getting paid. As a young person, one thing hard for me to understand was what skills you really needed for the work world. People talk about them in such vague ways. But I later realized that these internships taught me real skills. Being able to talk on the phone is a *serious* skill. I learned it when I worked in that press office. Vague things. Good writing skills, good communication skills. These are all real things. It's only been in recent years that I've understood how truly important they are. In my job now, the vague skills are the *only* things I do. Radio is about strong writing skills, good communication skills, talking on the phone.

My junior year I worked in the school cafeteria as a dishwasher because I just needed to *work*. After the D.C. internship, it was *such* a relief—you'd get sweaty and smelly, you had a *task*. Being in the cafeteria took me entirely away from school three mornings a week. The people I worked with were college students, but the supervisors were people that lived in the town. Being in college, I felt so disconnected from the patterns of *life*; I *longed* for the kinds of relationships that real life gives you.

That winter, I went to England for a semester. I was there until June and then I needed a summer job. I saw a little flyer advertising for people to teach English in Poland in exchange for living expenses. The association was run by this old, drunk Polish man who had escaped to England during World War II. It was completely unstructured. I took a bus to Poland—*thirty-five hours!* We arrived in Warsaw where someone was supposed to pick me up and take me to another little town. No one arrived. Three others were also left stranded. We found out what town they were supposed to go to, and I went along with them.

My impression of the job had been that we would live with a family and teach them English through conversation. It turned out they thought we were English professors who were going to teach *classes*. We had *nothing*: no lesson plan, zilch, *nada*. And I had *no* idea how to teach the English language. Thank God I had brought one little grammar book with me. It was surreal and scary and stressful. I had a class of fifteen people I was supposed to teach, four hours a day, five days a week, for five weeks.

Half the class were women who had previously taught Russian— you *had* to learn Russian in Poland until the collapse of the Berlin Wall. But it was no longer required, and everyone wanted to learn English. Unless these women learned English fast, they were going to be out of work. All of a sudden I felt this tremendous sense of responsibility. There was so much riding on it. I didn't get angry, and I couldn't allow myself to feel taken because I had to give these people *something*. Fortunately, there were three guys in my class who already spoke decent English and wanted to learn an American accent. They were my saviors. We all tried to teach the women. The guys were better teachers because they'd already had to learn the language.

The other problem was that you couldn't get supplies, like chalk or notebooks. So I made up games every day. This experience changed my ideas about work. Just the summer before, I had been in Washington,

D.C., trying to make something out of nothing and I couldn't get anywhere. And here, I tried my damnedest and definitely created concrete things. It made me realize that there really could be something at stake in certain kinds of work. This was *real*—it was connected to these people and their lives and their future. Some of the women planned on teaching English in the fall and literally could not speak a word of it. In the end, what saved me is that we liked and enjoyed each other. It was human. It was a real exchange. I saw a little bit of progress, and to me that meant more than any press conference I'd ever gone to.

For the first time I felt like work was part of life, that it mattered. It's the same thing as understanding that knowing how to talk on the phone is a valuable skill. I got the sense that there's a way to make a connection between existing in the world and doing something productive with and for other people. In all of my struggles to dissolve the separation between school and work, and life and school, and life and work, this was the first time that these things felt like they were in one place, in one little circle, connected to each other. Work *should* matter. Work should be a creative and constituting kind of practice, not something you do just for the money.

When I returned from Poland, I went back to school and pretty quickly decided I needed a break. For much of my life I had used school as a way of defining myself. Being good in school was the beginning and end as far as how to make it in the world. I knew that going to professional or graduate school were ways to move ahead, but I had no interest in either. I suddenly realized that I didn't know what I was doing: [anxiously] "I *can't* be finished with college yet, because what the *hell* is going to happen to me afterwards?" I was under the impression that after college you made a choice about what you were going to do for a living and that determined everything from then on. I've learned since, that's bullshit. It's important, in that it starts you on a path—but it's not determining. By not getting my degree, I put off geting the "real job," making the real choice. I was afraid of getting stuck.

I went and lived with my mother and worked in a bookstore. It was a relief—concrete, task-oriented. But after six months it started driving me crazy. "I'm working nine-to-five and there's nothing in this work, *nothing*." I ended up taking a waitress job at a small family restaurant. I had never waitressed before, and it was great, though I've had plenty of bad waitress experiences since. There's a certain pleasure in being able to do things really fast, and when it's busy and crazy it's a total high. You feel like you *earned* that money. It was concrete: I was serving the food, doing the work. I started to see that I was making my own decisions about *how* I was doing my job—this was the kind of waitress *I* was going to be.

There was a halfway house down the street and an old people's place up the street. It was the kind of restaurant where lonely old people or lonely crazy people came—all regulars, except on weekends. I got to know these people a little and started becoming interested in their stories. I started to think about becoming a writer. I didn't want to write fiction, I wanted to write about real people. That was the beginning of wanting to be a journalist. I remember thinking, "What I like about this waitressing job is going to figure into what I do with my life—this is going to take me somewhere."

I heard about a man who needed people to work with mentally handicapped adults, to help them with living skills. I ended up working with a woman in her thirties who had Down's Syndrome and had just moved into her own apartment. Three days a week I would take her shopping. I really liked her and started thinking about her in terms of story. I was intrigued by describing her movements and gestures and things she said, and I started writing about her.

Finally, I was ready to return to school. I took a nonfiction writing class and was seen as being really good. I thought, "I can go with this, I can be good at this—I can *do* this." Then I graduated. "Wow, this was what I was terrified of and this is great. So . . . what next?"

My nonfiction writing teacher connected me with an internship at WFCR, a little public radio station in Western Massachusetts. I worked two days a week doing spot news. I read the papers in the morning, looked at the wires, made some phone calls and got soundbites for the afternoon news. I hadn't been an NPR [National Public Radio] person

before, didn't even really know what it was. I started listening to
"Morning Edition" every day, it became a part of my forming sensibil-
ity.

I saw working there as a way to make concrete some of the things I
was interested in, in terms of observing people and doing stories. I was
really lucky at that job because the woman I worked for, Pippin Ross,
was *great*. She was good at what she did and had a sane approach to
work. She had a little boy and every day she left at four-thirty. "See ya."
Her attitude was: I'm going to be good at what I do, but I'm not a slave
to this. She was one of these people who was able to teach you a little bit
and let you go a long way with it. She wasn't interested in overteaching,
she wasn't worried about controlling everything.

My first day was Martin Luther King Day, and Pippin was about the
only one around. There was no news, but there had been some floods. It
was like, "She told me how to do it, and now I'm gonna do it, all in one
day." [She grows increasingly excited, as though re-experiencing the
learning moment.] We sat at the reel-to-reel machine and she said,
"This is how you cut tape." Then, "Call up the weather guy and do a
little piece of spot news about the floods"—so that was what I did. All I
had to do was get the soundbite, write a line in and a line out of the
piece, and that was it. My very first piece.

I did spot news for a few months, and then I started to get a little
disillusioned. Pippin said, "Well, why don't you do a feature?" So I did
my first feature . . . It would be embarrassing to hear it now. It was
about these men who lived in a single-room occupancy [SRO] unit. I
remember the anxiety of feeling I had to find some kind of news in order to justify the story. There was a little bit of old news because a college had wanted to buy the property and turn the SROs into dorms or
somesuch thing. I went and interviewed the college financial person.
But when I sat down to write the piece, all I wanted to write about was
these guys and why they lived in SROs. And Pippin let me do it. She
said, "I don't care about the financial officer, just write what you want."
So I did!

I did the first story for free, but after that she paid a hundred dollars

for each one. I became an independent reporter and producer. I didn't
know that's what I was until their newsletter came out and I saw myself
listed! [Laughs.] Then they gave me a summer contract to do two days
of spot news and one feature a week. I started to use my voice. Instead
of just putting together the spot news, I was the one reporting these
forty-five-second and one-minute stories. And my boss didn't demand
that I justify them with news. I learned about not getting too tied down
by rules because *she* didn't.

Pippin liked to do special little series. We did a back-to-school series,
and I spent a day with a blind high-school senior, a girl. The story
was about not being able to see and how hard that is as a teenager.
At one point I had the recorder on and she wanted to know what
I looked like. She had *never* seen, so I didn't know how to describe
myself. I said, "How do you figure out how people look?" She said,
"Well, I ask if I can touch them, but most teenagers won't let me." We
were sitting very close to each other and I said, "Well, you can touch
me." It was this . . . moment. There was all this really personal, raw
stuff and my boss kept saying, "Whatever you want to do, just do it."
So I *did*.

That job was a great start. And it *felt* like a start, even though I had all
these other little waitressing jobs to help support myself. I learned so
much from Pippin. I remember one day, she was applying for other
jobs. She was looking at her résumé and said, "God, I haven't really
done anything in my life." That shocked me. I said, "But, you're so
happy—you have such a good life!" She said, "Well, I guess that's
true . . ." She had this nice marriage and this kid and this job. That
wasn't a model I'd had before. For some reason, I had thought that you
had to work harder or be more miserable or be more *something* to have a
good life. But she had balance.

I left that job to move to Chicago because my boyfriend lived there.
When I knew I was going to move, I started asking people if they knew
anyone in Chicago. I wanted to work in radio and I started to call
around, to cultivate connections. I wrote "Hello, here's who I am" letters to independent producers I admired. I didn't think it was necessar-

ily going to get me anywhere, but I wrote—not asking for anything, just saying, "I'm moving to Chicago and I'm trying to find a way to do this kind of work. What do you think?" It's scary—it was not an easy thing to do. I fretted for a long time before I sent them out.

Someone who works for Soundprint* called me back and we talked about how much we both liked radio. Again, having good phone skills was helpful. I felt articulate and relaxed. To tell you the truth, I have no idea what he told me to do. I think he said, "You could do a documentary for Soundprint." I felt like that was way out my reach, and I still do in some ways—that's a goal for me, to do documentary work. Though that conversation didn't lead anywhere concrete, his calling me back made me feel believed-in, made me feel almost part of a community. If I wanted to do a documentary for Soundprint right now, he might not immediately remember me. But if I said, "I called you four years ago, and now I've done X, Y, and Z, and I have this idea—what do you think?" it could be valuable. It's a personal connection.

It's rare that you'll *immediately* get anything concrete from connections. What you get in the moment may be knowledge or enthusiasm or support or one more sense of what direction to go in. And it's often through connections that you eventually *do* get concrete things.

I didn't hear back from any other people except Ira Glass, an NPR reporter. I knew his work, I knew he was in Chicago, and I found and wrote to him at the NPR bureau. I didn't hear back and I didn't hear back—and then the first week I was in Chicago I received a postcard: "Give me a call." I called and he said, "You want to come cut tape for me?" He was putting together pilots, trying to get funding for *This American Life*.†

Previously, I hadn't had to do much complicated editing, and Ira taught me a lot about it. He also listened to my stories and critiqued them and asked me to critique his. I felt fumbling and stupid, but I tried.

---

* A radio documentary series.

† An innovative weekly radio program which, in 1998, its first year, won radio's prestigious Peabody Award.

I could tell right away that he felt I had something to offer. Every time that happens, it's kind of a revelation. "Oh, I do?" I *still* feel that way at times.

After a few months I needed a real job. I had made a few connections, but didn't know how to turn them into anything. The only place I wanted to work was at WBEZ, the Chicago NPR affiliate. All this time I'd been looking in the paper every morning, circling jobs. Looking in the papers is lonely—it's so distant and scary. You feel very vulnerable. You circle things and try to get excited about them.

I applied for maybe fifteen or twenty jobs, sent out that many cover letters. I was probably a good candidate for many of them. Most didn't call me back. I found an ad asking for teachers: "Do you like children, do you like to read? Call us." It was a reading-skills program for first grade through adult; the program was divided into five levels, and you were asked to teach all levels. You traveled around to various high schools and taught two classes a day, five days a week. Some of the resources they had were great. It was different from Poland: here they actually gave me a way to teach. I liked it . . . one time through!

The pay was decent and I had health insurance, but it was a *lot* of work—it was stressful, and you had to drive all over. In a way, it was too much action and not enough reflection. Were I a different person, it might have been great. I saw other people getting more of a charge out of it, and I started to feel guilty: "Why isn't this enough for me?"

By the summer, I started thinking, "They're asking a lot of me and not paying *that* much." They'd started asking people to do things like go out of town two days a week, stay overnight in a motel. I said no. Also, the place reminded me of college in that it became very much a *group* activity—and I was one step back from that. I believed in teaching this method, but I wasn't going to talk about it at dinner. They had a lot of barbecues with everybody, and I didn't want to go. Soccer games, football—not for me. I wasn't a team player.

Then they laid me off. They said not enough people had signed up for the classes. That was a shock. I was the only one laid off. It was the first time I felt like I got fired. I said, "How come me?" The director of the program said, "Because other people said yes to these things, other people gave more of themselves." I thought, "*Hmmm*—interesting lesson . . ." So those are the people that get laid off. It's OK to say no to doing certain things, but it can cost.

I felt very hurt, but relieved. My crisis was that I had no income. I temped. I had to get dressed up, and I *hated* that—and for the first time I felt a little ashamed. There's nothing wrong with being a secretary, and I feel snobby saying this, but I felt like, "I've gotten further than this."

During the time I was a teacher I did my first piece for WBEZ, for "Chicago Matters," this series they do every year. That year's topic was immigration. Earlier, I'd written to Johanna Zorn, the series producer, and sent her a tape. She invited me to submit a story idea. I ended up doing a story about a Cambodian boy. There was a lot at stake, a lot of unknowns, and the people I dealt with were new to me. When it was over, I decided I didn't want to work in radio anymore because that experience had been so stressful.

But around the time I was laid off, I heard about a temporary job opening at the station—as the reporter for the following year's series. I felt confident about getting the job and felt I'd be good at it. I forgot all the anxiety—[laughs] but I was *still* nervous. It's like that at every job. You have to start over: it's a new set of people to create working relationships with, to assure and impress.

When I first went in, I said, "I need a reel-to-reel machine." There were none. WFCR was so not up-to-date that we worked on this weird thing with knobs, it wasn't a *real* board. When I saw the WBEZ board I was like . . . "I don't know what button to push! No one's ever taught me this and how am I going to ask?" I felt I was supposed to know certain things. I *still* feel that because I never went to journalism school. But you learn on the job, you just have to ask questions. Of course, you have to be lucky enough to be around people who are willing to teach. The first time Mary Gaffney, one of the engineers, and I were sitting in front of the board, I sheepishly admitted I'd never seen anything like this in my life. She said, *"You haven't?!"* And then she taught me. "Well, all you do is . . ." and "It's easy, just press."

You can't worry about what someone is going to think of you for asking questions. And it's important to know *how* to ask, because there's different ways of asking. You need to be purposeful. It's good to ask questions in context. It's good to give yourself the space to try something and make some mistakes and ask questions to fix them. Recently, an intern started asking me all kinds of questions—all at one time. I thought, "You *cannot* be processing all this information, so don't ask it all at once—ask me one thing at a time." Ask questions in situations where you're going to learn the answer in context.

It's great to find people like my first radio boss, who was willing to give me room to make mistakes. The people I choose to work with, when I *can* choose, are those willing to give you some space, those that don't need to make *everything* that you do exactly like what they would do. When you're starting out in your work life, it's important to recognize when people are trying to over-control you—to understand that it's *their* problem and not yours . . . to not feel like you're a failure, that they *have* to be so controlling because you're not good enough.

After the series job ended, I filled in for someone who was on maternity leave and I did a whole different set of skills. I started doing all the voice-overs for the station. That was a job I felt and *was* entirely unprepared to do. I was not very good, but they let me do it—I learned on the job, and I got better. At first, I felt very vulnerable: I *knew* I was bad. Being vulnerable and being willing to be bad at something is very much a skill. I still struggle with that a lot.

Since then, I've filled in for various people, again been the "Chicago Matters" reporter, and filled in as acting news director. I've worked hard, and I'm good at what I do, but I also feel lucky to have had decent opportunities. I don't have a lot of complaints, and as I get older I don't *want* to have a lot of complaints. [Laughs.] I'm taking stock, trying to figure out what I want to do next. I want to move forward from where I am.

I'm young and I *know* that I have a lot to learn. Radio is so ephemeral: you can touch a book, but you can't touch a radio story. But in many ways radio is touchable in the process of making it. Learning how to edit and mix on the computer is tangible . . . it's a skill. You're making something that other people are going to experience in *their* world, where they're listening to the radio while washing their dishes or driving their car.

Of course, there's a certain amount of tension in making your life be about other people's lives. What I do feels a little like stealing. When you interview someone, you have a certain kind of power—it's not always an even exchange. Sometimes I make decisions fast: what to use, what not to use, how to characterize a story. You never know if you're totally accurate. What's accurate?

I don't know if I'll do radio my whole life, but I'll be doing some version of what's appealing to me about radio. The people part, the thinking, writing, reflecting, putting things together, editing part . . . I *love* coming up with story ideas and exploring the world, talking to people, observing them. On one level, it's the easiest part: it's about putting yourself in the world and gathering information. Sitting down and writing about it is lonely and scary and difficult. It's a puzzle: there's a sense of having to convey action, actually replay action, with context and description and a hell of a lot of editing. [Laughs.]

When I do stories, I'm trying to interest people in something that interested me. Sometimes it's not that interesting to me by the time I sit down to write it. Sometimes it's difficult to keep the connection between what happened in the world and this isolating process of re-creating it. You have to remember what *originally* interested you. That's where reporting is ultimately not objective—there's *no such thing* as an objective reporter. At the same time, you've got to strive to be true to something. I try to be honest, but I don't even know what that is. What I'm interested in is making sure I stay engaged in those questions.

JEFFREY MARCUS

A high-school museum internship started Jeffrey thinking about careers in the nonacademic educational field. Also significant was a summer wilderness journey: "That trip probably had as much influence on what I ultimately want to do with my life as anything else." After college, Jeffrey took a year to earn money and take stock before moving forward in pursuit of a career. He managed and taught at a gymnastics gym, and found supervising older, often long-time workers, an uneasy challenge. "There was some attitude: 'Who's this snot-nosed, punk kid right out of college coming in telling me what to do?'" After the relative freedom of college life, adjusting to the demands of a full-time job wasn't easy. Later, a summer job leading wilderness trips solidified his interest in the environment, after which he decided to fashion a career to reflect his varied interests. At twenty-three, in his last year of graduate school, he looks ahead. "I should be thinking more about how to market myself, of how I can set myself apart."

Both of my parents are doctors. My mom is a pediatrician; my dad, when I was growing up, taught tropical medicine at a university—he currently has a traveler's health practice. One thing I really credit my parents with is not pressuring me to become a doctor. They were always very open and willing to say, "Whatever's going to make you happy, that's what you should do." But it was always assumed I would go to college, that was a given, and after college decide what I wanted to do with my life. In high school, there was a career guidance center where I took one of those aptitude tests. It wasn't very helpful. Honestly, it made no impact at all, I don't even remember what it said. People should take those things with a grain of salt.

I had a job in high school on the weekends. I worked at the local drugstore, collating newspapers. The Sunday papers arrived in sections, and I'd have to piece them all together. At the end of the day my hands were *black*. That was really the first time I had to wrestle with ethics. We were allowed fifteen-minute breaks in the back of the store—but sometimes people would stretch it into twenty-minutes or half an hour. When we were supposed to be stacking shelves, or going to the back of the store and getting stock, there were opportunities to slack off and not work. Some people took advantage of the situation whenever they could. Also, it was fairly easy to shoplift things from the back, and people would do that. The trouble is just how easy it is to rationalize something like that: "I'm only being paid $3.25 an hour, and I deserve a little extra perk." I'd think, "Do I tell my boss?" But I didn't—I didn't snitch. These were my peers, and I guess I was still too immature not to be complacent about those sorts of things.

My other high-school work experience was wonderful. Senior year, they allowed you to have an internship somewhere, and I volunteered at a science museum. I worked in the Discovery and Human Body Rooms—interactive exhibit spaces where the public can participate. They're typically staffed by volunteers who are there to help explain and facilitate.

That was my first experience working with really good supervisors who encouraged me, and allowed enough personal freedom to explore and try new things. They let me develop some new exhibits for the place and design some training sessions. In high school, I had torn a ligament in my knee, and so for one exhibit I put together a little educational exhibit on knee injuries and what they were all about. It was an *extremely* positive work experience. The supervisors were good role models because they were very energetic, very involved with the exhibit floor and the volunteers—they were constantly coming up with new ideas. They were upbeat and seemed extremely happy with their work. I'd never been exposed to that type of job before. It made me think I'd like to get into the field of education, working with people and museum-type learning.

That volunteering experience led to my first paying job: the following summer I supervised the volunteers at those same places. Some of the volunteers were young, but a lot were older, retired people. It was an energetic and enthusiastic group; they were there because they *wanted* to be there. I was never really tested in my ability as a supervisor because it all ran so smoothly. That experience led to my decision to become a psychology major in college. I saw that as a way of heading toward education; I would be looking at early childhood development and this sort of thing. Toward the end of college, I developed an interest in biology as well.

I'd always enjoyed being outdoors and when I was in high school, I'd taken a six-week camping trip, backpacking and canoeing through the Pacific Northwest. It was the first time I was exposed to spectacular wilderness areas and became aware of the many threats to them. I saw the need to actively protect the environment, and I thought I'd like to somehow combine my interests in biology and education.

Through wilderness trips, I was exposed to other types of jobs, such as park ranger. I started to piece things together: "Here's the types of things I like to do, now what are the kinds of jobs that will allow me to do them?" So I took all that and went on to become a gymnastics instructor. [Laughs.]

I had been on the gymnastics team all through high school, and been captain. Summers, when I was home from college, I worked in a local gym coaching little kids. When my boss knew I was close to graduating, she asked if I wanted to manage one of her gyms. This was early in my senior year, just as I was starting to think about what I might want to do—and I was still quite confused as to what exactly that might be.

In a sense, she made me an offer I couldn't refuse. I enjoyed teaching gymnastics, and this was a teaching job that would also give me responsibility, in terms of being a manager. This would be my first full-time, forty-hour-a-week job. Financially it made a lot of sense, and it was a decent opportunity. I could live at home and save money, and that was some incentive. I didn't see the job as a career move, but as a way to get some work experience and make some real money for the first time in my life. I decided to do it for at least a year and then reevaluate.

It was a difficult job in a lot of ways. Number one, the hours. She was paying me decent money, but she made sure I worked for it. I worked six days a week, fifty- or sixty-hour weeks. During the day, I taught back-to-back-*to-back* classes. I'd start work around eleven in the morning and leave the gym a little after nine at night, but it would vary. Some days I taught straight through for four or five hours. I wouldn't have a chance to take more than, say, fifteen-minutes to grab my dinner while one of the other coaches led the stretch and workout.

My first priority was to be up and energetic for the kids, to make sure they were safe and having a good time. That required constant mental alertness, as well as physical energy—I had to be able to demonstrate for them and lift them and everything else. I became physically exhausted at a certain point, from not having enough downtime. But being so young, and this a first experience, I was a little hesitant about saying anything to my boss. I wanted to prove myself: "I can work as hard *and* do the job as well as anyone else." I didn't want to seem like a weenie—"Hey, I'm tired . . ."

We had a maximum class size of about eight kids per instructor. Ideally, you want to have four or five, so you can have high-quality interaction. To some extent, I felt nervous talking to her about these sorts of things. But I'd make myself do it because I felt a responsibility to the other instructors, to the kids, and to myself. I wanted to make sure I wasn't completely overwhelmed and rundown. I would suggest she trim the classes, but from her perspective of, "this is a business, I need to make money," she always pushed toward more.

I wasn't teaching constantly: there was also office work. I walked into an awkward situation when I started. There was a full-time secretary who had been coordinating things for the gym. When I was brought in to manage, the boss wanted to cut her hours. There was a real standoff between the two of them, and even a little bit of resentment from the woman toward me. I was coming in and taking her money, if you want to look at it bluntly, and this was a woman with a family.

For a little while she *wasn't* working—I guess you could say she went on strike. So I had to do all of that work. So then the question was: "Well, do I need to hire someone temporarily to help run this gym?" The last thing I wanted was to get in the middle of their dispute, but at the same time I *needed* to keep things running—and *I* couldn't do it *all*. Finally, they worked it out and she came back. It took a little while to settle into "OK, *you* do this and *I* do that"—but we worked those things out.

For the first time I really felt my age: middle-aged people worked there, people with families, people who had worked there for several years. I'm coming in and want to make improvements, want to make this gym the best gym I can. But people often get entrenched in what they've been doing and *how* they've been doing it. Perhaps some of my ideas were better, but perhaps not. I probably didn't have as much appreciation as I should have for "the way it's always been done." So much of my frustration came from trying to reconcile my big ideas with the tried and true. I was coming in with "This is the way it *should* be done"—and it's hard to shake things up, particularly as a *young* manager. What credibility did I have to rock the boat?

Teaching the kids I *loved*, and the gymnastics part was great. But trying to be assertive and yet at the same time respectful, *really* learning how to be a good supervisor, wasn't easy. In your psychology classes you learn all these things about what motivates people; but to take it from the textbook into an actual real-world situation is a lot more difficult. I was twenty-one, twenty-two, and I didn't have a good template for how to deal with it, because I had never been in that kind of situation before.

I didn't have anyone to talk to about the job. I didn't have any close friends in the area, and I didn't vent a lot of these things to my parents. Maybe that's because they wouldn't vent about *their* jobs too much. I was following the pattern of "Well, you're supposed to work hard and do your job, but not complain about it or bring it home." And also feeling like, "I'm a big boy—I gotta work this out."

When I was well rested enough, I could approach each situation and think it through: "OK, what do we have to do to get beyond this?" Work it through in a rational way. But the days when I was overtired, I couldn't deal with things nearly as well.

I fulfilled my year contract, but decided this was not what I wanted to be doing the next year. To some extent, it was a good first job—but it was a lot more difficult than I expected. It was a baptism by fire into the real world, where you have to deal with long working hours and everything else. The real world, in terms of most of your life, is your job.

In college, one of the nice things was being involved in one activity or another: movie-making, gymnastics club, classes, going to different lectures. And it was nice to have a big social life, get to do a lot of different things. Here, my life was my job: I went to work, I worked all day, I went to sleep, woke up, sat down and read the paper, got myself ready, and went to work again . . . On weekends, I was so exhausted I didn't feel like going out, so I didn't have a social life. Even when I like my job, I want to have *something* of a life outside of it. This job helped me realize that as well.

After I quit, I took a summer job leading wilderness trips. That was when I decided to make a shift to the outdoor, wildlife, environmental field. So I started looking around at the options. I came across the Student Conservation Association, which sets up volunteer opportunities at various national parks. I started volunteering down in Big Bend National Park in Texas.

I took a three-month volunteer position. I started with a job that wasn't *exactly* what I wanted to do—I worked the front desk a lot. But I did get to lead nature walks, and design my own—which I definitely enjoyed. I even volunteered to work with a wildlife specialist on days off from my *other* volunteering! [Laughs.] That helped open the door when the Americorp program came along: they had some five-month positions, and the wildlife manager knew I was interested in one of those. We got along well, so I got the job. That position gave me more experience and helped open the door to graduate school.

I started searching through newspapers and magazines that listed environmental-type positions. I didn't have a precise focus, but I knew the general types of things I was looking for. I realized I didn't know enough about being a naturalist, about the natural world and biology. Several of the jobs I was interested in required a master's degree, so I thought, "I'd better get myself back into school." Through the five-month Americorp position, I earned a minimum-wage salary. They give you an educational stipend to put toward future schooling—that helped pay some of the tuition expenses.

To get into graduate school in wildlife biology, you can't just say, "OK, I've got the grades, I want to be accepted." You have to find a professor willing to sponsor your work, usually someone who has a research project and funding.

At the moment, I'm being paid to help with a project concerned with improving wildlife habitat on farmland in North Carolina, and looking at what role predators play on these farms. So, for example, we're trying to convince farmers to leave at the edges of their farmland small narrow strips of grassy- and weedy-type habitats for birds. Usually, farmers plant their crops right up to the edge of the ditches. Anyone who has big brushy weeds growing in their ditch is considered a messy farmer, so it goes against the grain of what the local landowners and farmers have been taught—it goes against the culture.

Certainly, some of the things I learned at the gym have been useful in this work. Such as the importance of *listening* first, rather than coming in and saying, "Hey, this is what I think you should do and this is what you're gonna do." Before you go in like a big ball of fire, stop, and say, "How are you doing things now? What are your concerns? What are your problems? What do you think needs to be changed?" The professor I'm working under is very good at finding common ground. Environmentalists are often seen as confrontational: they're seen as working *against* loggers, trying to stop this or that development or growth.

We're trying to find common ground, work *with* the landowners, farmers, and hunters—trying to keep everyone on the same side.

This is the first time I'll actually be looking for a career-type job, something I'm going to do for several years down the road. I doubt I'll be in the same position for my entire lifetime—it just doesn't seem to work that way anymore. And wildlife biology jobs are hard to find—it's a very competitive field. I imagine the most successful people are the ones who plan ahead and look at the job market while they're still in school, the ones who position themselves for different opportunities, and even more important, make connections.

To be sure of getting a position, you have to be willing to move where the job is. I look at people out there—they're *very* mobile. It's a much different culture now, and to some extent I think there's something that's lost. Being in one place and feeling a sense of community is something I've been lacking.

Being in academe and working at a university, I don't see that. My professor was trained as a wildlife biologist, and nowadays more of his time is spent writing grants, balancing budgets, and dealing with administrators than is spent actually out in the field. To some extent, you have to stay at the bottom of the rung to be in the really interesting positions. It's the low-level grunts that get to do all the fun stuff, actually get out there and muck around in the outdoors. The more you work your way up and become successful, the more you're supervising other people who get to go out and do the fun stuff. I don't want to turn into some bureaucrat or administrator somewhere—which is why I want to avoid academe, and will probably want to avoid working for the federal government too. Which actually eliminates about seventy-five percent of the jobs that are available in my field!

I have to acknowledge that I may change as well. There may come a point where I don't want to be waking up at five A.M. and getting tick and mosquito bites—some point where I'd rather be working in a cushy office, be in a position where I can make broader-scale changes, such as initiating an entire research program. That's where a lot of the difference is made. Or I might even want to get in the political arena. I don't think it would be fun lobbying, or helping to write legislation, or push bills, but when you look at where you can really make a difference in the world, that's certainly one way.

I'd like to make a difference in the world. That's one of the reasons I like the idea of education, because that's where I think you really *can* make a big difference—with a young generation, with children—by introducing them to new things and ideas, and instilling in them solid values, especially about the environment.

KATE MCFADYEN

Kate, twenty-eight, thought about becoming a banker and interned at two different types of banks. She's a proponent of internships: "As an intern you discover things about work environments. You're learning, you do the best you can, you have fun." She graduated with a psychology degree, but felt ill-equipped to launch a job search. Through connections, she was hired at a bank—and realized banking was not for her. A job at a mail-order catalog company awakened her to the importance of work environments and bosses. "I thought, I just haven't found the right place, it can't all be this bad." She concluded that first jobs "are about paying the dues and getting something on your résumé." She looked into herself: what did she enjoy, what was she good at? Marketing seemed the right direction. After a positive experience in that field, she returned to school. "The really successful people I had seen all had MBAs. I figured that was probably a good thing to do." Through successive jobs, she's continued defining her work goals: "Whatever it is, as long as you're building skills all within the same arena, you can't really go wrong."

My mother was a schoolteacher for a long time, later a fund-raiser. Then she got her master's in social work and is now a social worker–therapist. My father's a banker. He gets to work at six-thirty in the morning and leaves at six at night. I learned from him that work does come first, the work ethic. I learned that you make up your mind what you want to do and you go wherever that takes you. Never be limited. We moved around a lot because of his work. I went through high school in three different states. After college, I moved back to Boston because I could live with my parents rent-free, and I didn't know what the hell I was doing. [Laughs.]

Did I have any idea what I wanted to do? No . . . No, *no* clue. Didn't care, didn't really think about it. The advice older people gave me was, "Kate, you're not supposed to know what your career is going to be in college. Relax, have a good time, learn as much as you can, get out, and then decide what you want to do." I took it to heart. When I started, I thought I'd be a business major, but instead I became a psychology major. I went to a liberal arts college and there *was* no business. [Laughs.]

Senior year, I wasn't anxious about what I'd do next, but my father and I wound up getting in a big fight about it. Before graduating, students had to do a project, sort of a senior thesis. I did one and it was going great—I got an award from the department. My father kept saying, "You have to start a job search." And I kept saying, "You have no respect for the work I'm doing. This project is important." And he kept saying, "It's *not* important, you have to get a job—*that's* important."

I'd done two summer internships during college at two different banks. It's different being an intern than actually working. You know it's not forever; and then, of course, the first two months of *any* job are interesting. Everyone's nice to you, not all that much is expected of you, and you don't get involved in the politics.

The first internship was at my father's bank. I worked for a woman in the marketing department who had no one else working under her. I ended up sort of managing their bonus-point award program. For every four dollars you spent, you got one bonus point and you could collect them and order from a catalog. All these invoices came in, and I had to xerox and make binders for them and double-check the billing. I'd never done anything like that, and it became my little baby. I also helped with a phone survey, learned the Lotus computer program, stuff like that. . . .

One thing internships provide is the opportunity to learn *how* to work in an office, what that involves, how people react, what the word *politics* means. Once, one of the executives asked me to type something up quickly, he needed it in ten minutes. I said, "I'll try," but there was *no way* I could do it because I didn't yet have the skills. One of the secretaries said, "That guy's *such* a jerk!" I realized, "Oh, people think people are jerks here." Oh . . . It dawned on me . . . Being in an office doesn't mean people leave their personalities at home. Some people are jerks and other people realize that. I guess I had imagined that everything would be very proper.

I was invited to birthday parties and learned what office friendships are, and office dialogues, and how you can become attached to people you work with. You're probably not going to be best friends forever, but you can still become very close. You learn some of the simple skills: how do you answer a phone, how do you get to work on time, how do you make friends in the office, how do you dress, how does a filing system work? [Laughs.] And just what does that word *politics* mean? You get accustomed to the idea there's a hierarchy. My boss that summer had a cubicle—she wasn't at the right level to have an office. The only empty work space was an open office, and it was right by her. *I* got the office! [Laughs.]

You learn that you have a boss, you have to get things approved—there isn't always a lot of autonomy. Actually, I had quite a lot of autonomy at that job, because my task was menial. They weren't going to sit over me at the xerox machine. There was one very dynamic guy I really liked. He came in one Friday in jeans. I said, "What's up with the outfit?" He said, "I'm taking a vacation day." "So why are you *here*?" "Because I want to get some work done without being interrupted." I thought, "Oh . . . isn't that interesting. This is how it works, this is what some people do." I also thought, *"You're crazy!"* [Laughs.] He wound up quitting. He said, "Because I'm not appreciated enough here." Only years later did I realize what he really meant: that he wasn't allowed the creative freedom he wanted. It made me question how organizations work, how people are evaluated and valued.

The next internship was in the consumer loan department of a bank that, as it turned out, was on its way to dead. The first bank was *so* tight—very professional, very well run, people got things done. And at this bank, I wasn't working with the high-level executives. I was doing a lot of mundane tasks, working with other people who did a lot of mundane tasks. We had one project where we had to get all the files out of storage. I had to dress in jeans and come in and pull files. And then we prepped them so they could all be microfiched. Well, the boxes sat around for two weeks after we pulled and got them prepped. Then the company decided they didn't have enough money to do the microfiche. [She shakes her head.] Highly efficient.

But it was interesting to be in that environment. It was so foreign to me to be around people in their thirties or forties who were basically working clerkship jobs. Everyone at the other bank, and everyone in my family, has always been very ambitious, go as far as you can go. You're always trying to get to the next level, do the best job you can, never stop, never rest . . . One of the guys I worked with was a great guy, about forty, having a good time, going to Cape Cod every weekend with his family, da da da. All I could ask myself was *why?* Why doesn't he try to do more? Why is he happy doing this? He may have been bored, but he seemed *happy*.

One of my jobs was to run the microfiche department when the woman who handled it went on vacation. It was the worst—*worst!* All you did was file microfiche by number—and we're talking *nine-digit* numbers. [Laughs.] *All day!* That's *all* I did. The woman came back from vacation, and I got to talking to her. She'd had a baby when she was thirteen, didn't even know she was pregnant. Everyone at this job was so different from the people I was used to. I learned there are *huge* differences between organizations, between corporate cultures. It was an eye-opener in terms of, well, they're both banks. A bank's a bank, right? [Laughs.] But, nooo . . . Huge difference.

When I finished college, I had no clue how to go about a job hunt from scratch. Nobody sat me down and said, "What are you interested in, what do you want to do? Let's talk about how to target and find the right people to talk to at those companies—let's talk about making up a "to do" list. The first thing is to think about your ideal job. What do you *want* to do? If you're not sure, who can you talk to who will help you? Someone who can tell you the good and bad parts, the fun and not so fun parts. "What's it like working in a bank?" "Well, you really have to wear the dark blue suits every day, even if you're a woman"—things like that. I came to realize I didn't want to wear a dark blue suit every day, I didn't want to be uptight all the time. When we have meetings at the advertising agency where I now work, we all joke around, gossip, trade stories about our love lives. It's all women on the account, which makes it a very interesting dynamic.

I graduated from college, and meanwhile, my parents had bought a house on Cape Cod. I went there while I was looking for work. The only way I knew how to get a job was to either look in the paper or do the who-does-a-friend-of-the-family-know thing. Of course, my father gave me the name of all of his friends and contacts. You're always told it's not what you know—it's who you know; and connections certainly do help in terms of getting your foot in the door. There was no job placement at my college, I mean *nothing*. Whatever you did, you did on your own.

I didn't know about cold-calling, targeting a company, targeting an organization. I would go to the beach, read the paper, and send out fourteen, fifteen letters a week. We had a P.O. box, and I made friends with a lady down at the post office. Every day, "Hear anything, Kate?" Now, one thing I didn't realize is that mail is a *bad* thing when you're looking for a job. [Laughs.] If you get the letter, don't even open it, just throw it away. If they want you, they'll *call*.

At the beginning of the summer I was like, "Oh, well . . ." I didn't want to be working yet anyway. Near the end, though, I was like, "Oh, *nooo*. What am I going to do?" And then I got seven rejection letters all in the same day. That was disheartening. [Woefully.] "I didn't think it would be *this* hard." I'd sent out maybe 200 résumés. I applied to anything that sounded interesting.

At one point I interviewed with a private detective agency. It was basically work on a freelance basis, which I wasn't too excited about, and it sounded kind of slimy. They explained that I'd be going into an organization, working there, becoming friends with people, figuring out who's stealing, and ratting on them. And then there was the, "You might be involved in a drug bust. We'll arrest everyone, and then, of course, we'll let you go." I thought . . . [Looks askance.] "I don't know about all *that*." I finally got a job behind a department store makeup counter.

I almost took that job, but then I got offered a job at a bank. Of course, my father knew the vice chairman there. I know the word was sent down: find this girl a job. I said, "Cool—got a job!" I applied for one position, but I didn't like the woman I would have been working for and interviewed poorly. I didn't get it. They brought me back to interview for a job in customer corporate service, and that one I got—and it was *horrible*.

They made a *big* production out of training me. Basically, as a customer corporate service rep, you're answering the phones all day for corporate customers. They can be a little mom-and-pop shoe repair or a medium-sized company. I went through this training period for three weeks—and, really, the training period should be two days. Everyone said, "Wow, you caught on quickly!" [Laughs.] Fifty percent of the calls are, "Can you tell me what my balance is?" Well, that's really hard. There were maybe one or two interesting calls a day. It was heinously boring. You're a human robot for the most part.

I did this for eight months, started looking for another job after three. But I have to say, I had a great time there. I made friends with two of my co-workers, Ben and Charles, and we had a blast. We would play pranks, rearrange each other's desks, stuff like that. Someone had given me a teddy bear for Christmas, and they strung it up by rubber bands between Ben's and my cubicles. It was like this tetherball. We'd whip it at each other's head. [Laughing harder and harder.] You're on the phone and all of a sudden, *whoosh*—it flies by your head. We'd tape the receiver down so when someone tried to answer the phone, it'd just keep ringing and ringing. Just to kind of get through our day. The first order of the day was to critique what the other people were wearing. That was a ritual. "Ben, do you have a mirror?" [Laughs.] "Charles—your iron broken?"

There was one supervisor for every three employees, it was *ridiculous*. The supervisors, from all I could tell, did nothing. Everything was monitored: they knew how long you were on the phone, how many calls you had gotten, how many calls were in queue. If there were calls in queue they would scream out, *"We have fifteen calls in queue!"* You'd think to yourself, "Then answer the goddamn phone . . . *Hello!* I'm already talking to a customer." [Laughs.]

You were told that the object of the game was to satisfy the customer, but really it was to get the customer off the phone as fast as you could, and sometimes you'd *want* to. I'd been there maybe a month when this guy called, "I need to get a balance on the account." I asked for his last deposit amount. It was one of the pieces of information needed to give him account access. He screamed, *"You stupid bitch, if I had that information I wouldn't need to call you in the first place!"* and hung up! I was like, *"Oh, my God . . ."* I told Ben, who said, "I know who that was." Ben called the guy back, and when he answered Ben took the phone receiver and banged it on the desk four or five times. [Laughs.] We did some terrible stuff. I remember one Friday afternoon, four-thirty, I couldn't *wait* to get out of there. I get this call from a woman who was pretty much screaming. "I've been transferred to *five different people!"* I said, [sympathetically] "Uh-huh," and I . . . [she mimes very gently placing the receiver in its cradle]. I just couldn't help it. Oh, that was awful—I would never do that now.

The job was terrible, but they tried to make it as good as they could in some ways. They were like, "Kate's really smart, so we're going to make her the head contact person on this difficult account." They said, "Kate, when they have problems, they're going to call you—OK?" I was like, "Yippee . . ." Oh, I feel *so* blessed now . . .

Some people had been there for, like, five years. A lot of them had no ambition and an attitude of, "Well, there isn't anything better out there—why bother?" My feeling was, "This sucks! Get me out *now*." I realized this was a dead-end job—this was not your open door into the rest of the bank. And I also realized I didn't want to be a banker.

My next job was in the marketing department of a mail-order catalog company. For the first six months it was great. I basically worked on Lotus 123 all day, doing sales analysis and reports. I managed two of the catalogs and the mailings, wrote up the instructions on how to do the merge–purges, made sure they were done right. But that soured after a while, too, because I stopped learning.

This was a family-owned company, and I realized there was no upward mobility—this was *it*. It was a very unhealthy place, by which I mean that not many people liked working there. And there was a *lot* of competition. I had a friend in merchandising who was vying with another girl for a promotion. She would write my friend memos and backdate them, then stick them in the *bottom* of my friend's "in" box. Then in front of the boss she'd say, "Well, why didn't you do that? I wrote you a memo." My friend would say, "I didn't get that memo." "Well, let's look in your box. Oh, *there* it is." *Really* ugly.

Also, I made some mistakes. I was very idealistic; I wasn't as politically smart as I could or should have been. I didn't realize how controlling the family was. I thought I would have more creative freedom, more room to say, "We could do this, we should do that." I tried and I was shot down—*oh*, was I shot down! [Condescendingly.] "Kate, I don't pay you to *think*." My boss told me that! "I pay you to be my worker bee and to catch mistakes."

During my year review she said, "You have made friends with the wrong people in the company, you have wasted enough of the company's time." She was so harsh and horrible, I broke down in tears—and I *don't* cry. I wasn't expecting a shining review, but my work had been impeccable, she couldn't criticize my work. She was criticizing my *attitude*. She had some points, but what she lacked was the ability to look within herself and say, "Why? Why has Kate's attitude changed over the past five months?" The work had gotten boring, there were no new challenges. And things like, when I'd have to ask a question, because otherwise I couldn't proceed with the work, she'd wave me off: "No, no, not now." So I'd figure, OK, fine—I guess I'll go out and smoke a cigarette . . .

The first six months were great, the next three were shaky, the final three horrible. I had two good friends there—or so I thought. I told them both I was interviewing for another job. Someone told my boss.

I've always wondered how that got to her. Since then, I'm *much* more careful. You can't overestimate work relationships . . . unless you don't care who knows what.

At that point, I had been working for almost two years. While looking for another job, I had a revelation: when you're first out of college, it's hard to get a job if you haven't had one—when your résumé's blank, it's tough. So maybe those first two years are about paying the dues and getting something on your résumé, just so you can get someplace *else*. I thought, "I've been in two sucky situations, I don't want to go there again. . . ." For the first time I said, "What do I want? What am I interested in? What are my skills? Where does that put me?" I thought about it. I said, "Well, I like psychology, I like research, I like business . . ." I decided I wanted to work for a market research company.

A friend of the family's had gotten me the second job, and I thought, "Let's *stop* going with that route." In the yellow pages, I found the addresses for all the market-research companies within a twenty-mile radius. I wrote each president a letter, sent a résumé, and got four interviews. I was offered a position as the director of field services at a market-research company. I *loved* that title—I was title-drunk. Of course, I was completely underpaid. . . . [Laughs.]

It was a small market-research company run by a woman who had started it out of her attic maybe ten years earlier. My job was to oversee all of the projects from the moment they came in the door up until the data was collected. I had thirty part-time telephone recruiters, and their supervisors, working under me. I worked there for two years and it was *great*. I mean, it was lousy in some ways, as any job is, really—and I think you have to realize that: there are lousy parts to any job. But we were all around the same age and we hung out together, even after work, there was just so much camaraderie.

I had a great deal of responsibility and autonomy. The first six months I was learning the job, but after I got the hang of it, I was basically left on my own, nobody watched over my shoulder. If we got a new project in the door, it'd be like, "Here, go ahead." I looked forward to going to work to a certain extent. I enjoyed being there and being responsible for things. I mean, this is your project, your budget—if you're under budget or over budget, it's 'cause of *you*.

But there was basically no place for me to move up in that company. The next thing up was, what? A vice president? *That* wasn't going to happen. The president hired bright people out of college and didn't pay them much. Bright, ambitious people will take a lower-paying job and then get out. That's what she wanted—that was part of her business model.

I decided to go to business school because I knew that in order to go where I wanted to go, wherever that *was*, I needed to fill in some gaps. I wanted to stay in the marketing arena—although in what context, I wasn't really sure. I didn't have a lot of what that took: the accounting, the finance, the formal marketing education. And I was thrilled to go back to school. [Laughs.] After working—*absolutely!* I completely invested myself in learning and mastering everything that was taught, I worked my *butt off*. It was *so* different from college. Going to college, for me, had been expected. It was a lot of fun, and if you were interested in something you did a great job, and if you weren't, you sort of got it done and who cared?

I graduated from business school, and to my surprise, found the next job hunt difficult. I thought, "I've got an MBA, I've got work experience, the market's growing—what's the problem?" It was a hell of a lot harder than I thought it was going to be. I still used a lot of who-you-know tactics, which are important. But I was more focused. I said, "I'm looking for a marketing job in a consumer products company or service company. Who do you know, what companies do you recommend I look at?"

I sent out a lot of résumés, I got a few interviews . . . for jobs I didn't want. I had a much clearer idea by then: "This isn't the environment I want, the job I want, or who I want to be working for." It's nice when you're in a position not to *have* to accept the first job offered. When you can sit back and say, "Is this *really* a person I want to work for?" This person is going to be my mentor, my teacher, my boss. This person is going to have a great effect on my life, well-being, and happiness over the next X amount of time. You have to work for a while before you start to recognize qualities of people in organizations. After awhile, when interviewing, you learn to look around the office, assess the environment. Arrive early so you have a chance to sit in the waiting room and observe. See people's comings and goings, how they dress, how they act, how they interact—are they very formal, is it a friendly environment, how does it feel?

While I was looking, I wound up temping for two weeks, making pretty decent money—thirteen dollars an hour. If I did an hour's work, that was a busy day. But I felt like *such* a loser. "Here I am with my MBA and look at me! I'm a temp, a secretary!" Then I got an interview at an ad agency I'd sent my résumé to a couple of months prior. They offered me a job as an associate account executive, which is sort of the lowest rank on the account management side. They offered me *way* less than I wanted, and I was doing menial stuff and bored out of my mind. I knew I wasn't going to like it when I took it, but I desperately needed a job. I figured, I can jump ship. They promised me a promotion within six months, and of course, once I got in the door my boss started talking about promoting me within a *year*. I started looking for another job after a couple of months.

A friend told me about an advertising agency in New York. They offered me a job and I took it. I'm an account executive, working on the direct side of the business for a new product launch. General marketing is most of the TV advertising that you see; direct marketing is all direct response. I've worked there for over six months.

I had a crazy boss from hell the first three weeks. She was very, "You don't need to know that, you don't need to understand, just do this." She quit, thank God. Even after she left, when I called to ask her a question, she said, "Well, *you* don't need to understand that"! [Laughs.] I tried in the nicest way I could to say, "Well, yes, I do." "No, you don't—if you can just understand this part, you're better off than most people." I wanted to *kill* her!

I've learned how the agency works. There are so many different departments: creative, production, media, traffic . . . You need to know how everything gets routed, and who you talk to, who knows how to do what. It was different at the other agency: they held your hand to go sharpen a pencil. Here it's "Go figure it out." Everybody should be thrown into the deep end. It's challenging. Sometimes it's frustrating and it sucks. But at least you feel you're using your brain. When it's all done, you can say, "I figured that out. *I* got that done."

My advice is to never stay in a situation where you're unhappy. Never. If people say you can't get another job or there's nothing out there, keep looking and be inventive. Look in the yellow pages and write to every single one of those companies. A co-worker at my last job worked as an associate account executive for two years and *hated* it. Hated it, hated it, *hated it!* Stayed for *two* years. Then moved over to the other side of the company and did the same *thing* for nine more months. She waited almost *three years* in this shit position before getting a promotion. You know what? That's a hell of a long time when you're young. That's wasted time. You're not making any money, and you're not doing anything interesting and you're not happy! That's *ridiculous*. Life's too short. I kept asking her, "*Why the hell* did you stay there for so many years? What are you, *crazy*?" She'd shrug her shoulders. I don't know how she did it.

Think carefully about the doors that are open for you. Always look for more. And definitely *never* take a job as a secretary: you don't move up because people forever think of you as *just* a secretary. One of the smartest people I know has been a secretary for years and it kills me. Some of those jobs are easy to get and have good benefits, so they're very tempting. But my friend got stuck. She became the *executive* secretary, but you're only going to make so much more money, you're only going to do so much more interesting stuff.

I read a book called *The New Rules*.* It tracks fifteen different Harvard MBAs and their careers. What they found was that people who

---

* John P. Kotter, *The New Rules: How to Succeed in Today's Post-corporate World* (New York: Free Press, 1995).

jumped around a lot wound up doing better. I think it's important to figure out what *kind* of stuff you want to do. Like, for me, if I want to be in marketing, well, you know what? I'm damn glad I worked in the mail-order catalog company—I learned a *hell* of a lot. I'm glad I worked at the market-research company—I learned a *hell* of a lot. I'm really glad I got my MBA. I'm really glad I'm at the agency now. But it's all walking down the same path, it's all walking in the same direction. So, if you're interested in music, do everything you can in music: go work for a label, find a band, do whatever—as long as it's all in the same arena of industry and you're learning skills that can be helpful in other areas.

Sometimes it takes a long time of piecing the pieces together before you get to where you want to be. I was talking to someone who's about to graduate from college, and she was all excited. I said, "It's great that you're done, and I don't mean to put a downer on you, but the first couple of jobs you get probably aren't going to be ideal. You're probably not going to figure out what you want to do right off the bat. Your first job might really suck. You have to be ready for that and realize it's part of your learning process."

Job hunting is something I hate. I *hate* it. Though I'm looking for a job now, and sort of enjoying it—because I don't care. I have a good job, I'm not dying to get out, I'm just exploring my options. I'm not as challenged as I was, and I want to make more money. I might stay in the agency business for another year or two and then skip over to the client side. Go work for Revlon or Estée Lauder or Procter and Gamble, work in their marketing or advertising department. How do you get to the client side? Well, you can make that jump fairly easily if you've been at the ad agency for a couple of years. It's not that hard to piece together your options. You don't have to know exactly where you're heading, but know enough not to put yourself in a dead-end situation. For example, I heard about this great job when I was looking—to be someone's personal assistant, making $43,000 a year. But what do you do after that?

A lot of people's mistake is they don't keep their eyes open, they pigeonhole themselves. When they realize they're unhappy in a situation, they get upset, they feel trapped. It's important for people to realize, "Hey—life is fluid." I almost married this guy from Scotland and moved over there. What the hell would I have done over there? Raise sheep? Who knows? Life is fluid, forever fluid. You never know what's going to happen.

ROBERT RICHMAN

Robert, twenty-seven, is up front about his academic history: "Me and school have never been the greatest jibe in the world. There's always been some other thing that I enjoyed more." A serious tennis player, he gave up sports in high school and turned his energy to student government and organizing students in civic and community service activities. After serving as a page at the Democratic National Convention of 1988, he was hooked on the excitement and logistics and intricacies of political work. "So much of politics is managing relationships — and it attracts strange and different kinds of people, with interesting habits and backgrounds and idiosyncrasies. It's given me a larger perspective, it's made me more accepting and open-minded." He sees campaign work as a young person's game, but feels confident in his ability to do whatever work he chooses. "What I've gotten from politics are useful skills, some of which I may never use again, some of which I use every day. In politics, you meet people in all walks of life who can help you do whatever you want to do."

Until I was fourteen or fifteen, I wanted to be a professional athlete. I got into tennis at a young age, and it was everything to me for a long, long time. I would go to school, and afterward play tennis for hours and hours and hours. I played tournaments and was ranked and toured around the Midwest.

The thing about tennis is that it's an individual, and very psychological, sport. You learn how to control your emotions, how to push *yourself.* You can't lean on or hide behind anybody else. It's just you out there. There are severe codes of conduct: you can't scream and yell, you can't throw your racket, you can't curse. Those are hard lessons to learn when you're twelve, thirteen, fourteen years old, especially with a whole lot of people watching you. You have to act mature. I learned self-reliance and discipline and how to work very hard—in the summers eight to ten hours a day, out there in the sun. Even though I loved it, it still involved a lot of discipline. I'd rather have been sitting around watching TV or going out with friends. You do have to give things up.

The tennis coaches wanted me to give up all other sports, but I wouldn't. You learn a whole different set of skills playing on a team. I often use things I learned about sports and teamwork in working with a campaign staff. Campaigns are results-driven: you win or you lose. There's the adrenaline rush, the competitiveness, the teamwork.

In 1996, I was the campaign manager for Darlene Hooley, a Democrat running for Congress in Oregon's Fifth District—huge, diverse, a *crazy* district. In staff meetings, I'd find myself paraphrasing my high-school soccer coach—and I'd thought he was *insane*. [Laughs.] He would say, "You gotta want it, you gotta breathe it, you gotta live it, you gotta love it, it's gotta be *everything*." He said that to win you have to *want* it more, what means as much if not more than skill or speed or size is *desire*. I would talk to the campaign staff about the sacrifices you have to make; about how you have to put the good of the greater interest over your own.

A campaign is very different from most work environments because it's completely consuming—it becomes your entire life. To win, you have to have workers who are pretty much willing to give up everything. It's very hard and very demanding, and you get burned out. Part of the manager's job is to motivate folks to keep pushing. But really, when I found myself directly quoting my soccer coach, it was kind of scary.

I gave up my dream of being a tennis pro freshman year in high school. To be quite fair, I was never the best—I wasn't a prodigy. But you have a dream and you fool yourself. But that year I seriously hurt my back, and I also grew eight inches in thirteen months. I was overwhelmed—and I realized I wasn't willing to sacrifice every other aspect of my life to play tennis.

In high school, I spent a lot of time organizing. A friend and I started a Students Against Drunk Driving chapter at the school; we put together community service opportunities for students. If there weren't opportunities out there, we'd create them. I was involved in different aspects of student government. Since students are a big part of the school, I thought they should have some voice in what happens there. Part of all that activity was about me and my buddies looking for ways to get out of class. Part of it was that I always felt school should be about more than just books.

I had a blast in high school and was fortunate enough to skate by without too much trouble—other than the fairly regular "you're not living up to your potential." I used to refer to myself as "Potential Boy." [Laughs.] I think it was more a question of having something I really wanted to do. And math and science and English and social studies and history were never things I really wanted to do. I was always skeptical about how school actually applies to what you do in the world.

In my family, it was assumed you went to college and then figured out what you wanted to do. My mother worked part-time as a college career counselor. My father's a professor, and the director of a university-affiliated research group for child welfare. My parents complained about things, but they never said, "God, if I could, I wouldn't be doing this."

Toward the end of high-school senior year, in the summer of 1988, a friend of my parents offered me the opportunity to work as a page at the Democratic National Convention. I thought rather than just going to the convention, I'd spend the summer volunteering in the state Party office. It was just something to do. You're kind of weaned on politics when you grow up in Chicago. I watched the news some, and '88 was a pretty big political year. I mean, for all of the life I could remember, Ronald Reagan was president. So the idea that, "Hey, there could actually be a *different* president"—was pretty cool.

My first day, I walk into the office of the state Party downtown, sit down, and wait for somebody to talk to me. I'm seventeen—I'm *terrified*. There are no private offices, just one big open room. All of a sudden, an enormous hollering and *unbelievable* ruckus erupts in the office. These two people are absolutely *screaming* at the top of their lungs. One is standing on a chair, cursing like you wouldn't believe. Then the other says, "I *quit*." The guy on the chair says, "*Good!* I would have fucking *fired* you if I had the chance!" The guy on the ground storms off. I'm looking around and I turn to someone walking by and say, "Is this normal?" And he says, "You should have been here *yesterday*. Somebody bit the boss!" [Laughs.] My first exposure to life in politics . . .

In the course of a typical day, I did every piece of scut work you could ever imagine. I xeroxed and filed and figured out room assignments in hotels. I did what nobody else wanted to do. Then we went to the convention. As a page, your jobs are as glorious as fetching orange juice for delegates, making sure the office is staffed, making sure that everybody gets their newspapers, has their schedules. . . . Mostly you're following orders. But having volunteered all summer, I had gotten to know the staff, and as a head page was given a little more responsibility, and more interesting jobs to do than the new volunteers.

It was grueling. We were up at five-thirty or six every morning and weren't in bed before two or three every night for a week. The hours between twelve-thirty and three were mostly spent partying, going to huge fund-raisers and glamorous events. But the rest of the day we worked really hard. With your first exposure to politics being a national convention, and with all the excitement and energy, glitz, and glamor that goes along with it—how could I *not* be hooked? I was on the convention floor when Jesse Jackson gave his "Keep Hope Alive" speech and when Ann Richards gave the "Silver Spoon" speech. At that time, Dukakis or Bush was on TV every night. You felt some remote connection. Even though I was just fetching papers and making copies, I felt part of a larger thing. It was real; it was as real as it gets.

There wasn't anything complicated about a lot of the work I did; it was mostly fitting pieces of the puzzle together. One thing was to help give out credentials, which are those little passes people wear around their neck. That's your status symbol: if you have a certain color you can get somewhere, if you have another color you can get somewhere else. I learned very quickly how that works and who you have to keep happy. I learned about the hierarchy of politics at every level, down to the staff and pages. It was all logistics, and while it wasn't overly intellectual, it *was* sort of challenging and fun. I remember sitting at the convention thinking, "I don't ever want to miss another one of these, this is a blast!"

That fall, I went to college. The following summer, I was back working for the Party. Michael McGann, then–executive director of the state Party, told me, "We believe that part of our job is to train young people on how to do this." I was fortunate in that I stumbled on a group of people interested in teaching and in giving me more responsibility than I probably was ready for. I'm sure part of the reason they liked having me around was that my parents could support me and I was free labor. [Laughs.] I now exploit people the same way.

In politics, everybody always wants something from somebody and because of that, relationships are incredibly important—it's a whole lot easier to get things if you have good relationships. The whole idea that you're representing something other than yourself is weird enough, in and of itself. When you're out there and you're in a meeting, what you say reflects back on how people view the Party. The implications of what you do are critical, and you can really screw things up by saying something careless. But there's politics in everything. People say, "*Ew*, politics is gross." I say, "Tell me how your office functions. How different is it from what you're pooh-poohing?" The same pettiness and interoffice politics are everywhere. And relationships are important in all work places.

In most political organizations, there are one or two people in charge of maintaining relationships with various groups. It's hard to explain what we do. . . . It's multilayered. For example, say the president's coming and we need to deal with the Secret Service, and get ten thousand people into a room four days from now. To explain what's really involved in getting something like that done, how hard it is, what skills you need, is complicated. It took probably six, seven years before my parents had a real understanding of what I did, of how much I was responsible for, of how hard I worked.

In the summer of '89, I worked as an intern for the field director of the Party, Chris Meister—he's a trial lawyer now. He was in charge of the grass-roots piece, of working with the local Party units, right down to the precinct level. He made sure we kept in touch with the black ministers groups, or the Hispanic political groups, or organized labor. I was his Boy Friday—and I can honestly say, he very much enjoyed having a Boy Friday! [Laughs.] Meister had been weaned on politics, he was a natural—and I looked up to him, he was impressive. You hear stories about colorful figures who love to yell and scream, and he was one of those. He has what people call a "large personality."

That summer, we started a survey project designed to see what shape the grass-roots organization outside of the city was in. It was a *huge* undertaking, hundreds and thousands of dollars. Nothing like it had been done before. I was on the ground level, doing mailings to the committeemen, but also involved in figuring out how to go about it. The logistics were complicated. The people I worked for always explained things: "Here's what you're doing and why you're doing it, and here's how it's part of a bigger picture"—which was really important. Otherwise, it would have just been stuffing, sealing, stamping . . . They taught me a *way* of thinking about things.

They tried to talk me into dropping out of school so I could keep working for them. Something I love about politics is that it's one of the few workplace situations where you have cross-generational relationships, where people of *all* different ages work on a level playing field, work with a lot of mutual respect. And while there's structure, it's not the corporate ladder: you don't move from this to that, you don't always know where you're going to go next. So I wasn't judged by my age, I wasn't judged by my appearance—I was judged by what I produced, and they liked what I produced. They even offered to pay me! [Laughs.]

In school I complained when this one professor would give us essay questions like, "How could World War I have been prevented? Answer in two pages." He said, "If you can't write it in two or three pages, it's not worth saying." Well, in politics, it's got to be done in two sentences. There is *no* wasted language, *no* wasted thought. And it's not you writing to get a grade. The stuff that I was doing—there were real people on the other end of it.

I finished out the school year, but took a leave to work for the Party during the spring, summer, and fall of 1990. I was given a title, the whole thing. I did the same kind of work, but in a staff position. One day I was sitting around the house and Michael McGann, the executive director, called to tell me that Chris Meister had to leave in order to manage an important campaign—that of a woman running for a state office. The thing about politics is that you start to think strategically. To have the foresight to say, "This is not necessarily good for what we're trying to do right now, but it's important for other reasons." Part of it's sacrificing, part of it's strategizing—standing back and seeing a larger picture.

I said, "Who's going to be the field director?" He said, "*You* are." I said, "Yeah, right!" He wasn't kidding. I said, "This is ridiculous! I'm nineteen years old, I have *no* idea what I'm supposed to be doing." He said, " I'm going to tell you what to do. We think you can do it." So all of a sudden I was the field director of the state Party! Of course, they didn't pay me more to become the field director—so I had a second job delivering pizzas!

Then there was a change in Party leadership and priorities. The survey was dropped, and I was out of a job. It was April and I couldn't go back to school until the fall anyway—not that I wanted to. [Laughs.] I had an opportunity to be the campaign manager for an Illinois Senate race. Campaign work was something I enjoyed and felt good at, I felt like it came naturally. Taking the job seemed to make sense. But when I looked more seriously into the guy running, I realized he was *sort* of pro-choice, but not really. He was a moderate, but nobody knew exactly what he stood for; and he refused to release his financial disclosure forms. I had some real questions, there was something in my gut that didn't really take to him. But the sheer ability to jump up a notch and be a player was very seductive.

Michael McGann took me aside and said, "You're now a very dangerous technocrat. You understand this world, you understand the technology, you understand *how* to do it"—by which he meant, I knew how to put together a grass-roots organization, how a campaign is run, how money is raised—the nuts and bolts, the tools. He said, "But you have no clue why you're doing it and what you're doing it for. What you are now is a very dangerous sort of automaton. You need to figure out why, you need to find some center, some values and beliefs and reasons to do it." It took me by surprise. I said, "Well, I'm doing it because I'm a Democrat." He said, "It's got to be more than that. What do you believe in?"

Shortly after that, someone called and said, "How'd you like to come work for a liberal who doesn't have a prayer in hell of winning?" This was for Paul Wellstone's U.S. Senate race in Minnesota. McGann had told me: "A good organizer can go anywhere in the world, parachute out of a plane, land on the ground and be able to organize." The nature of campaigns, for people who do it for a living, is itinerant. You go to different states, some to different countries, to find campaigns to work on. I thought about what McGann had said to me about values and beliefs, and said, "Sure." I ended up on the Wellstone campaign.

The campaign was not run by professional political people: it was grass-roots, a whole different political world. And it turned out I had more experience than most. The Wellstone campaign really gave me faith, and I think it would have even if we'd lost. We beat a guy that spent eight to ten million dollars; a guy who ran sleazy ads and a sleazy campaign; a guy *nobody* thought could be beaten because he was so well funded by oil and tobacco and conservative Republicans. I remember calling McGann at some point during the campaign and saying, "Now I know what you were talking about."

And then I went on and worked for lots of liberals that couldn't win. [Laughs.] Still do! In 1994, I stayed in Minnesota and was the political director and deputy campaign manager for another U.S. Senate race that we lost, which was crushing. But actually, I've been very fortunate in that I've had a number of winners. I can't complain. And at this point,

I don't understand how somebody can be in politics and campaigns and not have a driving belief. You have to have some sort of gut reason besides money and power. Because, unless you're a James Carville, you don't make a lot of money doing this kind of work.

I saw *The War Room*.* I wish campaigns were really like that. I would *love* to put my feet up on the desk and say, "I think we should do this," and have fifty people make it their life's work to make that one sentence happen. If you see *The War Room* and you want to go into politics because you think it's going to be like that . . . Anybody going into campaign politics because they think it's glamorous is in for a big crash. It's *not* glamorous.

When I interview somebody for a job, one of the first things I try to find out is why they're doing it. You're not going to be in the spotlight working on a campaign. You're not going to be in the paper. If anybody on a campaign I run is quoted in a newspaper without my permission, they're fired. If you're doing it for glory, you're going to be miserable . . . unless you have a really demented version of what glory is. If you really want to be *in* politics, to work on campaigns to get people elected, it *ain't* glamorous. I would much rather have somebody who is going to roll up their sleeves and work incredibly hard, be committed and passionate and have a lot of common sense than somebody who has more experience or more education. If someone asks me, "How often will I get to travel with the candidate," I'm not going to hire them.

Some people really love doing advance work, but most of what that involves is holding the rope for the president or candidate, or making sure everything's set in the room, or figuring out how to move a candidate from one place to the next when you only have two minutes in each room. Ninety-five percent of what ninety-nine percent of the people working on campaigns do has *nothing* to do with the candidate. It's sitting in either too hot or too cold rooms, with lots of paper and

* A documentary about Bill Clinton's 1992 presidential campaign (dirs. Chris Hegedus and D. A. Pennebaker, 1993).

envelopes and a phone. It's coordinating volunteers. It's going out and talking to old people and young people. It's knocking on doors and asking for money. Even when you're walking around with the candidate, it's not glamorous. It can be fun, but most of the time it's drudgery.

Campaign politics is very much like a disease. It's not a healthy lifestyle: you're eating pizza four times a week, you're drinking too much coffee, and you're surrounded by tons of people who smoke. But there's *nothing* else like it. The adrenaline rush is *huge*. And it can be huge both ways. I tell people, "Never get too high, never get too low." If you do, you're going to drive yourself nuts. There are so many victories and so many defeats that can come, literally, within hours of each other. You can have ten adrenaline rushes a day.

I decided that what I wanted to do in '96 was be a part of trying to take back the House. That it was at least remotely possible, and really, really important. So I went out to Oregon and campaign-managed for the first time. Darlene Hooley, the candidate, was a county commissioner. She'd been able to win countywide in a swing area, so people thought she *might* be able to win a statewide election.

One of the things that's fun about politics is that there's no typical day. You walk in the door of your office, you know what you'd like to have happen, but you have no idea what's actually *going* to happen. I would often start my day on the phone in my apartment at six or seven in the morning, in order to catch people in Washington, D.C. early in their day. I'd spend maybe forty-five minutes doing that, then go into work by nine-thirty, and usually get home around midnight—that's a normal day. Generally, I'd be on the phone anywhere from six to eight hours. I'd get a massage every Friday night. [Laughs.] Oh, what a great thing . . .

I'd talk with people at the National Democratic Party, labor, different organizations. I'd talk with media and direct-mail consultants, pollsters. We'd talk about anything from how we'd been attacked that day to what we wanted to do proactively to how much money we needed to raise. The Democratic Party can only focus on so many campaigns. As the campaign year progresses, the list of those they focus on to win goes from a hundred to seventy-five to fifty to twenty-five to ten. Your job as a campaign manager is to make sure you're always making the cut. As a first-time manager, I spent a lot of time running things by people and getting advice. It was essential strategic work. I believe very strongly, if you don't know then *ask*. In a campaign, you don't have time to make mistakes.

The number-one thing my job involved was making sure the candidate was doing what the candidate needed to do. I give Darlene Hooley a lot of credit because early on she said, "I don't know how to do this. What I need to do is surround myself with people who do know and then listen to them." When my parents came to visit, we had dinner with the candidate. Darlene kept saying to my mother, "He's twenty-six years old. I'm fifty-six and I'm letting him tell me what to do!" That saved a *lot* of headaches. But the first couple of months, I was *scared*. I'd always been a number-two person, which was great because you had input on all the decisions, but you didn't have to make them. And then it's *your* ass on the line, and it's terrifying.

One thing you learn in politics is how to sleep no matter what's going on, because you have to. But when I first realized the gravity of what I was doing, I'd wake up incredibly anxious—it was just overwhelming. My girlfriend, now my wife, was also working on the campaign. I give her a lot of credit for helping me through that while she was working for me and living with me. She has a *whole* different story. [Laughs.] But one of the things you learn in politics is how to shut out the emotion, because in a time of extreme crisis and heightened tension you have to be completely focused and totally dispassionate.

There's nothing on this earth like an election night. Your entire life for the last ten, eleven, twelve months is judged up or down: did you do it right or wrong? People say it doesn't matter if you win or lose, what matters is that you fought. And it's true to some extent: there are fights worth fighting whether you win or lose. But whether you're talking federal or state elections, it's about a vote: that vote is either going to be there for the thing you care about or it's not.

In Hooley's Oregon campaign, the opponent was one of Newt

Gingrich's freshman incumbents. He was on the appropriations committee, a very powerful player. Had he won the election, he would have been in Congress voting *against* freedom of choice, against gay and lesbian people, against people of color, and voting *for* big business, oil, and tobacco, the insurance companies and defense contracts . . . And instead, there's going to be a representative who votes the opposite way on all of those things. It makes an *enormous* difference.

People say, "You can't be a part of the system because we have to change the system." But the reality is, in the Senate, if you get fifty-one votes you make a law. If you change one of those votes, it changes how that's going to happen. It's important that people stand on street corners and yell and scream and make life difficult for politicians. We have to push for change from outside *and* from inside. You could have a million people pushing for change from outside, but if you don't have anybody working for change on the inside, it won't happen.

I love doing this, but being a campaign manager is not my life's work because I don't think you *can* do this for a lifetime. It's too hard. Eventually, I want to have kids, I want to be a father. Running campaigns is a young person's business. That's why I was able to move into a position of authority in my early twenties. Next year, I'll have the opportunity to run a major statewide campaign. Why? Because people in their early-to-mid thirties who have already done it are hanging it up. You need a new generation.

I can see working in politics for a very long time, perhaps as a consultant for organizations. But I'd also love to work for a professional sports team, or do event management. I've planned big events—the skills are very transferable. What's hard is for me to imagine putting on a tie and going to work in an office every day, being a nine-to-fiver. Right now I'm a consultant. I've got four clients, three political, one environmental. I set my own hours, and I *love* working out of my home.

I'm a guy that has never planned his life more than six months in advance, a year at the outside. I *like* the fact that I don't know what I'm going to be doing two months from now, that I've gotten to see different parts of the country. I like change. One of the great things about politics is that you get to know an incredible variety of people, people who live in other parts of the country and think differently. A lot of people go through their whole life, they're straight, they've never known anybody gay; if they're white, they may never have met a black, whatever. I have great friends from all walks of life. I value that. Politics isn't the only way to get that kind of experience, but for me it is because that's all I've ever done. [Laughs.]

When I got into politics I was shy and didn't like talking to people. But you deal with the press and you learn how to watch yourself, how to be careful, how to convince people. If you can convince someone to vote for a candidate, you can convince someone to buy a product, or contribute to a cause. The skills really *are* transferable.

People come out of college, and often they've got the whole world in front of them to choose from, they're not directed in any certain way. You come out of politics in the same kind of way. But I think you can do anything and go anywhere. Of course, you have to have the skills to do whatever you want, but the people I know in politics who have gone back to school for further learning have all done exceptionally well. School is a hell of a lot easier than a campaign. Pretty much anything is easier than a campaign. [Laughs.]

I may run a couple more campaigns, definitely one more in '98. And I'm thinking about 2000, a presidential year. It's going to be a huge moment for our country, for what direction we're going to go in. I've seen a presidential campaign from the very bottom. I'd like to see it from a higher level.

MARC SPIEGLER

In high school, Marc, now twenty-eight, apprenticed in carpentry and construction, giving him his first experience in the satisfaction of hard work and perseverance. After college, a market-research job gave him insight into what he did and didn't like in a work environment. Following lessons in starting a new job, public relations, and the etiquette of resigning, he left. A chance conversation gave him an entirely new direction: journalism. After graduate school, he dove into freelance writing and also worked at a small Chicago newsweekly. He sees freelancing as an acquired skill, involving lessons in self-esteem, in balancing life and work, assertiveness, and foresight. When offered his own column at Chicago's largest monthly magazine, Marc changed jobs. Dealing with increasingly powerful members of the community held new challenges, and gave him the opportunity to reflect on the importance of networking and accountability. For Marc, "there are the jobs you love . . . and there are gigs. There's only one purpose to a gig and that's to make money. By definition, a gig is not a great thing to have. By definition, you want work. If you're going to spend eight hours a day on something, it should be something you love. Why? Because one day you'll wake up and ask, 'Where did fifteen years of my life go?'"

To the extent that my job as a journalist has to do with freelancing, with pitching ideas, with not really doing the nine-to-five thing, my mother's work experience was more important to me than my father's. My dad would go to work someplace else, but I would *see* my mom working. Both parents are academics of one sort or another, and my mother is also an artist. When we were young, she did paper-cuts*—it was something she could do from home. Despite the fact that she was this intellectual, feminist woman, it was important for her to be around my younger brother and me while we were growing up. She's been, to one extent or another, freelance for almost ten years now. Freelance is a particularly tough thing. I learned a lot about surviving as one from her experiences.

In high school I worked in the summer, forty hours a week, doing construction with my history of architecture teacher. His summer project was to work on people's houses. I did different kinds of labor: landscaping, masonry, construction. The job paid three dollars an hour, and I was *ecstatic*. I don't think it's bad for kids in high school to work—I think it's bad for them to work too much. During the school year, I'd work maybe ten hours a week. I don't know how anyone is supposed to work in a convenience store twenty or thirty hours a week and still learn anything. It's better for kids to focus on schooling when they're in school. The two hundred bucks a month they make working in that convenience store is going to cost them two thousand a month for the rest of their lives. It's a simple economic decision.

That job created in me this faith that there's a value to working hard and focusing, that there's a return on the investment of time. Summers, we'd work eight, ten-hour days. My first job was to sand the steps of the risers for a cherry staircase. Cherry is a very hard wood and I would have to hand-sand it with four or five different grades of sandpaper.

You put your head down and focus on the task and when you leave, more exists than when you started. I worked on a number of projects, and I would go around and look at various things I'd built. You're very conscious of having accomplished something. It would be much harder to feel that satisfaction flipping burgers, or waitressing, or stocking shelves. When you build something, there's a physical result to your effort. When you build something, it's *built*.

I learned that outdoor construction in winter was sometimes a bad,

* A paper art form known as Scheerenschnitze, in which one cuts images out of paper then displays them on a sheet of uncut paper.

bad thing. I remember being up on a roof and trying to close off a bay during an unexpected snowstorm. I suddenly realized I was standing on a piece of wet plastic with an open sixty-foot drop in front of me . . . "OK, this is *bad*." I remember mixing loads of cement while standing in a pool of water and holding a metal-tip shovel, feeding gravel into a mixer with a frayed electrical wire. You'd get a little shock if you put the shovel in wrong. Once you've mixed twenty-five loads of cement in an hour in the middle of the August heat, there's not all that much that's going to scare you in terms of hard work. There's this feeling that nothing can break you. You have a belief in yourself.

But long-term, the problem I have with manual labor is that my mind wanders. Once I understand how to do something, I go on automatic pilot. I can't do that with journalism because I'm constantly talking or writing. You can't separate yourself from the task.

In college, I was a political science major. When I graduated, I thought about going to law school but decided not to because lawyers have the highest retention and dissatisfaction rate. A bad combination: a job you hate and can't leave. I thought about being a political operative because politics is fascinating—it's about psychological manipulation and communication, getting out a message. Finally, I thought, "OK, I'll go enjoy life in New York while I think about what to pursue." I took a market-research job with a company called the Daniel Yankelovich Group. He's one of the founding fathers of public opinion research.

First job you get worth any kind of money, you blow more than you make for a while. The first three or four weeks at a new job you're always exhausted. Your brain is processing stuff: "Where's the copier, how do I use the phone system, who is this person and why do they hate that person, is it OK for me to wear jeans?" It's sensory overload, it wipes you *out*. Most bosses won't expect you to be worth shit for about six months. If you're smart, you don't try to do anything else while you're starting a new job. If you're stupid, like me, you fall in love with a woman who's about to leave the country for Switzerland, like I did. . . .

This firm had a very intellectual way of measuring the changing values of America. It was done with anthropologists. They wouldn't ask, "What color car do you like?"—they'd ask, "How do you feel about religion?" I'd hoped it would be a job where I did a lot of political assessment, but it was more along corporate lines. I learned about statistics and how focus groups work. I had the chance to watch client management, to understand how you tailor a pitch to a particular client. These are all skills I use now. I learned about selling, selling, selling. I learned not to compromise the quality of your work *ever* because that always comes back to haunt you. Basically, my understanding of the business world comes from that job.

But the *biggest* thing I learned was that I didn't want to work in that part of the corporate world. I became tremendously frustrated with the corporate system—which takes someone who has a decent intellectual capability and makes them photocopy stuff just because everybody before them photocopied stuff. It's idiotic to have overqualified people doing mindless work. If you need someone to photocopy, hire a high-school kid.

I worked there for almost two years. I got in a rhythm and had the suits, ate the same breakfast every day, walked the same ten blocks to work. Everyone has the urge to create order out of their lives. Some people hone a routine and they're happiest once they've figured out how they can work forty hours, make their money, go on vacation, and get their dry cleaning and shopping done. Other people hone a routine and start going nuts because they wake up on Monday morning and know exactly how their whole week is going to go. I'm in the second group. I loved New York, but on another level I thought, "This is not enough."

I learned another valuable lesson in the process of leaving. A friend of mine had worked there for two years and busted his ass for the company. He'd show up early, take work home. He applied to the graduate school of management at MIT. The president of the company knew, because he'd asked her to write a letter of recommendation.

People kept asking, "Did you get in?" He was accepted at MIT and he planned on continuing to work through August—he was making over two grand a month. [Sourly.] They told him to stop working a month earlier because business was slow . . . When it came my time to leave, I had a friend write my recommendation and I gave them two and a half weeks' notice. I prefer a policy of openness, of frankness, of not screwing people over. I wasn't proud of leaving them in the lurch. But when you see your boss screw someone over, you learn they would do it to you. If they have a history of being good with employees, you owe the same to them. But never be loyal to a company that would fire you at a moment's notice. You have to remember: companies don't own you, they *rent* you.

It's comforting for people to feel like wherever they are is where they're meant to be. Journalists do this all the time: you take the final conclusion and build a progression leading to it. Either you have this theory that there's a hell of a lot of randomness in your life, or you have this theory that everything is fated and it just looks like there's a hell of a lot of randomness. It doesn't matter. No matter which way you look at it, the bottom line is this: coincidence plays a huge part in your life, and every choice you make leads to a different consequence.

How I got into journalism was through talking to an acquaintance. I thought journalism was the coolest profession, but I thought, "Well, I screwed up, I didn't work on my college paper . . . I can't be a journalist." I thought there was this progression. Little did I know that journalism is one of the last few meritocracies around, where if you can do it, you can do it and that's that. I had met a woman who was applying to journalism grad school and said, "I guess you wrote for your college paper." She said, "No, you don't have to have done that, not as long as you have a writing sample." I said, "Well, I've got *tons* of those." In college, teachers had always remarked on the fact that I wrote well, that I enjoyed turning a phrase.

I applied to journalism school. I thought that no matter what I did, journalism would be interesting: I'd be writing, I'd be talking to people. I wanted a profession that I might be happy in, even if I wasn't wildly successful. I took a route that was deliberately risky, and I liked the fact that I wasn't sure I would succeed. Terror is actually a big part of my decision process.

I'm like a broken record when people ask, "What should I do to get into journalism?" I tell them, "Freelance! Freelance for publications that are good and then it'll get seen. Don't take some trade job you're gonna hate." People say, "But I really want to work for such-and-such." I say, "Well, write for them freelance, because then they'll know that you understand what they're trying to do." People have this idea that they're going to come out of college and immediately work for a big-city newspaper. Well, that's not the way it works.

Before graduating from journalism school, I interned at *Windy City Sports*, a midsize Chicago sports magazine. But I did a freelance piece for *New City*, an alternative newsweekly. A friend told me about how skateboarders, because there are no hills in Chicago, go into garages and ride down the ramps. I called *New City* out of the blue, I had the name of an editor over there. I said, "There's an interesting thing about skateboarders in garages." She said, "Go ahead and write it." I spent hours and hours—it ended up being the cover story!

A couple of days after the story appeared, a friend said, "Are you going to apply for their staff writer job?" I had no idea there *was* one. I hadn't been reading the paper's ads! [Laughs.] I wrote *New City* and laid out all my bona fides: I'd been at the Washington Bureau for the Medill News Service, I'd covered Capitol Hill, I had clips from all over the country—I'd done stuff. And I had that cover story. They ended up hiring me, half-time, a hundred and fifty a week, no benefits.

Eventually, I cut a deal where I worked thirty hours a week for *New City* and freelanced on top of that. I was a freelancer with one very stable job, which gave me health insurance. The job didn't pay that much, but it was a great deal. There was a period, where if I was awake, I was thinking about work. I worked seventy, eighty hours a week, weekends, nights. As a freelancer, you have to have self-respect because you're never secure enough—there's *always* more you could have done. After a while, you learn the rhythm that works. You don't walk around feeling you should have done more that day. You say, "OK, I had a good day, I got enough done—I'm going to go relax."

I'm still very hard-driving, but less so than I used to be. If you're in a creative profession, your brain has to do other things, you have to get some down time. You have to see people, you have to be in touch with the society you're writing about, and not just by writing about it. And life is short.

After I broke up with a longtime girlfriend, basically because I was working so hard, a friend said, "If you're young and talented, yeah, you have to push your work forward. But it's more important to do a smaller amount of really good work than to just pump stuff out, do lots of pieces for lots of people." It's better to do higher-quality work, because what really gets noticed is that one great piece, not all those lesser pieces. Volume is not enough.

People think if they're busy, their career is moving forward. That's not necessarily true. It's more important to think about where you want to be three or four years from now. As much as you're dealing with each day's crisis, you also have to put time aside to meet the people who can make things happen for you three years down the road, to develop other contacts within your industry. You have to take the time to dream a bit, to think about what it is you want to do.

I worked for *New City* for two years, but eventually got a better offer. I took it, in part because I'd done what I could do at *New City*. It's better to leave a job too early than too late. The job was as a columnist at *Chicago* magazine, a glossy monthly. I walked back to *New City* after they made the offer. I was thinking, "What am I going to do?" I had this weird feeling in my stomach—I was afraid I wasn't going to be able to do the job. I'd only been a practicing journalist for three years. I'd done good work, but I didn't have the political connections, I didn't have the media connections, I damn sure didn't have the business connections. I said, "I *have* to take this job!" [Laughs.]

It's a good job. I'm a senior editor, which is a good title, and I get a decent salary. I don't have to actually edit anything, which is great. At one point at *New City*, I was promoted and started doing a lot of editing.

It was a higher-status job, but I didn't like it. I wouldn't want to be the managing editor of *any* publication. A managing editor has to pay a lot of attention to detail, has to traffic copy, keep track of how and when people are paid.

My column for Chicago magazine, *Power Lines*, is two pages every month. It has a mix of media, business, and politics. I'm writing in a monthly, and I'm covering the same ground as both the weeklies and the dailies. I can't do anything that's breaking news. I can do speculative stuff, behind-the-scenes stuff, analytical stuff. I spend a lot of time trying to come up with story ideas. Sometimes it's tremendously frustrating. I'll know a lot of really interesting material but I won't be able to write it, because by the time I write it it's old news.

Most of what I do is to point out the foibles and failures, the behind-the-scenes chicanery of powerful people. I cover people in a non-pandering, nonfawning way. I said when I got the job, and I was only half-kidding, that my plan was to make enemies for two years and skip town. That's hyperbole and it's a nice line, but I think it's true. In Washington, good newspapers won't let someone stay on the Pentagon beat for too long because you make too many friends and you make too many enemies. One of the beauties of journalism is that it's sort of accepted that every two or three years, you'll refocus your career.

I don't dress up to go and sit at work and be on the phone. If I'm doing certain things, I wear a tie or a suit. I dress up if I'm going to interview a guy who wears a suit every day, because if I show up in jeans, there's going to be automatic mistrust. Journalism is, to some extent, the process of seduction and abandonment: you're trying to suck people into talking about themselves, but then you don't have time to continue to be as good a friend as you've suddenly become. If you're in the process of trying to get people to reveal things or explain how things work, why throw up another obstacle? So, though I don't own any blue pinstripe suits, I'm not going to wear a zoot suit. The "routine" people are just as happy to wear the same thing every day and happy to cite corporate culture as the reason for doing it. But the bottom line is, in almost any organization, there are people who don't play by the rules and get ahead just fine. If you're really good at what you do, that's what you'll be judged by.

I became aware of the political nature of work early, when my father was blackballed in a university tenure fight. In academia, the pursuit of truth is often a camouflage for politics. What makes academic politics so ugly is that it's *not* naked and raw: it's about tenure, which is about money and security. My own job is political. My job is about making friends, keeping friends, not burning bridges you don't have to burn, helping people out, giving people information. You learn to choose your fights. My father has an intellectual's approach, which is that if you're right, you're right, period. Sometimes you can be right but be wrong to press that advantage. Sometimes being right isn't enough.

The better you are at something, the more likely you are to make enemies. The more a target you become, the more you have to watch your ass. I'm someone who's firing at big targets. If I'm a smart campaign manager, the first thing I do is have opposition research done on my opponent. Then I have it done on myself, so I know every negative thing that someone can say about me. That's the game I play with myself. The question you need to ask yourself when you go outside the rules or open yourself up to criticism is not, "Would my mother buy this defense?" What you need to ask is, "If I hated someone, what would I do with this ammunition? Could I defend this action if people found out about it?" Lots of times they won't, but you've got to think a few moves ahead.

The real secret anyone learns is that there are *no* secrets. If you're going to do something and you don't want people to know about it, do it *alone*. It's important to think about consequences in your professional conduct and in your personal behavior as well. The more responsibility you have, the more consequences you have to think about. It's not just a question of what if you get plastered and throw up and someone from work sees you? It's more subtle stuff. "I've got a big day tomorrow—do I want to sleep enough or do I not care?"

But you can't let work rule your life. Too many people start working and stop living. There's the old maxim: you work to live, you don't live to work. There's a lot of validation and challenge and intellectual content that can be found in work. Work can be a great thing. But for a lot of people I know, that is their life, and the way they measure their life is by how much money they've got.

Money is the easiest form of reward to measure. Because money comes in measurable quantities, you can say, "I'm ten percent happier this year than I was last year because I'm making ten percent more"—in fact, you may be miserable. That's what's great about knowing people outside your job. It's important to remember there are people outside your industry, outside your city or country, who are happy. That's the value of keeping a wide variety of experiences flowing into your life, because you're exposed to different ways to be happy. Sometimes it means you reconsider your work, or where you live.

But a lot of people, they get into this sleep-work-eat-sleep routine, over and over. Americans have this insane attitude toward work. The American dream says anyone can make it. The flipside is, if anyone can make it and you don't, you're a failure, it's *your* fault. Well, not everyone can or wants to be the CEO.

What I've learned is there are the jobs you love, for which you're willing to sacrifice time and money and work for less than you're worth. And there are gigs. There's only one purpose to a gig and that's to make money. By definition a gig is not a great thing to have. By definition, you want *work*. If you're going to spend eight hours a day on something, it should be something you love. Why? Because one day you'll wake up and ask, "Where did fifteen years of my life go?"

I can't imagine leaving journalism, because I love it. What did I do today? I went to work, I made some phone calls, I talked politics with some guy. I wrote, I went to a press event, kept track of who was in the room, met some new people. Essentially, I took a two-and-a-half-hour conversation and lunch break. But, you know what? Sometimes doing lunch is the most important thing I do. That's where I meet people, that's where people tell me things.

Over the years I've made a lot of friends. When I've met someone I've liked in the industry, I've kept in touch. Some people are scared of

the schmoozing thing because it seems fake. And there is fake schmoozing, but it really doesn't go very far. Most people are smart enough to
ignore you if you're just trying to talk to them because of their power.
It's important to remember good schmoozing doesn't necessarily and
shouldn't mean that you're nice to people you don't like. What it means
is, if you find someone you like who's in the same industry, talk to them.
What it means is, find people you like, that you want to help, and that
could help you. Life is too short to have friends you don't enjoy. People
are people, no matter what their position or social standing. That's the
secret to successful schmoozing.

Don't target people—target results. Don't say, "I want to know X
and X at this company"—just say, "I want to know more people in this
industry." Meet people in that industry, read the same publications they
read. If you're going to talk to business people a lot, it helps to be able to
cite some *Wall Street Journal* article you've read. Information is critical.
Taking the time to keep up on what's out there puts you so far ahead,
because you speak the language, you speak the jargon. I try not to call
anyone until I've read at least one, if not both, daily papers. Often, it's
where you start the conversation. "Did you see such-and-such? Can
you explain that? Why is this guy running for that office? Why did they
fire that guy?" Then, you get around to your real agenda: "Oh, by the
way, I'm doing a story on . . ."

I have a lot of friends in politics. Not politicians, because they're too
hard to get to know, but operatives. They're people I can sit down and
have a beer with. Maybe we like films or basketball or roadtripping.
Maybe we like to laugh at the same things, mock the same people. You
can't build an affinity that isn't there; you can only recognize the affinity
and cultivate it.

When I was twenty-three and trying to decide what I wanted to do
with my life, my uncle, a very successful doctor, gave me some good
advice about work. He said, "The important thing is to do things that
lead to your finding the career you'll really like. When you're forty, it's
not going to matter if you're doing what you've been doing for twelve
years or for fifteen, or twenty, or eight. If you're doing something that's

good, that you want to do, that you love, you will succeed." It's better to spend twelve years figuring out what the right career is and eight years doing it full force than to choose something, do it for twenty years, and then realize that, really, it's not at all what you wanted to do.

Time spent considering what you want to do is a good investment. It's not bad not to know what you want to do with your life. A woman friend who went out with a lot of guys once said to me, "I knew it wasn't going to work out with most of these guys. I knew they were this way or that way: unfaithful, or not as smart as me, or much more into their band than into me. But from each one, I learned something about myself, about what I can and can't take." In the same way, I think that with each job prior to journalism, and even with this job, I learned what I need out of a job and what I can't stand in a job, what I'm willing to sacrifice, what I'm not willing to sacrifice.

I was talking to another fairly successful writer here in town—he's busy all the time. He told me, "If you want to do the big stuff, you've got to prove you can do it. First you do little stuff, then you do big stuff, then you do big stuff for bigger people." What I haven't done is take the leap of being fully freelance and pitching just the big stuff.

I like writing for a lot of different magazines. Part of the reason is practical: not having all the financial eggs in one basket. Part is that I like writing for different audiences. Part is, there's always a market: any idea I come up with, I can find someone who'll probably buy it. What it means is that I'm not hanging out waiting for something to happen: I have an idea and then I try to sell it.

I can make enough money as a writer to live quite happily, and although the more stable route is editing, it's not satisfying to me. I like working on *my* project, not sixteen other projects. If what you want to do is have a routine, then climb to the highest title possible and perch. But if you're someone who demands challenge, you gotta think, "What are you learning? What are you doing?"

If you don't like your job, think about what it is you don't like and make sure you're not in that situation again. If you don't like the job but there's something you like *about* it, try to make sure the next job has more of that and less of what you don't like. Think: who you are as a person is not going to change that much. You're not going to suddenly develop a great organizational skill or become someone who loves a routine. Figure out who you are in relationship to work and then look for a career that fits that, rather than trying to *bend* yourself into a career you think is high-paying or socially acceptable or whatever.

The people I know who are fulfilled in their work situations are those who constantly ask, "Am I happy with this?" and make a change when they're not.

Epilogue: Where Are They Now?

I intended to finish the book in 1998. But, like Grace Tilsit, who opted out of medical school to tend to her ailing mother, I was reminded that life sometimes disorders even our most ordered plans. My own father took ill and passed away during the course of this book's creation, and for a time I put aside my work to tend to him and then to my grief. The delay proved beneficial in at least one way: since all but one of the interviews took place in 1997, it was interesting to learn what had transpired for my young acquaintances during the intervening two years. I spoke or corresponded with my collaborators during the fall and winter of 1999.

T. J. Devoe is attending college and working nights at a gas station. He's home so rarely that his grandmother, Peggy Terry,* relayed a message from him. "He told me to tell you the gas station is 'a stepping-stone up,' then laughed and said, 'No, actually it's keeping me alive.'"

Gina Parks is in her fifth year at Delaney High School. She has applied to doctoral programs in higher education, and writes, "I am frustrated with the number of inner-city students who work so hard to get accepted to college, only to fail out after one semester or one year. My

---

* Peggy Terry appears in several oral histories by Studs Terkel, among them, *Working*.

goal is to do research around retention of inner-city students and what postsecondary institutions should be doing to support them."

Troy Graham's next job was at a small software company, where he did "everything from sales to technical support." Early this year, he moved on to a sales job at another software company, this time at a significantly higher salary.

Max Leonard, when I spoke with him, had just returned from two weeks spent teaching literature and composition to students in Alabama. He had indeed worked for the software company for a year. "I became intrigued by the process of business." He was successful, enjoyed it, and got raise after raise. He feels his real strengths are in the areas of negotiation and organization. Max is a sophomore in college.

Jenny Petrow recently returned to the States after a two-year stint teaching English in Madrid. Late in the fall, she moved to New York City and is working as a curriculum developer at an online learning site where she speaks Spanish all day long—"A lot of my colleagues are native Spanish speakers."

Karen Hurley has held four jobs since moving to Arizona in the spring of 1998. She is still drawn to the health-care field and plans to become a Doctor of Naturopathy.* She hopes to finance her medical education by joining a new broadband-technology firm where she will be eligible for stock options. "It's a gamble, a leap of faith," she says.

Gil Santoscoy, Jr., moved to Los Angeles in the spring of 1999. He currently entertains at children's parties and is compiling an audition reel in the hope of landing an agent.

Ray Mancison left Paradigm after it merged with another label and decided to venture out on his own. He and two partners created MCM, Inc., a multimedia company consisting of a production division, a corporate marketing division, and Modern Art Music Unlimited, a record label division. For now, he is free of mergermania.

Gabrielle Lyon resigned from the Small Schools Workshop last summer, and is now the director of Project Exploration, a not-for-profit

---

* A system of treating diseases, largely employing natural substances.

foundation she and her husband created to, among other things, directly involve students and teachers with scientists and their research. "Did you know, there's not one African-American paleontologist in this country? There's not even one graduate student!" Not for long.

Carl Valentin is a second-year medical student at Rush Medical College. "I don't know that you're supposed to enjoy medical school, but to the extent that it's enjoyable, I'm enjoying it." He was elected by his class to give this year's first-year medical students their welcoming lecture, and is president of the Emergency Medicine Club.

Mary Henderson received a master's in social work and took a new job, in part, to build her résumé, but also because she felt it necessary to move on. "I'd started there as a kid a year out of college with no direction, and when I left I had my master's and five years of research experience. But I think it was hard to escape being viewed as 'the kid.'" She's currently running an alcohol- and substance-abuse research project at a state agency.

Isabel Lucero had to find a new job after the Latino organization for which she worked folded due to funding difficulties. She currently has a city job involving workforce development. "It's policy-wonkish—a ton of fun for me!"

Gillian Moore writes that she's temporarily left teaching, frustrated by "the bureaucracy, the emphasis on standardized testing, the disregard and disrespect for students." She's pursuing a degree from art school, after which she expects to return to the classroom. "I do love teaching kids."

Grace Tilsit gave birth to her second child in 1998. She has given up her dream of becoming a doctor, but contemplates starting a business she can run from home.

Julie Baxter joined a new literary agency as a fledgling partner in the fall of 1998 and is happily thriving in her new position.

Mick Betancourt's voice sounds years older on the phone. He speed-talks: "This is my third twenty-hour day. I worked at Home Depot and rehearsed, had a meeting with my production company, and if the five hundred flyers for my show are ready, I gotta get out and put them

up all over town." During the past two years, he's produced and per-
formed in numerous comedy shows around Chicago. He recently
graduated from Second City's conservatory program, and has already
turned down offers from two management companies. "I'm hoping to
get taken on by a higher-level management firm so I can attract a good
agent." He and his wife, Kate, plan on moving to Los Angeles in the
spring.

Chico Pinex continues working with the NCC and still dreams about
driving that big truck.

Credell Walls was recently hired by the Garfield Park Conservatory
Alliance as an educator—instructor. He is glad to be working with children and hopes to continue his college course work in the future.

Cesar Rivera, after graduating from business school, got a job as an
emerging markets portfolio manager at a well-established Wall Street
firm—he was working there at the time of the interview. As emerging
markets investments cooled down, the firm began laying people off. Cesar didn't see a bright future. "My hair is the wrong color—I'm too
young." Still yearning to be a trader, he's temporarily stepped away
from Wall Street and taken a job with a West Coast technology company's finance division. He describes the company as "humane." About
the change, he explains, "I'm a big believer in, if you're in a bad situation, leave and start over." In five years, he hopes to return to Wall
Street as a trader. "I measure my success in cash, and I don't understand
the kind of career where you work hard and there's no chance of ever
getting rich."

Iliana Roman's hair salon business is doing fine and keeping her busy.
She's still thinking about getting a real estate license.

Emily Hanford's husband was hired as a Professor of Communications Studies at the University of North Carolina, Chapel Hill, in 1998.
Through an internet professional publication, Emily learned of a position at Chapel Hill's public radio station, WUNC. In June of 1999, she
became WUNC's news director.

Jeff Marcus finished a degree in Wildlife Biology and was hired by
the University of Nebraska to work on a conservation project involving

two endangered species, the piping plover and least tern. He hopes to find further funding for the project after its two-year grant expires.

Kate McFadyen followed her inclination to switch over to the client side. After a more lucrative but stressful experience with a difficult boss at a cosmetics firm, she moved on. She now works in marketing at a high-end cosmetics company, has a great boss, and is enjoying a good salary and additional responsibility.

In 1999, Robert Richman and a partner formed a consulting company called Grassroots Solutions. He took a leave of absence from the company to work as the national field director for Bill Bradley's presidential campaign and, as of this writing, was very, very, very busy.

Marc Spiegler left his job and column at *Chicago* magazine and moved to Switzerland to be with his girlfriend in 1998. He is again working as a freelance writer.

ACKNOWLEDGMENTS

I would dearly like to take the credit for coming up with the idea for *Help Wanted*, but I can't. In the work world, people claiming credit for the ideas of others happens all the time. But I want to set a good example, so I relate that the idea for this book came from my esteemed publisher, André Schiffrin. I thank him for suggesting I do oral history work in the first place, and then quietly feeding me one book idea after another.

For the most part, friends and business associates led me to my subjects, but a few were people already known to me through one work circumstance or another. For their excellent leads I thank Bill Ayers, Will and Michelle Brink, Meg Blackstone, Jim Desmond, Jamie Kalven, Kecia Lynn, Matt McDonnell, Harold and Marlene Richman, Migdalia Rivera, Rachel Stewart, Adria Steinberg, and Peggy Terry. For giving me some insight into current guidance counseling methods, I thank Hope Cracut, and, for leading me her way, Steve Grossman. I very much thank Mike Spock for all of that recycled paper, as well as for giving new meaning to the concept of a flexible work schedule. Special thanks go to Rick Ayers, for providing valuable feedback on an early draft of the introduction, and to Ted Byfield, for doing likewise on the manuscript as a whole.

I thank the people whose generous and thoughtful interviews made this book *this* book and not some other. (Two thirds chose to use their real names, the rest preferred the blanket of a pseudonym.) To those whose interviews I was not able to include, I offer my apologies and my thanks for their time, stories, and insights. Although their words do not appear in print, they are very much a part of this work.

Writing a book can be a solitary activity, but I'm very fortunate to have had the moral support of a number of people while this book came into being. For their care and concern I thank all of my Chicago pals, as well as the Wednesday night group; also, those geographically distant friends who are close in mind and heart; and my much-loved mother and her duck-feeding compatriot in New York. I also thank my late father for his sound and heartfelt advice about the world of work.

Writing a book may be solitary, but it is in many ways a collaborative endeavor, and my terrific editor, Ellen Reeves, has been the finest of allies. Her comments, suggestions, and enthusiasm made all kinds of difference and for that I am immensely grateful. Also at the New Press, my thanks to Barbara Chuang, Leda Scheintaub, and Hall Smyth of BAD.

To Studs Terkel, who for many years has been an inspiring and most remarkable teacher as well as a kind and generous friend, I offer my respectful, appreciative, eternal gratitude. I humbly bow my head in his direction. To his late wife, Ida, whose blithe spirit is so sorely missed, goes my appreciation for the time I was fortunate enough to spend in her graceful and grace-filled presence.

Finally, to anyone I've ever worked with or for, I offer gratitude, apologies, forgiveness.